DISRUPTIVE
SCHOOL
BEHAVIOR

DISRUPTIVE SCHOOL BEHAVIOR

Class, Race, and Culture

JUDITH LYNNE HANNA

HOLMES & MEIER
New York   London

Holmes & Meier Publishers, Inc.
30 Irving Place
New York, NY 10003

Great Britain:
1–3 Winton Close
Letchworth, Hertfordshire SG61 1BA
England

Book design by Dale Cotton

The paper used in this publication meets the requirements
of the American National Standard for Permanence of
Paper for printed Library Materials, Z39.48-1984.

Library of Congress Cataloging-in-Publication Data

Hanna, Judith Lynne.
  Disruptive school behavior

  Bibliography: p.
  Includes index.
  1. School integration—United States—Case studies.
2. School discipline—United States—Case studies.
3. Educational equalization—United States—Case studies.
I. Title.   II. Title: Disruptive school behavior.
LC214.2.H36   1988   370.19'342   87-11947
ISBN 0-8419-1134-7 (alk. paper)
ISBN 0-8419-1164-9 (pbk.) (alk. paper)

Manufactured in the United States of America

For Shawn and Aaron and all those
children who enjoy or endure the adventure of growing up
and the process of desegregation

For the parents, teachers, and school administrators
who truly care

CONTENTS

PREFACE

The message of this book bears directly on the crisis of confidence in the quality of education and the debate fueled by the release of three major studies in 1983: the National Commission on Excellence in Education's *A Nation at Risk,* Goodlad's *A Place Called School,* and the Twentieth Century Fund's *Making the Grade,* and the continuing disclosures.[1]

America's schools received a failing grade. Trouble exists on every front, from teacher competence to classroom violence. About 40 percent of seventeen-year-old minority youth in America can be considered functionally illiterate; the figure for all youth is 19 percent. In addition, by 1980 violence had become extremely widespread. In the Los Angeles public schools, violence reached such magnitude that the California attorney general charged Los Angeles officials with subjecting children to cruel and unusual punishment by forcing them to attend unsafe schools.[2] Detroit schools are rife with children killing children.

By 1985 the Congressional Research Service/Congressional Budget Office and Children's Defense Fund reports had sounded yet another alarm. Poverty among children had increased and become more widespread in the last decade. Nearly half of all black children are being raised in poverty, and the poor are increasing in number at a faster rate than the middle class. For children in families headed by single women under thirty who did not complete high school, the poverty rate was more than 90 percent. Almost three-and-a-half times as many black families (43 percent) as compared with white families (13 percent) are headed by women.

All these related educational and social problems have come to the fore precisely in the decades when desegregation was supposed to be solving many of them. School segregation was "the sign and symbol of black inferiority."[3] As a remedy, U.S. courts mandated desegregation plans for equal educational opportunity. The issue changed from

xi

whether blacks should have equal protection under the law and equal opportunity to how these principles should be realized. School desegregation created a new situation with great potential for improving the lives of blacks in U.S. society and for the reduction of interracial tensions.[4] In some cases, desegregation has had a positive impact; in others, there are problems that no one is paying honest enough attention to. These problems cause desegregation to have little or no benefit and even to lead to interracial hostility where none previously existed.[5]

Since the 1954 Supreme Court decision that led to school desegregation, the representation of different cultural groups has increased in many educational institutions. Student–teacher and student–student misunderstandings and confrontations are, of course, common; a mixed cultural environment complicates (and may increase and/or magnify) some types of academic and social problems because of the clash of attitudes, values, and behavior.[6] Such cross-cultural misunderstandings and different behavior patterns reinforce existing prejudices against minorities. Misunderstanding and dislike of different behavior may also alienate individuals and groups and foster the inability to develop trust and rapport.

Moreover, these communication misunderstandings between individuals and groups negatively affect the upward mobility of members of minority groups. The "gatekeepers," those individuals who have the authority to make decisions about the social mobility of others, are usually white. Education, which depends on effective student–teacher and student–student communication, is usually critical to access to a range of opportunities for life satisfaction as well as occupational choices. Communication dissonance may keep some minority group members out of classmate "old-boy" networks. These informal channels of information help people obtain positions in the workplace, maintain them, and to advance in their chosen field.[7]

Psychologists have found that an individual who is misunderstood and misunderstands others may experience stress. Although stress may motivate an individual to overcome problems of faulty communication, it more often leads to a negative self-image; distorted or disorganized thoughts, values, and emotions; frustration; and failure to achieve his or her goals. Disruption in school and society are often linked to individuals sending messages of stress about themselves.

If we believe that one's experiences shape attitudes that in turn affect behavior, we should examine the actual implementation of national laws to protect the rights of minorities—implementation, that is, as it occurs not in the courtroom, but in the classroom and on the playground. What are the recurring social experiences children have in many schools? We know little about the everyday life of children who come together in a school. How do they take heed, inspect, address, move toward or away from, parade before, lay claims on, insulate themselves from, and adjust to each other and their teachers?

What is overlooked as aggression, play, or children "horsing around" in structured or free play *and* formal classroom settings can reveal, when examined with the anthropological lens, a great deal of social life ordinarily hidden from adult eyes and serving purposes unrecognized by adults.[8] Aggression and play teach children lessons that may subvert formal education. Adults often underestimate the complexity and subtlety of the social knowledge a child needs to operate in school, and especially in a multicultural one. These pages throw light on such facets of student life, help to explain them, and suggest remedies for some of the problems that confront our schools.

This book describes what it is like to be a student in the desegregated "Pacesetter" Hamilton Park Elementary School (HPES) in Dallas, Texas. The story comes from students' reports and experiences over a period of a year. The HPES case is then considered within the broader American social chronicle and comparative view of schools with low-income populations that reflect their groups' situations in society.

Although this book began as a general study of a magnet desegregated school, a central theme emerged from the children's concerns: a counterculture of disruptive behavior, verbal and nonverbal aggression called "meddlin'" by some youngsters, and the need to do something about it. Formal schooling often takes second place to the challenges of coping with meddlin'. Indeed, disruptive behavior can counteract such changes as more difficult curricula and qualified teachers intended to improve education. American adults have for several years perceived disruption and the lack of discipline to be major problems facing the nation's schools.[9] Children share this concern.

The school I studied appeared to be nearly an ideal setting for making desegregation work. *What happened in this school reflects in small part the variety of unwanted student behavior now occurring in less ideal settings, both segregated and desegregated, with greater frequency than ever before.* Much of what is now taken for granted would have been shocking twenty years ago. Wanting to show their success, principals play down as many offenses as possible. In an attempt to maintain control of their classes, teachers have given grades for good behavior as well as educational achievement.

Because disruptive school behavior precludes much academic teaching and learning, short- and long-range solutions to problems that occur in desegregated schools, and also in homogeneous schools with low-income populations, are proposed. Of critical importance, this work treats an aspect of experience civil rights activists had designated as taboo for fear of reinforcing extant bigotry. Yet by not disclosing the experience and attempting to deal with it constructively, we shackle millions of youth to a life of poverty or crime.

For many readers, this book will evoke a wide range of emotions: denial, surprise, empathy, despair, and hope. Some people react viscerally to a discussion of negative aspects of a minority group even by members of that group and consider such a discussion tantamount to insult, smear, blaming the victim, and perpetuating racist stereotypes. Recall the reaction in 1965 when Daniel P. Moynihan reported his analysis of the black family. Twenty years later, people had finally begun to address the problem. Glenn C. Loury, a member of the new black conservative movement, speaks about the behavior of the black lower class, something black leaders have been reluctant to do.[10] They feared, as did white leaders and scholars, that such a discussion would lend support to racist claims that blacks are somehow unworthy or inferior. However, the result of taboos on talking about real problems is apparent in the statistics I have mentioned on the plight of poor blacks in America. The reader who wants a rosy picture of schooling in America should not read further.

Disruptive School Behavior rests on the conviction that equal opportunity for formal education is necessary but not sufficient to enable people to achieve socioeconomic success in adult life. There are unintended consequences of good-faith efforts in public policy and the practice of conventional wisdom. The findings of my study do not leave the burden of responsibility with teachers as do other investigations. The purpose of these pages is to reconcile the goals of equal educational opportunity with the realities of children's social experiences and life opportunities that will affect their attitudes and behavior as adults; to ease the burdens placed on children, parents, and school personnel during novel intercultural contacts and adjustments; and to make participants in schools with low-income student bodies more aware of the dynamics of their conflict and in doing so to suggest how their differences might be harmonized or eliminated. Consequently, the following account will focus on problems in education with the hope of challenging Americans to devote time and energy to work toward eliminating the festering sores.

The study's significance lies in considering public policy, children's realities, and the dynamics of not only black/white, but also low/middle socioeconomic class, neighbors/strangers, and children/adults. Consequently, the results and proposals for change challenge conventional wisdom that sometimes guides research, parents, teachers, civil rights activists, and policy makers.

This book is written for educators (including parents); for students of public policy, communication, social interaction, urban problems, ethnic relations, American studies, and play; and for all those individuals in a variety of institutions attempting faithfully and in good will to realize equal opportunity and justice. Most of all, the book is for our children.

Because I have written with a broad audience in mind, some may find certain sections familiar or even elementary. I beg their patience; the sense of the familiar, I hope, will offer the specialized reader a comfortable map before moving into less explored territory.

NOTES

1. In the following two years, there were more than 30 other national studies of education, 290 state commission and blue-ribbon task force reports, 2 network television documentaries, and widespread newspaper and magazine coverage of public school problems, reflecting near hysteria over the plight of our schools (Lefkowitz 1985).

2. *Newsweek* 1980.

3. Comer and Poussaint 1975:217.

4. The term *race* is not used here as a biological concept referring to populations but as a folk concept referring to political behavior. Policy makers often viewed desegregation as a key means of improving relations between black and white (National Advisory Commission on Civil Disorders 1968, Read 1975, Wisdom 1975).

5. According to St. John's (1975) review of more than 120 studies up to 1974, the results of desegregation are at best equivocal. Subsequent assessments by Bradley and Bradley (1977); Stephan (1978); National Academy of Education (1979); Hawley (1980); Wax (1980), Wolf (1981); Dentler and Scott (1981); Yarmolinsky et al. (1981); Schofield (1982); Cook et al. (1984); Wolters (1984); and Marek (1985) do not provide a sanguine picture.

A panel of distinguished authorities on the sociology, law, and politics of desegregation divided deeply over the historical reality, contemporary meaning and effects, and future portent of that lodestar (Cook et al. 1984). Debate occurred over what kind of racial distribution in a school was best. St. John proposed a 14 to 40 percent minority enrollment as optimal for a minority large enough to exert pressure yet small enough not to constitute a power threat to the majority. Cataldo et al. (1978:100) found that the key feature of desegregation in seven Florida school districts contributing to avoidance by whites was a threshold of 30 percent black in an assigned school.

6. The United States has long been viewed as a haven for people from various parts of the world who would be assimilated by the "melting pot" of a dominant American culture. Speech would become more homogeneous, patterns of dress more standardized, and so on. In the 1970s, these views were

reassessed, and persisting, coexisting differences in values, beliefs, attitudes, and means of expression and communication were recognized, even celebrated. This celebration gave legitimacy to some characteristics of the counterschool culture.

Some people attempt to ignore differences, but they must become aware of these differences to understand and deal with them. Individuals must also know the appropriateness of their behavior in different situations in order to engage in harmonious social relations. And they need some reason for wanting to do so.

The consequences of misunderstanding face-to-face interactions can be fatal. When an innocent bystander failed to respond to a Chicago gang member's hand signal, the youth gunned down the bystander. Another bystander was shot and killed when a gang member mistook his arm gestures for the signals of a rival gang.[7] Every small group has its independent and unique patterns of understandings and interactions: each family, each neighborhood, each classroom. Children's general past experience leads them to expect similar social relations in the future. Once this process of learning from experience begins, it may become a self-perpetuated system of preferences, expectations, and actions capable of persisting indefinitely.

7.   Erickson (1975, 1979) found that if a counselor and student shared ethnic background, cultural communicative style, and special interests, the student was more likely to be given useful advice and evaluated positively for advanced and improved positions. In his work with hard-core unemployed black trainees in Chicago, Hall (1974:7) found that some of their spontaneous behavior could be wrongly interpreted by an employer as showing disinterest, cockiness, or lack of confidence. Employers did not know what would trigger antagonism or suspicion in applicants. See also Davis 1982.

8.   Sholomo Ariel, Matia Kam, and Irene Sever, in the Study Center for Children's Activities in Kiryat Tivon, Israel, found that children created a system of rules among themselves that were unlike the rules of the adult world. "Children's play world is a world unto itself, with its own peculiar wonderland laws and customs" (quoted in Larson 1980). Fine and Glassner (1979) suggest that children's culture at deeper levels is secret from adults. Goodman (1970) and Spradley and McCurdy (1972) suggest how play may subvert formal schooling. See Duncan and Fiske (1977:252–53) on children's experiential learning and Damon (1977) on integrating concepts.

Children, who have their own minds, senses, and unique historical era, independently respond to situations in which they find themselves. Of course, they also reflect parental culture—comprising the values, beliefs, and practices of a group.

9.   See Rubel 1977, Maeroff 1981, Patchen 1982, and the Gallup Polls in the 1980s.

10.   Loury (1985). Many school administrators are not concerned with growth and development to meet current needs. If matters appear to be going well on the surface, they choose not to bother with research that might uncover problems that should be solved. Clark's study (1977) of school riots in desegregated schools suggests that if there had been an investigation of the sentiments and behavior of school participants from different economic and racial groups, contentious issues could have been spotted and worked through. These riots were reported. In many other instances, conflicts of varying degrees of severity are hushed up, and black and white children continue to abuse each other and be abused by adults.

ACKNOWLEDGMENTS

I gratefully acknowledge Holt, Rinehart, and Winston for permission to use previously published material in "Public Policy and the Children's World," in George D. Spindler, ed., *Doing the Ethnography of Schooling*, pp. 316–55, 1982.

My appreciation goes first and foremost to my sons, Shawn and Aaron, and my husband and colleague, William, who lived through the research behind this book. The youngsters catalyzed this study by sharing their thoughts, observations, and experiences at HPES.

The research could not have been possible without the cooperation of many people. I thank them all, although for reasons of space, they cannot all be listed. Phyllis Owen, one of the coprincipals of HPES, to whom I first spoke about the things I had heard from children and parents at HPES and across the nation, recognized the need for the study. She and the other coprincipal, James O. Griffin, not only gave permission to conduct the study, as did the Richardson Independent School District (RISD) administration, but they gave generously of their time and themselves, shared their experiences and insights with me, and cooperated within the constraints of RISD and Texas Education Agency guidelines. Charting new paths, the principals were eager to have visitors witness life in their school, identify strengths and weaknesses, and learn from the visitors' view how improvements could be made. As one of the students at the school remarked, "They care about kids to have someone [me] interview us."

I wish to thank HPES teachers and parents who shared their feelings, thoughts, and experiences. I appreciate the cooperation of second-grade teachers Marilyn Blankenship, Kathy Erfurth, Marilene Meneley, Lydell Seward, Sylvia Wheeler, Kathy Westfall, assistants Alexis Clayton and Jean Brock; fourth-grade teachers Suzi Gibbons, Marcia Johnson, Janette Perry, Anne Wilson, Norma Young, assistants Surinder Kane,

Kathy Martin; sixth-grade teachers Gai Andrews, Elise Bergeron, Sue Mann, Helen Schnuelle, Vera Simpson, Janet Taylor, assistants Bobbie Woods, Jill Trask, special education teachers Helen Green, Carole Kilduff, Carol Millis, Laura Muckelroy; speech teacher Clarice Mason; educational diagnostician Charlotte Garner; counselors Teta Smith, Fannie Fair; discipline room counselor Paula Thomas; Extended-Day Program director June Baker; music teacher Jeannie Alley; art teacher Kay Lueck, Susan Yonely; Spanish teacher Diane Strickland; librarian Gloria Gray; audiovisual specialist Bhajan Chehal; computer proctor Kathy Watts; staff members Mary Ebey, Georgia Cantrell, Jessie Smith, Sherry Webb; and public relations person Margie Carter. Babs Rakofsky, Ann Hampton, and Thelma Van Dyke, teachers in other grades, were especially helpful.

Of course, my greatest debt is to the children who told me what it was like to be a student at HPES.

Not only did RISD, through Richard F. Hays, assistant superintendent, elementary instruction, give permission for the study, but in pursuit of the goal to provide excellent education for the total child, it also provided partial support. The University of Texas at Dallas (UTD) and University of Maryland, College Park, are acknowledged for their contribution. I am grateful to have been awarded a National Endowment for the Humanities fellowship at the American Enterprise Institute for Public Policy Research to complete a draft of this book and extend my work on public policy and urban education.

Assistance with the history of Hamilton Park developments came from Aletta Scuka, library associate, history and social sciences division, Dallas Public Library; Irving Statman, deputy director, Department of Housing and Urban Development, Dallas; and George W. "Gus" Fields, long-time Dallas resident. Jane Tyler, now deceased, led me to research studies and assisted me in editorial matters.

Marla Maybry, Dolores Davidson, Eve Hoag, and Eileen Tollet assisted in transcribing tape-recorded interviews.

Allen Sullivan, deputy associate superintendent, Dallas Independent School District, and Harold Childs, professor of sociology at the University of Texas at Dallas, with their experience as black minority members in dominant white America, trainers in multicultural communication, and educators, acted as sounding boards for my observations and as sources of information and further references to literature that explored some of the problems I identified. Kent Skipper and Ernest A. Gotts, professors of special education (UTD) and Ronald D. Henderson, team leader, desegregation studies team, National Institute of Education (NIE) provided useful insights.

Helpful critics on earlier drafts of the study report were: Harold Childs; Ernest Gotts; Judy Nassif, a native Dallasite and parent of two children at Hamilton Park Elementary School; Pat Magruder, artist, filmmaker, psychiatric nurse, and UTD graduate student; Roslyn Joffee, a Maryland teacher; Remi Clignet, professor of sociology; Stephen Elkin, professor of political science; and Jean Grambs, professor of education, University of Maryland; Robert Wegmann, professor of sociology, University of Houston at Clear Lake City, and George Noblit, professor of sociology, Memphis State University; Iris Volkman, American Enterprise Institute; William Julius Wilson, professor of urban sociology, University of Chicago; John Ogbu, professor of anthropology, University of California, Berkeley; Irving Spitzberg, J.D., executive director, Council for Liberal Learning, Association of American Colleges; Nathan Glazer, professor of education and sociology, Harvard University; and Michele Teitelbaum, Public Action and Human Consequences Series editor, Transaction Books; editors Katharine Turok, Marilyn Buckingham, and Gavin Lewis at Holmes & Meier. My greatest debts of gratitude are owed to George D. Spindler, professor of anthropology and education, Stanford University; and William John Hanna, professor of community development, University of Maryland, whose continuing encouragement with this project is most deeply appreciated.

DISRUPTIVE
SCHOOL
BEHAVIOR

1

RETREAT FROM NAÏVETÉ

STEMMING from but going beyond a case study of a desegregated school, this book considers low-income-student counterculture behavior that impedes success in mainstream America. In this chapter, I comment first on desegregation, race, and class; then on the origin of this study; and finally on some concepts that help us understand the dissonances of black and white, low income and middle class, friends and strangers, and child and adult that are part of the story.

Desegregation, Race, and Socioeconomic Class

The U.S. courts have been mandating school desegregation since the 1954 *Brown et al.* v. *Board of Education of Topeka* decision by the Supreme Court that separate educational systems for different races were inherently unequal and therefore violated the Fourteenth Amendment of the Constitution of the United States. School desegregation remains an issue; indeed, the landmark case was reopened in 1979.[1]

Requiring school desegregation with prescribed racial ratios has led in some instances to equivocal results, unfulfilled expectations, and new dilemmas that perpetuate some of the very inequities American policy makers wished to eliminate. School desegregation is the domestic policy issue in recent years arousing the strongest feeling and most widespread political activity, and many studies explore the propriety and effect of court actions.[2] Questions are being asked even where calm prevails: In order to solve societal problems in the grown-up world, are adults placing undue hardship on the pioneering children who experience school desegregation with its new kinds of multicultural interactions?

1

What are the benefits and costs? Should a few involuntarily be subject of experiments that have shown little success?

The desegregation process has become logjammed.[3] Court action seems to have contributed to "white flight" or determined where people live.[4] The causes of dramatic shifts in the black/white public school ratios are multifarious and affected by social trends, such as differential birth rates and the movement of many white-collar jobs to suburban areas. Between 1970 and 1974, nearly two million more Americans moved from cities than to them, reversing earlier trends. Whatever the cause, the results are the same. Minority-group students outnumber whites in all but eight of the country's twenty-nine largest cities, and the trend of decreasing white-student enrollment in urban public schools appears likely to continue.[5]

By 1982 the nation had become more conservative. President Ronald Reagan's policies and proposals braked the forward direction of federal government activism in civil rights and education. The administration attempted to restore tax-exempt status to educational institutions that practice racial segregation. Under siege for all intents and purposes, busing for school desegregation—the keystone of the civil rights movement—was out of vogue. Mandatory busing, largely in popular disfavor because it violated the tradition of parents determining through residential choice the school their children attended (assignments being made on the basis of proximity of school to home), gave way to voluntary desegregation in Chicago and St. Louis.[6] Federal aid to education to help the underprivileged was cut. At the local level, shrinking student enrollments led to school closings and reassignments that some people argue parallel the white-flight movement to avoid attending desegregated schools. In 1984 the U.S. Justice Department argued for the first time that a local school board (in Norfolk, Virginia) could abolish a completed busing program ordered by a court to achieve desegregation and return to neighborhood schools even if that increased racial segregation in the schools.

Yet history attests to setbacks and resurgences; the judiciary has its measure of independence, and the American people show progress toward egalitarianism. Indeed, polls indicate that a majority favor desegregation. The key issue, however, persists: how to help the growing and increasingly neglected population that has acquired, from the injustices of the slavery era, styles of action that impede both success in school and work in majority America and how to make academic efforts have a better payoff for low-income blacks and others.

After more than a quarter of a century of desegregation plans that have not fulfilled expectations, the actual experience of life in a desegregated school has just begun to be closely examined.[7] Broad-ranged studies of academic achievement, self-concept, or prejudice fail to capture the complexities of the school environment. Moreover, most tests do not measure what some people consider important aspects of academic achievement (for example, the ability to write an essay, debate a proposition, innovate, and understand and participate in the arts).[8] Because the educational process itself, daily school life, is ignored, educators and policy makers may take inappropriate action toward educational improvement.

Although I present a case study of life in a desegregated school, HPES, and discuss some of the problems and possible causes and solutions, the issues are relevant not only for currently desegregated schools, but for future ones and any city school with a *low-income*, especially black, student body. Hamilton Park Elementary School was typical of many schools in the United States, neither the best nor the worst. There were enough black students at HPES to be more than an unwanted appendage or a visible but inconsequential minority. The school is located in a black community and was integrated under court order in 1975 as a "Pacesetter" magnet school; *magnet* refers to attracting students to a school because of its special features. Although there is a history of immigrant children mingling in dominant-culture American schools, the court-ordered integration decision caught the population without a model for strategies to mix groups whose races, social classes, and neighborhood origins differ. It is noteworthy, however, that the school district and administrative staff, for a variety of reasons, were strongly motivated to make desegregation work at this particular school.

A key problem that surfaced was the high correlation between color and socioeconomic class. The latter, based on hierarchical differentiations in society, refers to a group of people who have relatively similar income, education, occupation, and potential to exercise power through status, prestige, or affiliation with an institution. One of America's most cherished myths is that we have only one class, namely, the middle class.[9] However, the United States definitely has a class of poor people and a wealthy elite, as well as a middle class.

Disruptive school behavior seems to be disproportionately but not exclusively found among low-socioeconomic populations. Their expressive behavior differs from middle-class behavior largely in response to perceived restricted economic opportunity. Even though a small percentage of students commit a large percentage of offenses, the behavior sets low-income populations apart and makes them unable to be assimilated into the working world. This dilemma occurs throughout the United States as well as in other countries.

According to a survey of the background characteristics of the school's student body, black HPES students were, with few exceptions, from low-income families, whereas the whites were from middle-class families. The few middle-class blacks in the school manifested attitudes and behavior different from low-income blacks and similar to middle-class white students. Evidence of this similarity presented later comes from comments by some of the middle-class black youngsters, their classmates, parents, and teachers in addition to my observations and meetings with middle-class black parents.

The U.S. Census and other literature attest to differences in black middle-class and lower-class lifestyles. There seems to be general agreement that both race and socioeconomic class reverberate within a child's life. Race has defined and restricted blacks, while class has created divisions within racial groups. Students of ethnic groups and pluralism in the United States have documented both variation and common patterns. Ethnic group members frequently behave toward each other differently from the way they act toward outsiders. When they interact with representatives of mainstream American culture, minorities often manifest the recognized dominant culture behavior. While middle-class blacks and whites are likely to have distinct attitudes and styles of behavior as a result of their own histories, there seem to be dimensions of a shared culture in middle-class black and white children's deportment in school that is associated with academic success.

Although quantitative data on black elementary school children are scarce, major national studies show the importance of socioeconomic class for academic achievement.[10] The landmark 1966 Coleman report found that schools did not have as much impact on student achievement as did the characteristics of the children who attended them. Advantaged children from two-parent families do better in school than poor children from broken homes.[11] Later national longitudinal studies show results for blacks and whites that are consistent with Coleman's findings.[12]

On academic measures, middle-class black students do better than lower-class black students, although middle-class black students do less well than middle-class white students.[13] Race appears to have an impact, but findings from the National Assessment of Educational Progress (a longitudinal study ongoing since 1971) and from the College Entrance Examination Board demonstrate a consistent reduction of the black–white gap during recent years due to the enormous post-1960s social changes affecting blacks and benefiting middle-class blacks the most.[14] The civil rights movement occasioned, over three decades, dramatic increases in the number of blacks attending elite colleges and universities; entering professions; engaging in successful enterprises; and associating with whites in residential areas, restaurants, and public facilities, even though discriminatory hiring and seniority practices persist to the disadvantage of blacks.

These studies of student academic achievement and background characteristics imply that middle-class white and black children share attitudes and behaviors requisite for academic success in American schools.[15]

Types of disruptive school behavior associated with low academic achievement have been described for low-income students in a variety of black and nonblack settings (for example, among whites in Boston, West Virginia, and England, as well as in seven desegregated schools.[16] In dramatic contrast, for an eighty-five-year span, the all-black, elite, middle-class Dunbar High School, in Washington, D.C., sent nearly all of its students to college and counts among its alumni distinguished professionals (for example, the first black general, Benjamin O. Davis; the first black federal justice, W. H. Hostie; the first black Cabinet member, Robert C. Weaver; the first black U.S. senator since Reconstruction, Edward W. Brooke; and the discoverer of blood plasma, Charles Drew). Students came to Dunbar from throughout the district because of the school's reputation for academic rigor.[17]

Thus, reference only to race or class as explanations for school behavior would be false. We cannot ignore either the legacy of discrimination prior to the 1960s, the impact of the civil rights movement since, nor the history of middle-class black achievement.

The presence of large numbers of middle-class children is necessary to convince many white and black parents that their children will receive a good education.[18] In the 1960s, affluent, civil-rights-oriented parents pledged themselves and their children to a life far less isolated than they had known as rural or suburban children; their offspring would know poor black children. These parents were at the schools volunteering to tutor, raise money, build a playground, and engage in similar activities. But they began to retreat ideologically and in practice as they discarded embattled convictions hard won and long held because of their own children's experiences.[19]

James Meredith, the young black man who sparked white riots by integrating the University of Mississippi in 1962 and was shot for walking old southern back roads to protest segregation in 1966, was preaching in 1985 that integration is a "sham . . . young Americans were guinea pigs in a disastrous social experiment that involved mixing children from different classes in schools when these classes did not mix anywhere and never had."[20]

In liberal Montgomery County, Maryland, a government lawyer

whose white daughter was bused to an elementary school in a black community, said that the child, who has black godparents, has begun to perceive black children in negative terms. He attributes this to the enormous economic and cultural differences separating affluent whites from Chevy Chase and the lower-income minority children who live in the area surrounding the school. "Our kids over there are a white fig leaf," he insists. "There is no real integration. It didn't work. It doesn't work."[21] "I object to making five-year-olds the grunts [footsoldiers] in an intellectual, ideological war over appropriate ways to achieve desegregation."[22]

Observers of lower-class black and middle-class white kindergarten children in a North Carolina public school during instruction periods and playground recess found that middle-class white children talked more, whereas low-income black youngsters were more aggressive (they hit, pushed, verbally threatened, commanded, and took objects). Children had clear preferences for working and playing with classmates like themselves.[23]

Historically, whites have enrolled their children in private or suburban public schools to avoid what they perceived to be the problems of desegregation. Now, there are numerous blacks removing their children from public schools; middle-class blacks also move to the suburbs or enroll their children in private schools so they can associate with other blacks or whites who share their values and behavior.[24] Moreover, there are low-income parents who at great sacrifice put their children in private schools to provide them with what they perceive to be education of a higher quality.

Whites fearing accusations of racism and blacks fearing charges of having betrayed their ethnic group if they spoke about the disruptive school behavior of disadvantaged youngsters avoid desegregated schools rather than try to change them. Compounding the situation of desegregation's outcomes are some poor or lower middle-class whites' fears of and hostility toward blacks. They resent blacks' success in finding a protest movement that attracted attention and held out hope of help.[25]

Odyssey to Discovery

There are descriptions of children's lives in inner-city schools, schools where blacks are a minority or a majority, a middle school where there is a close racial balance, and schools in the first year of desegregation. My book reinforces some findings of these case studies. Whereas most school desegregation research was conducted in schools with ado-

6

lescents during the year of transition from segregation, I report on the third year of a desegregated elementary school with preadolescents.

This study of children's perceptions and descriptions of their behavior within the context of the family, community, school, and current and past history has its roots in my concern for social justice and equality. The immediate motivation was my experience as a parent with a problem, and this impetus fit in with a long-time research interest in how communication influences attitudes and behavior.

But this book is not a parent's autobiography. Although my role as parent catalyzed the study, my role as researcher and former teacher in several school systems led me to design the study using systematic objective procedures for collecting and analyzing information and to be aware of ways in which my personal involvement might affect my research.

I have tried to present the duality of parent and scholar as each experience seemed to influence the other and led to opportunities and insights that would otherwise not have been possible. I did not study my children as the noted psychologist Jean Piaget did his; my youngsters were part of the parent–child, child–child, and child–school complex that I explored. When researchers investigated only exotic societies in faraway places, they wrote their reports as distanced scholars; such distancing is less plausible in our own society even if it has the diversity of races, socioeconomic classes, neighbors, strangers, and generations.

My husband and I had learned about HPES from university and research colleagues. Before we enrolled our children (nine and seven years old) in the school, we visited the place and liked it. All the children appeared happy. The teachers appeared to be caring and to stimulate productive learning experiences. The principal for instruction described the most noticed differences between blacks and whites: Blacks were more physical. We thought our sons were physical.

As casual observers, we did not detect problems among children or between children and school personnel that later surfaced during my year's involvement with the school as a serious listener and observer. Adults passing through a school do not always see or feel what children experience. Similarly, the life of other institutions is hidden from the passerby: A visit to a university department does not automatically reveal the vicious infighting that may exist. Men often do not observe the sexual harassment their female coworkers are subjected to. In fact, much social interaction among peers is outside management's purview.

The neighborhood school our sons attended before we moved to Texas was mixed, with Afro-Americans, Filipinos, Chinese, Koreans, Greeks, French, Germans, and Italians of varied educational background. Our children frequently played with black houseguests. The boys joined me at predominantly black dance classes in New York City. But when they began attending HPES, they asked what "honkies" meant; they said their classmates talked about their gangs, the "honkies versus niggers." Shawn, in the third grade, had never heard these epithets before attending HPES and did not know their meanings; but he did know it was "whites versus blacks," and there were gang leaders. Sometimes, he said he belonged to the "white gang." Both my children began speaking negatively about black children at HPES. Such statements as— "They get me in trouble," "They're dumb," "They're mean," "I don't like HP," "I'm sick. I can't go to school," "It was so noisy in class I got a headache and spent two hours in the nurse's office today"—were common, as were reports of black children's misdeeds. For several months I dismissed these comments. Children often fluctuate in their attitudes toward peers. I emphasized to my sons that we should accept people on the basis of personality rather than color.

When I reported what I was hearing, one of my black friends said that I was anxious about the implications of the youngsters' comments, knowing the conventional wisdom that children commonly reflect their parents' values, and I might be accused of prejudice. But our children were not reflecting our attitudes and behavior, nor were they continuing their former behavior.

I thought my children's experiences might be unique, so I broached the subject with other HPES parents. They, too, were uneasy about their children's attitudes and behavior. Some white children who had previously been in schools with blacks and had black friends were now expressing antipathy toward blacks; indeed, they were talking like racial bigots. When I spoke with other parents whose children were in other schools in Dallas and throughout the United States in the course of attending professional meetings and giving guest lectures, I found they had had similar experiences.

Black parents, too, were upset about "meddlin'" (verbal or physical harassment). A black educator and former president of the HPES PTA told me that her six-year-old child who had been playing with middle-class whites and blacks said, "Mommy, I don't want to play with blacks. They don't play nice." At twelve, he asked his mother, "Why am I not supposed to like whites?"[26]

Finally I realized that my children's problems were part of a wider problem facing not only HPES but the U.S. educational system as a whole. It was then that I decided to do a study of HPES, linking my parental and scholarly concerns to illuminate a general problem.

I spoke with the school's principal for instruction about my desire to conduct research in order to find out what was going on. As the recipient of discipline problems that teachers cannot handle and the mediator between the school and home, a principal is often more aware of these difficulties than many others. Partly for this reason, the principal encouraged my project—also because she told me she had just spent six weeks working with several black girls who had been disrupting the classroom by challenging their white teachers with insubordination, for example, insolently moving a shoulder away from the teacher or thrusting out a chin toward her.[28] Moreover, one of HPES's goals was to bring white and black parents together with its staff to work through many problems for which there are no easy solutions. As a parent and researcher, I was encouraged to try to help. My own questions and pursuit of scholarly understanding merged with the problem-solving needs of the school.

My initial hypothesis was that blacks and whites at HPES have different communication styles (especially nonverbal ones) related to how friendships are initiated, sustained, and terminated, as well as how conflicts are handled and did not understand each other's nonverbal communication. These group patterns appear when a minority representation reaches 50 percent of a classroom. After reviewing more than 120 desegregation studies, St. John had proposed a 40 percent maximum minority enrollment before the majority might feel threatened.[27] This suggests that when minority members were outnumbered in a school setting, their dissonant cultural expression might be inhibited.

But at the outset of my involvement in the school as a researcher, my observations and children's reports raised some questions that I never thought to ask. By way of illustration, "See what I mean? That hurt! And it would hurt you too!" My son Aaron, a star goalie on a championship soccer team and generally a good athlete, had just run after the ball. A black child also raced for it. Aaron reached the ball first. The other boy, taller and heavier, pushed him aside to grab it. Then the black youngster kicked Aaron's buttocks so hard that he lurched painfully forward and blanched. I was observing playground social interaction that day. On other days, I had observed this particular black boy, as well as a few others, behave the same way toward other children. Aaron had told me more than once over a five-month period that blacks did not "play nicely"; they were "mean." I had offered possible reasons for this kind of behavior and encouraged taking various perspectives on the problem. I had pointed out that all children of whatever color sometimes misbehave. But Aaron's own everyday experiences in the classroom, in the halls and lunchroom, and on the playground—such as that just recounted—convinced him that blacks—boys and girls—at HPES behaved differently.

9

I did not observe gang activity among the children in the fourth grade; however, I did stumble onto a third-grade intraracial fight involving two groups. Two black girls started arguing about a jump rope game. Rachel, known to be hot tempered, and Sheniqua, known not to take anything from anyone, began fighting. A circle of black girls formed around them. Some of the girls jumped up and down ecstatically cheering the combatants. Each contestant had an ally who entered the arena to hit her opponent. Two teachers broke up the fight, each restraining one of the contestants in a huglike hold. Too busy to find out the cause of the fight, adults treated the symptoms. Black and white children witnessed this episode.

I soon discovered that my initial hypothesis that children of different backgrounds misunderstood each other turned out to be only partly true. Children understood many of the messages. The problem was that they did not like them or how they were sent. These messages and modes of communication created anxiety and fear.

From my initial involvement in the school, these additional questions came to the fore: What are some of the specific problems in the educational setting that impede equalizing resources and consequent academic achievement opportunities? How do the initial and natural suspicions of strangers develop into negative categorizations? To what extent are victim and sender of aggressive messages and styles the same? How does the school devise means to protect the victims and promote teaching, learning, and civility?

The four contrasting pairs of black and white, low and middle income, neighborhood friendship networks and strangers, and children and adults that appear in the story are not always separated, but the reader should keep them in mind.[29] While each part of a pair initially locks a child out of other interaction groups, negotiational patterns often occur that interweave the pairs.

The origin of a study influences its focus; no study is bias-free. I am not the first researcher personally to be involved in a school she or he is studying. While being an insider provides access to knowledge not available to the outsider, the involvement creates biases that warrant introspection.

As a white woman with two children in a magnet school, which my husband and I chose as offering the best public educational opportunity, I bring a particular perspective to the study. As an adult and parent, I have been guilty of insensitivity to our boys' sensibilities and their ways of looking at the world. I sometimes lack empathy for their immediate feelings of pleasure, pain, and anxiety or view their world through my historical perspectives, personal background, and visions of change.

Nevertheless, having experienced some discrimination as a minority group member in sex, age, religion, ethnicity, expression of viewpoint, and color, I am at least *somewhat* sensitive to what others must feel as an outsider and object of aggression.

Having taught in junior high and secondary schools and consulted for the public school systems of Los Angeles, New York City, Philadelphia, Lansing, Englewood, Montgomery County, and at the private Gill School, I had first-hand knowledge of the difficulties that faculty and staff face in communicating subject matter, providing affective training, and relating to parents and administrators. I realize that we often inadvertently convey incorrrect messages. Anthropological training helps a researcher take both insider and outsider points of view and make sense of them. Thus my background provides me with a framework for understanding children, ethnic diversity, discrimination, and education.

This study offers some prescriptive strategies for solving the problems identified, but it does not offer a tested blue print. Raising more questions than it answers, my research allows the reader to make interpretations and reach conclusions as it brings together various threads of an intricate fabric that may improve both educational and multicultural enterprises that characterize much of America. In the remainder of this chapter, I briefly sketch the theoretical underpinnings that guided data collection, descriptions, and analysis of the study. The research methods and procedures for participant observation, interviews, and film analyses are then presented.

Conceptual Guideposts[30]

A basic premise in anthropology is the examination of the feelings, thoughts, and actions of human beings, not as isolated bits and pieces but in a holistic context. A child's perceptions and performance in the classroom or on the playground interpenetrate other aspects of life.

Creations of their family culture, children are also creatively adapting individuals with their own mind, sensory apparatus, and historical time in which they grow up. They are not passive receivers of intended or accidental instruction. Therefore, it is important to see the broad setting and particular incidents that motivate their actions and shape their attitudes. How children perceive themselves, each other, and the rest of the world determines priorities in the way they conduct themselves. They assess situations, then they select strategies.[31] "It's how you really feel inside," said the black coprincipal at HPES speaking about what will make integration work. True, this is important; but there is a

11

prior question: What happens to foster and shape feelings harbored deep inside? Anthropologists attempt to get inside the "native's" world of meaning. In this study, the "natives" are American children.

Another concern of anthropology is the comparability of all human cultures, not the behavior but the underlying processes. Thus, in examining schooling, I attempt to describe and explain why there are group differences in thinking, feeling, and—what is of greatest concern here—communicating.

Communication is the social process of an individual or group sending a message to someone who understands it, infers the meaning, and responds. Sometimes interference occurs to block a sender's message. As a word may have different and ambiguous meanings, so may a nonverbal act. If one person pats another, it can be taken as loving, patronizing, condescending, or pushing. People can simultaneously send what on the surface seem to be contradictory messages, for example, saying no with words while smiling, which indicates that the no is not meant seriously. The verbal no might be understood but the smile overlooked.

The nonverbal channel of communication may be more important when there are discrepancies between the verbal and nonverbal. Because human beings are multisensory, they occasionally talk and listen, but more often, they look, feel, or move. The simplest form of power, the body, is the first and most natural human instrument. Consequently, children are especially physical and somatically sensitive. Ontogenetically, people discover and master their bodies in time, space, and effort patterns. Sight and movement are specific ways of entering into relationships. The intimate experience we have of our own bodies influences our responses to other humans. We never stop "speaking" with our bodies, which can be continually "read" even when we do not intend to send a message.[32]

People belong to both speech and movement communities. Motor patterns demarcate social groups just as anthropologists have discovered humans use plants and animals in totemism, economic products in caste social organization, and language in class relations. Ideas of group distinction transform into eye-catching, moving configurations to promote self-identity, prescribe social roles, or serve as catalysts to social action.

Every group has a cultural code of standards for behavior that determines the range and substance of overtures and responses and places a value on them. Sometimes the rules are tacit or ambiguous. Social competence is the knowledge of what to do, where, with whom, how, and when within a cultural code in order to attain goals.

We know that a dominant culture's verbal language, in its reflection and creation of cultural values, restricts or enlarges the ability to benefit from the educational process, shapes patterns of social stratification, and preserves the status quo. Nonverbal communicaton also affects social relationships.[33] A gaze indicates dominance patterns in many cultures. Turning one's eyes away might suggest subordination; not looking at someone may mean shutting out the person. In dominant American culture, an interested listener leans forward, a displeased one glances away or grimaces. Use of space sends messages and has its rules of etiquette about avoidance and approach. Male adults usually differ in their response to the proximity of an attractive female and to an unknown beefy male.

Although many individuals develop the communication skills to behave successfully in more than one culture, communication is difficult when people have different codes that are not mutually intelligible and their experiences differ markedly. When these individuals are unaware that there are different learned codes in operation, social relations often become worse: Responses are unpredictable and erratic.[34]

For example, when a low-income black child speaks too aggressively, moves too close, or touches too soon in a relationship, a white or black middle-class child may become uncomfortable. Middle-class children generally initiate friendships with friendly behavior. They may fight, make up, and resume the friendship. The sequence may vary among some low-income children who first fight to establish peer ranking and then become friends. When they act aggressively toward a middle-class child at the outset of a relationship, it is unlikely that a friendship will develop. Cross-cultural communication becomes difficult if people make the questionable assumption that if they speak the same verbal language, they also share other modes of communication.

For the analysis of cross-cultural communication in the setting studied here, the most valuable conceptual tools are provided by the theory of symbolic interaction.[35]

The theory has three key premises: Human beings behave toward each other on the basis of meanings they construct; these meanings emerge through social interaction; and meanings can be modified through interpersonal negotiation. The theory seeks to explain principles that determine appropriate behavior. Of particular importance throughout this study are the following concepts: (1) categorization, (2) self-fulfilling prophecy, (3) impression management, (4) likes attracting, (5) dissimilars rejecting and stigmatization, (6) nature of social interaction, (7) maturation, and (8) play.

(1) Categorization, or labeling, facilitates interaction. Learned from instruction and experience, categorization may be based on a number of human characteristics, such as color and other distinctive body features.

The perception of physical differences and expressions (for example, the use of territoriality, posture, and touch) is the basis for much cultural stereotyping. Stereotypes are oversimplified, uncritical beliefs about the characteristics and behavior of racial, ethnic, sexual, occupational, and deviant groups.

How we categorize an individual's actions affects our interpretation of the behavior and our response to it. For example, how we respond to a blow depends largely on how we perceive the cause. Was it an accident? Was it a cruel act by someone habitually prone to such aggression? Was it a friendly joke? Did the person mean to hit someone else? Labeling someone as friendly inhibits hostility, whereas categorizing a person as unfriendly facilitates aggressive or avoidance responses. The broader the category, the more inaccurate it is likely to be. If on the basis of color cue, we categorize another person as dangerous, it becomes difficult in most cases to check for other cues that we might associate with attractiveness. An impenetrable wall is set up.

(2) To a certain degree, all people harbor some incorrect expectations concerning others either because they have not yet encountered contradictory evidence that would cause them to change their expectations or they did not notice or explained away contradictory evidence. A person inaccurately defining a situation and having false expectations of another may behave in such a way as to make those expectations a reality.[36] This phenomenon of the self-fulfilling prophecy has been studied in some schools, where teachers' expectations influenced students' performances: Students whom teachers expected to do well did so, and vice versa.[37] However, teacher–student interaction is a two-way process: "Often the student conditions teacher behavior providing clues and provocation as much or more than the teacher conditions student behavior." Expectation effects occur in only one of three types of teachers, the "overreactor."[38]

(3) Both verbal and nonverbal languages carry meanings acquired at home and are at the core of a youngster's self-concept. Reactions of important others also contribute to self-identity in a continual process. In complex societies where there are a variety of roles that a person plays, identity formation can be complicated and difficult. This is especially the case for blacks and white women, who face double standards and limited opportunities: Equality is for everyone, but statistics on racial and gender achievements show a skew in favor of white males.

The need to give the right impression occurs among children just as it does among adults who play different roles: lover, parent, office

worker, community participant. At times, children pretend to be something other than what they are, and others respond to their bluff. When
put to the test, these children must live up to the image they have created
or develop a new one and receive different treatment. Children often
play several roles that may be contradictory, such as when a child plays a
student role and also the role of being one of the group.[39] Reference
group theory presumes that children respond to the norms, performance standards, and rewards salient in the peer group to which they
belong. The group acts as a frame of reference for self-evaluation,
attitude formation, and behavior.

A group under stress with limited resources will attempt to create a
feeling of self-worth by confronting threats to its identity in "defensive
structuring."[40] The process involves subordinating the individual in
cooperative group activity(such as playing particular games, occupying
special places apart from other groups). The body and its use or adornment become especially important if a group has few material possessions and little power, as is the case with children.

(4) People tend to like those who are similar to themselves. Shared
values reflect unspoken assumptions about rules of behavior. Agreement
about values provides individuals with validation for their own attitudes,
beliefs, and behavior. Therefore, those who share communication styles
better understand each other and are more certain of having harmonious interactions. Most of our activity occurs within relatively homogeneous groups, and social pressures often constrain an individual
member who is open and receptive to dissimilar others.

(5) Fearing the unknown, people often dislike those who are dissimilar from themselves; this attitude makes hostility or withdrawal
more likely. Focus on the contrasting and sometimes negative features
often helps individuals define their identity. Interaction between those
of dissimilar cultures is fraught with possibilities for misunderstandings.
Even when the same language is used by both, meanings given to the
same words may differ.[41] Individuals who do not fit certain categories
within particular social settings are often ostracized or picked on. As
stigmatized people,[42] somehow discredited in the eyes of others, they are
avoided by those individuals for whom they may be easy scapegoats. This
is the defense mechanism of "magically" getting rid of evil by projecting
it onto a person or group and attacking this object.

(6) The nature of group interaction affects attitudes and behavior.
Competition in academic, physical, or psychic realms may lead to aggres-

sion, whereas cooperation may develop positive feelings and interaction. Groups thus form on the basis of shared sentiments of solidarity.[43] Increased tolerance between blacks and whites was found to occur when interracial contact involved two groups of equal status cooperatively pursuing shared goals with the backing of laws, customs, and local offices.[44]

In competitive situations, because of repressed hostility, anger, suspiciousness, language differences, and problems of social maturation common to all children, a black counselor reported that a black child often has a greater burden in finding assertive self-expression than the white child. "The usual black response in a state of anxiety has been passive or aggressive—either say nothing or become loud, threatening, and abusive."[45] Furthermore, blacks have the burden of interacting with several groups, each with its distinctive communication style (for example, conventional middle-class white, nonconventional white, middle-class black, street black).

(7) Children's level of maturation affects their social interaction. Young children's thought is phenomenalistic—that is, it is the direct outcome of sense impressions—and as they develop, their perceptions become structured through increasing cognitive sophistication. "With their coherent view of the dominance relations in their group, they do not have to fight with each member in order to know their own position in the hierarchy."[46]

Children develop perceptual patterns through emotional involvement with peers that can be generalized to new relationships or new social situations. Thinking, shaped by home, school, neighborhood, and the mass media, helps them interpret personal experience. Historically, minorities have not been treated well in parts of dominant America and in the mass media. If children's phenomenological and cognitive experience with minorities is satisfactory, it counters negative messages about them. If a child's experience is unsatisfactory, the messages reinforce the experience.

With maturation, children may be able to place themselves mentally in others' positions. This role-taking ability is important in overcoming egocentrism (children's tendency to believe that whatever they are thinking, feeling, or seeing, is also thought, felt, or seen by everyone else)[47] and ethnocentrism (the tendency to evaluate other cultures less favorably than one's own).

(8) Play, a form of social interaction in which children work through values, beliefs, attitudes, and social roles in their society, allows exten-

sions, exaggerations, and constrictions of these roles. Children deal with present conflicts and anticipate future contests in play. It is the first activity in which a child has a chance of finding a high place in a prestigious hierarchy. Thus play, including play aggression, has adaptive functions.[48] Play is not merely an imitation of life; it helps children learn to anticipate and test ways of coping in a relatively safe arena. Shock of the unknown may cause great stress. To counter this, Nigeria's Ubakala youth and adults used dance-plays to communicate aspects of their world view, to order social relations, mediate conflict, and introduce change.[49]

Approach to Knowledge

I used some of the standard ethnographic research methods common in traditional fieldwork settings in which anthropologists may be the first to study a particular culture. These methods involve learning as much about a site as possible, gaining access, living among and interacting with the people one studies, building rapport and trust with the community, observing behavior, and speaking with informants. Working in one's own culture required modifications to meet new ethical and situational requirements.[50]

Being a casual parental observer in the school for five months during 1977 alerted me to problems of multicultural communication that existed at HPES. A survey of the literature on multicultural education indicated that these difficulties loomed larger elsewhere. During the summer, I met with school and district administrators to outline the study. The school principal for instruction was enthusiastic about the study because she believed that insiders often do not see all problems and opportunities and are "lulled into a false sense of security and complacency."

A black educator had conducted a one-week in-service workshop to assist HPES with its new desegregation and continued coming to HPES once every six weeks for a two-year period. However, there was staff turnover, and some of the new teachers and assistants had little, if any, training to work effectively with multicultural student bodies. Moreover, since its inception, the school changed its emphasis in multicultural relations from working with staff adults to working with the children.

I used several data collection and analysis methods. Each method had its limitations that may unduly influence the data. The shortcomings of one technique may, however, be compensated for by using several.

Through participant observation, I became involved in the day-to-day activities of the school to formulate questions for further investigation. I had casual discussions with students, teachers, other school personnel, and parents and conducted systematic interviews with students. In addition, I used historical documents, videotapes, and films that an assistant and I made at the school, surveys of parent satisfaction with the school, and analyzed key incidents, only some of which came to the attention of the school administration. Because the school reflects the dynamics of the larger society and the creative interplay between children of different cultures, key incidents, "epitomize underlying relationships which quantifying methods never reveal."[51] By participating in and observing HPES life for three-fifths of the days in a school year, I was able to learn if children's perceptions in the aggregate had validity; that is, if youngsters actually did what was reported.

In September 1977, one of the principals distributed a letter explaining my presence to all school personnel. We invited teachers to speak about the study. Following this, the school sent my letter to parents explaining the study, which we decided to call Project Understanding, and requesting permission for prospective student respondents to participate.

On the opening day of the 1977–78 school year, I began the first phase of the study: observing school behavior and informal interviewing. One of my goals was to obtain a broad picture of the behavior of students, staff, parents, and communities involved with the school; another goal was to identify the patterns of black–white association. A third was to identify similarities and differences in communicative behavior and social interaction. After I conducted systematic interviews with students, I made a second round of qualitative observations to find out the extent to which children's perceptions of behavior corresponded to mine.

Observations of the complexity of naturally occurring actions of large numbers of people in a school setting have limitations. I was unable to record everything. Periodic graduate student assistance and audiovisual records (made by the HPES staff member for publicity) were useful in helping me try to counteract the tendency to selectively notice, record, label, and evaluate events. I also looked for data that undercut my developing assessment of a situation. I visited the five second-, fourth-, and sixth-grade classes while they were engaged in formal academic activities, approximately ten hours each. Over the course of the school year, I observed children in these and other grades at play, in the halls, at lunch, and on field trips. Although a single observation might be unique, repeated observations suggest a pattern. For this reason, I observed at different times, on different days of the week, and in different places over an extended period of a year.

I considered the quality of a behavior and its repercussion to be more important than its frequency of occurrence. For example, when Fred got into a few fights and established a dominant position, these incidents became school lore and served to guide children's interactions. Fred did not have to fight again, nor did he choose to because the principal threatened to expel him if he did. In short, systematic qualitative research to identify the issues is a necessary precursor to quantitative research. From analytic surveys of educational research, investigators have concluded that the kinds of variables researchers generally manipulate are in fact irrelevant or of small importance in this setting.[52]

I viewed interactions of "situational frames" (what happens in a particular instance), "action chains" (what happens sequentially over time), and history (prior situational frames and action chains). My observations occurred somewhere in the midst of an ongoing stream of behavior that might have begun hours, days, weeks, months, or years earlier. For instance, some fights among girls had their inception in resentment about boy–girl, black–white relations in the previous grade. Students' verbal reports complemented my observations and put them in perspective.

The results of my preliminary observations and informal discussions surprised me. Over the initial eight-week period, I identified alliance (groups of children acting in unison), patron–client (a strong child protecting a weaker one in exchange for respect or favors), and gang (an antisocial group) behavior. I expected such behavior among teenagers, not elementary school children. What I had seen differed markedly from reports of student activities made by some school personnel and parents.

After hearing adults deny the kinds of alliance, patron–client, and gang relations I had witnessed, I decided to conduct systematic interviews with the children to "get inside" their worlds of meaning. Perhaps adults misinterpreted the students' acts, were unaware of them, or knew about what happened but preferred not to admit it.

In September, I began developing the questions I would ask representative groups of students. I did not use classroom questionnaires. Since children's reading comprehension varied considerably and they often copied each others' answers or talked about them, I designed the interview to try to bring to the surface the main ideas in children's minds rather than imposing my own. The questions I developed after the first series of observations often evoked descriptions of key incidents that epitomized underlying problems. I probed when I was not sure what a child meant: "Could you explain a little more?" "What do you mean?" "Really? "What happened?" Such questions also sustained the flow of replies.

The questions I asked explored children's understandings of expressions of friendship and anger, social interactions among themselves and with teachers, likes and dislikes concerning the school and teachers, notions of appropriate behavior and how to handle misbehavior, causes of fights, and fears. I showed the questions to the principals, the district administrator supervising the project, and special education teachers who worked with slow learners for suggestions about content and speech usage that children from different cultures would best understand. After pretesting the questionnaire with black and white boys and girls in grades 2, 4, and 6, I revised it. Then I began interviewing 120 students in a random sample stratified on the bases of sex, race, and three grades chosen to obtain a range of levels of cognitive and social development. In this sample, students in each of the grades under study were identified according to race and gender in order to form four race–gender categories: black male, black female, white male, and white female. An equal number of students were selected randomly, each person having an equal chance of being selected, from each of the categories within each of the grades. This representative sampling helped discover and verify knowledge as well as generate insight that is inconsistent with the investigator's preconceptions or hunches. There were nine substitutions in the sample: One white parent did not want her timid second-grade daughter to participate; substitutions were also made for two second-grade black boys, a fourth-grade black boy and black girl, and three sixth-grade black girls and one black boy. There was some criticism that the school spent too much time testing and not enough teaching. Five of the black students whose parents refused permission to participate were reputed by teachers to be discipline problems and by their grade-level peers to be "tough kids."

Teachers informed me of the days and hours when it would be most appropriate for me to talk with their students so that they would not miss essential work. I was known to many of the children as a visiting mother who had participated in many school activities. At the beginning of the approximately fifteen-to-twenty-minute interview, I told each child I was writing a story about HPES and wanted to know from the student's point of view what it was like to be a student at this school. I asked the children if they would share thoughts with me. No one refused. I usually interviewed students in a room I called my "hidey hole" after a special place described in a children's story book. Carpeted on the floors and walls and usually used for special record and video listening, this room has the virtues of being generally available, unique, private, and quiet. The informality (I dressed casually, we had candy, and we sat wherever the child preferred—on the floor, cushions, or chairs—was conducive to free expression.[53] On exceptionally nice days, we chatted outdoors.

Because I am adult and white;[54] some children might have been reserved in telling their story about life at HPES. Given apprehension over being evaluated, we might expect the answers to be more in line with school norms in order to minimize risks of unfavorable assessment. Thus, the antischool behavior of aggression and class disruption might be greater than reported.[55] On the other hand, most children easily have rapport with, and confidence in, a pleasant, attentive stranger who tries to provide no cues of disagreement. Most children appeared to enjoy the questions and to speak frankly. When I asked, "What did you think about these questions?" one child told me he thought they were "nosy;" others thought they were "fun," "hard," "okay." Two children thought they were "weird;" only one black sixth-grade boy said they were "no good."

I taped the interviews, explaining to the children that I could not write as rapidly as they could speak and would spend more time than their teachers wanted them to be away from class if I tried. I assured respondents that their answers would be kept confidential and no child would be identified by name. At the end of the sixteen questions, I asked the children if they thought there were questions I did not ask that would give me an idea of what it was like to be a student at HPES. I asked the child whatever question was proposed. If children wanted to hear themselves, I played back some of the recording. The taped interviews were later transcribed and checked by someone other than the transcriber. The quotations in this book are verbatim and reflect both local expressions and the children's developing vocabulary.

There was remarkable consistency in answers among age, sex, and racial groups. There were some contradictions within a child's own answers to different questions. These appear to reflect the student's perceptions of what school authorities believe is appropriate and what actually occurs. If on their interview day, children had observed or participated in an incident relevant to one of the questions, they usually described it to me with great relish. Children's reports helped to focus further research observations. I especially tried to observe children who were nominated relatively frequently by their peers as being toughs and feared. They were the individuals who created behavior problems and caused some black and white children to denigrate blacks as a group. Children's perceptions are not always accurate, and some perceived the same situation differently. However, when these insiders tend toward a consensus that is validated by outsider observations and school personnel and parent reports of actual behavior, a more truthful picture begins to emerge than is possible to obtain from either insider or outsider views alone.

When a teacher was hired about a month into the school year to monitor what was first called a discipline room (and in September 1978, was referred to as an alternative room), I prepared a report form to be filled out for each student sent to her to work quietly, talk over difficulties, or develop a plan for improved school work or social relations. The purpose of the form was to try to identify what kinds of behavior were proving intractable for teachers to handle in the classroom.

What was the effect of my presence at HPES? Because the school was born in the limelight and continued to be watched, children and teachers were accustomed to being in the public eye. HPES had a continual flow of visitors and student teachers. Parents participated in parent–teacher activities, parent groups, special school trips and programs, and an organized volunteer program to assist the instructional process. Thus, in my role as parent, I was a natural participant-observer in the school community. I assisted on field trips, providing the extra necessary adult supervision, volunteered to send cookies for parties and exotic food for health studies, and brought in "dangerous" weapons (swords) for my children's show-and-tell period.

Youngsters not in the sample who returned permission slips allowing them to participate in Project Understanding frequently asked, "When are you going to take me, Mrs. Hanna?" Several children did not know what I was doing. Some teachers had not discussed the project, or the children had been absent when they did. I explained my presence, and children thought it was "neat" that adults wanted to hear what they had to say. A few proposed titles for the study report.

Most of the teachers expressed great interest in what I was learning and in reading the report. Their openness mirrored the principals' hopes for an outsider's perspective on what the educational enterprise was all about. Because there had been parents with axes to grind who monitored the school, some teachers expressed anxiety to the administrators and other teachers about my presence. Perhaps a few teachers were insecure about their ability to manage their own classrooms. An anthropologist who studied a school in her home community felt that some teachers feared sharing their children's affection with an outsider.[56] I became a sounding board for a few frustrated teachers and parents. Some teachers excused any problem and accepted difficulties as par for the course; others were less sanguine. Informal comments made in the hall or lunchroom as we passed were often revealing.

NOTES

1.   In 1979, eight black parents, alleging that after twenty-five years school officials in Topeka, Kansas, have failed to end segregation, requested that the Federal District Court reopen the historic case. Bell (1980) and his colleagues believe that the "resurrected Brown litigation speaks much for the persistence of those who believe even now that racial remedies are the answer and also reveals, unfortunately, their rigidity and their unwillingness to face facts long plain to all who will see." Ron Edmonds, a black educator from Harvard, has been especially vocal in arguing that desegregation is unimportant. He calls for deep reforms in the delivery of public instruction.

2.   In a detailed analysis of the *Bradley* v. *Milliken* court transcripts from the perspective of the logic and quality of the testimony on Detroit residential and educational segregation, Wolf (1981:250) shows the testimony from social science experts to be a swamp of illogic, inconsistency, distortion, and omission. She concludes that as the line between legal and ideological–moral issues blurred, the courts may well have been "willing victim of a well-coordinated ideological crusade" to use school desegregation as a practical mechanism to alter black–white power relations in the social fabric of the nation.

Wolters, adducing evidence from five school districts whose litigation was consolidated for the Supreme Court's 1954 decision, concludes that the court decisions have mostly resulted in a failed policy. He places blame for white flight, heightened racial tensions, and a general deterioration in standards of behavior and school work on disingenuous federal judges and naïve educational reformers who instead of interpreting Brown to require an end to racial discrimination took the ruling to prohibit racially neutral policies that do not promote a specified proportion of racial mixing. The courts did not rule on whether race was used to prevent children from attending public schools in their districts but on failure to take affirmative color conscious action to ensure an even dispersion of black and white. Illegal public assignment of pupils on the basis of race paradoxically became the rationale for pupil assignment (1984). See also Kluger 1976; Horowitz 1977; Marty 1977; Weinberg 1977; and on criticism of court action: Wollenberg 1977.

3.   See Wilking 1977; Rist 1979; *The Black Scholar*, no. 1 (September/October 1979). The new climate, in contrast with the turbulent agenda created in the 1950s and 1960s deemphasized the responsibility of government to resolve the problems. Fault and responsibility, it is argued must not be presumed to go hand-in-hand (Loury 1985).

4.   Wegmann (1977) speaks of "anticipatory nonentrance," which means acting to avoid a situation in which individuals would be likely to withdraw their children from a school. See also Frey 1979; Goodman 1979.

5.   By 1980 the proportion of white students in the Los Angeles school district had fallen from 56 percent in 1966 to less than 29 percent; in Detroit, whites comprised less than 20 percent of the pupils compared with more than 50 percent ten years earlier; in Chicago, the proportion of white students enrolled has dropped from 26.8 percent to 18.3 percent in five years; the proportion of whites in St. Louis was less than 20 percent, and in Houston, less than 29 percent. Desegregation planners have fewer and fewer whites to mix with blacks (Lindsey 1980).

6. The *New York Times*/CBS News poll in 1981 reported that 87 percent of white respondents opposed busing for desegregation and 59 percent of the blacks opposed it (Clymer 1981:B7).

7. Studies that begin to examine aspects of student life include Willie (1973), Schafft (1976); Silverstein and Krate (1975), McDermott (1976), Rist (1978, 1979), Metz (1978); and case studies supported by the National Institute of Education (see Wax 1980): Clement et al. (1979), Collins and Noblit (1978), Ianni et al. (1978), Scherer and Slawski (1978), and Schofield with Sagar (1978); *Anthropology and Education Quarterly* 9, no. 4 (1978).

8. See *Art Education* (special issue: Art and the Mind), March 1983.

9. McGrath 1978.

10. Note that measures of social class often fail to meld parent's education, occupational status, income, and—what may be of critical importance—number of parents in the household, parent–child interaction, religious institutional involvement, and immigrant/nonimmigrant status. A National Association of Elementary School Principals/Charles Kettering Foundation study found that children from one-parent families, children who have divorced parents, lost a parent to death, or been born to single women, are twice as likely to do poorly in elementary school and far more likely to have behavior and discipline problems. In high school, they were three times as likely to be expelled and twice as likely to drop out (Hechinger 1980). The census figures show that 50 percent of all black children live in single-family homes, 12 percent where neither biological parents is present, and 30 percent with no parent in the work force.

11. See also Hollingshead (1949), Heider (1971), Kunz and Peterson (1977), Bradley and Bradley (1977), and Scarr and Weinberg (1978).

12. See Crain and Mahard 1978:45–48. A positive effect of higher socio-economic status on academic achievement exists "at virtually every stage in the educational cycle" (Eckland and Henderson 1981:42–43, 93–98).

13. Biddle and Slade 1982.

14. Jones 1984.

15. For example, Hare (1977, 1978) found that differences in elementary school children's self-esteem were attributable to class rather than race. Five years after the national safe school study, a report from the first wave of the National Center for Education Statistics *High School and Beyond* (1980), a long-itudinal study of U.S. high school seniors and sophomores, found behavioral differences between low-income and middle-income students. Low-income status and misbehavior were associated with poor course grades. Moreover, the presence of both parents in the home who keep track of their child's activities in and out of school has the most inhibiting effect on misbehavior (absenteeism, use of drugs, class cutting, vandalism of school property, robbery or theft, verbal abuse of teachers, physical conflicts among students, conflicts between students and teachers, student possession of weapons, rape or attempted rape (DiPrete et al. 1982:37, 71). See also Kronus 1971 on blacks and whites at similar income levels developing similar life styles.

16. In Boston, Sennett and Cobb 1973; in West Virginia, Cosnow 1979; and in England, Willis 1977, Hakken 1978, Rutter et al. 1979; and in desegregated schools, Cassell 1978:9, Wax 1980, Schofield 1982, and Finkelstein and Haskins 1983.

17. Wolters 1984:58–59.

18. See Giles 1978, Maeroff 1981. After Federal District Judge W. Arthur Garrity, Jr., ordered busing in Boston in June 1974, white school enrollment

dropped from 58,000 to 29,000. This figure exceeded that predicted due to normal yearly losses by maybe 7 percent according to Christine Rossell or 50 percent from the estimates of the court-appointed experts Dentler and Scott (1981).

19. See Runkell 1977, Caditz 1976.

20. Quoted in Williams 1985.

21. Quoted in Muscatine 1981:B1.

22. Quoted in Burgess 1981:C1.

23. Finkelstein and Haskins 1983.

24. See Rubin 1976, Evans 1978, Hechinger 1979a, Williams 1979, and Feinberg 1980. In the 1970s the nonsectarian private school enrollment increased by 60 percent at the same time that the number of U.S. school-aged children diminished to 43.7, or nearly 2 million (Sewall et al. 1979). Black enrollment in Catholic schools increased from 4.8 to 7.7 percent (NCEA 1979). The decline of Catholics in the schools from 95 percent in 1970 to about 91 percent in 1978 is in great part due to the increased percentage of black students who are not Catholics. By 1986–87 black enrollment was 8.9 percent, and Catholic enrollment had dropped to 88 percent (NCEA 1987).

25. Coles 1967:275.

26. Contrary to the ideal desegregation model, the literature substantiates the fact that racial stereotypes were not reduced nor tolerance increased among children as a result of desegregation school experiences (Armor 1972; Stephan 1978). Sheehan and Marcus (1977) report that in the Dallas school district, Anglo (nonhispanic white) students in desegregated schools were more prejudiced against blacks than Anglos attending predominantly white schools. (Minority black and hispanic students became less prejudiced after increased exposure to Anglos.) Supporting this study is one of a Boston school (Useem 1977) located in a relatively affluent liberal suburb that volunteered for an integration program to which a small number of academically self-motivated blacks were voluntarily bused. White students who did not experience much interracial classroom contact were the most favorable. The Boston study concluded that those whites who ranked higher in the hierarchy of ability groups, grade averages, and socioeconomic status were less likely to have positive attitudes toward blacks on the basis of contact in the classroom. It was not a case of children being "meddled." It may have been the special attention given to the blacks, the change of pace to accommodate their needs, or the expectation that blacks would require these (see Rosenfield et al. 1981).

Researchers in Florida found little difference in expression of attitudes toward blacks between the whites who avoided desegregation and those who complied with this public policy. Although higher-class families tend to have more favorable attitudes toward neighborhood integration, they are concerned about their children attending schools where aggression is common: 45 percent of the compliers reported that their children had experienced aggressive incidents. However, only the higher-class families had economic means to send children to private school. Note that more than 80 percent of all the Florida white respondents did not believe that the government had a legitimate right to tell them where to send their children to school (Cataldo et al. 1978:44).

27. St. John 1975.

28. Long et al. (1976) argue for the need to observe what a child says nonverbally. The child learns that "the spoken word can be held against him as self-incriminating evidence." The dominant culture and its authority figures are

verbally oriented; nevertheless, their nonverbal behavior contributes to student learning [Galloway 1976; *Theory into Practice* 16(3) (June 1977)].

29.   I use the words *black* and *white* in this study. The courts mandated a fifty-fifty black to white ratio in each classroom at HPES for each sex. Adults often think in terms of *black* and *white,* and children do also (Taylor 1978). But as the school recognized, color labels are in many ways insidious misnomers. The school used the terms *neighborhood* for black and *volunteer* for white. Yet many children did not understand the meaning of these glosses. *Neighborhood* is a term that coincided with the low-income families that lived in the area surrounding the school.

30.   The theoretical perspectives underlying this study are derived from anthropological tenets as well as symbolic interaction. The inquiry draws on studies of communication approached structurally (Ray Birdwhistell, Albert Scheflen, Paul Ekman), sociologically (Dell Hymes, Erving Goffman), symbolically (Herbert Blumer, O. Duncan, Victor Turner), and ethologically (Robert Hinde, Michael Chance, Owen Aldis).

31.   Current theoretical models portray children as actively constructing social knowledge out of their unique experiences, conceptual abilities, and limitations (Shantz 1975; Glick 1978 et al.).

32.   The importance of movement in human perception is seen in language acquisition (Bloom 1976). Children of deaf, signing parents were found to begin using two-sign sentences six to ten months earlier than children uttering two-word spoken sentences (Stokoe 1976:507). According to a longitudinal study of four children, among the names of objects that children learned first were moving things, such as people, pets, and balls. Action events were named prior to static ones in language development. This pattern even has an analog in the origins of "new languages"—pidgins and creoles. As a child's speech develops, so does an extensive repertoire of nonverbal means of communication. Speech is actually serial motor activity built on a fundamental base of nonverbal communication.

Piaget observed that

> A symbolic function exists which is broader than language . . . language is not enough to explain thought, because the structures that characterize thought have their roots in action and in sensorimotor mechanisms that are deeper than linguistics. It is also evident that the more the structures of thought are refined, the more language is necessary for the achievement of this elaboration. Language is thus a necessary but not a sufficient condition of logical operations (1968:91).

33.   Cf. Lawton 1968.

34.   See Birdwhistell 1970, Szwed 1975, O'Malley 1977, Kochman 1981, and Halberstadt 1985.

35.   The theory that has evolved is grounded in the social psychology of George H. Mead and sociology of Blumer (1969). Concern is with discovering aspects of the empirical world: the creation, meaning, structure, and use of symbolic behavior in human social relations. Discovery occurs by naturalistically and systematically observing and ordering events as well as eliciting perspectives of participants in these social relations.

36.   Merton 1948, 1957.

37.   Rosenthal and Jacobson 1968; Word, et al. 1974.

38.   Brophy and Good 1974:12, 115–16, passim. See also Pilling and Pringle 1978; Wolf 1981:117–18.

39. Directing us to look at how individuals present themselves in everyday life, Goffman speaks of the process of fabrication, an "intention of effort of one or more individuals to manage activity so that a party of one or more others will be induced to have a false belief about what it is that is actually going on" (1974:83).

Bernstein (1970:30) pointed out that understanding children's involvement in their roles as student must take into consideration family, age group, and school work and show the relationships among them.

40. Siegel 1970.

41. Cf. Thompson 1973:115.

42. Goffman 1963.

43. Cf. Vincent 1974; Hanna 1979, 1986b; and Hanna and Hanna 1981 on the creation of ethnic identities.

44. See Allport 1954; Pettigrew 1971; Useem 1977. In their assessment of the social psychology of heterogeneous schools, Pettigrew (1974) noted that black college students performed best when they anticipated comparison with other blacks, less well when they anticipated comparison with whites, and least well when no comparison at all was anticipated. However, the acceptance of blacks by white classmates and teachers was found to have "a social facilitation effect upon their ability to learn." Thus, the social context of perceived threat or acceptance is critical to achievement.

45. Cheek 1976:65.

46. Omark and Edelman 1976:121.

47. Piaget 1926.

48. Aldis 1975.

49. See Sutton-Smith 1977, Erikson 1977, Schwartzman 1978, Hanna 1976, 1988a. New Mexico's Mescalero Apache Indian children reflected traditional cultural patterns in playing tag (Farrer 1981). In contrast with Anglo-American tag in the same school, circularity characterized their game movements. Traditional homes and dance patterns were circular; the society was egalitarian, as was the circle pattern (tribal decisions are made by consensus). Bodies touched during the tag game. In Apache culture, friends often touched each others' arms when speaking; they sat with their bodies touching at the hips, arms and shoulders; and women danced shoulder-to-shoulder. Apache children did not negotiate or call out rules during the game. A child who misbehaved was ignored or restrained if the infraction was great. Mirroring the strong Apache family orientation, participants in the game were usually cousins. The implications are that teachers should draw on Native American understandings and resources to educate Apache children more effectively. Teachers, for example, might provide role models so that children learn by observation, use the disciplinary tactic of removing an offending child from the group, permit physical closeness and group work among relatives, and arrange desks in circles instead of rows to provide security in the educational setting, which is in many ways distinct from the home.

50. Spindler 1970, 1982; Wiseman 1974; Dillman 1977; Cassell 1977.

51. Leacock 1977:155.

52. Averch et al. 1972; Torbet 1981.

53. Cf. Smith and Geoffrey 1968:6, Wax 1980:20, Silverstein and Krate 1975:152.

54. However, Williams and Morland (1976), in their summary of studies of

children's perceptions of race and color, found no difference between responses given to black or white interviewers.

55.   Although a student might try to aggress by shocking, it does not seem likely, given the nature of the interview and the number of children who reported contrary behavior, much of which I also observed.

56.   Schafft 1976.

2

TERRORISM, FIRE BOMBING, AND CREATION

SCHOOLS in the United States do not exist as isolated entities. As part of the public education tradition of local control, they tend to reflect the values and experiences of the communities that surround them. Schools may also reflect the communities of the students who are bused to them. Therefore, a brief overview of the development of the Hamilton Park community in Dallas[1] will illuminate the case study material that follows.

Having characteristics of the South and West, Dallas is an island of recent economic and cultural development. It is more traditional than many other cities of its size. Dallas and the adjacent city of Richardson accept the use of adult authority to discipline children, dislike federal intervention, and have a short history of public conflict about different ideas. There is a German immigrant religious tradition of ritualistic pietism, an ethic for being optimistic, and fear of the pessimistic (Ernest Gotts, personal communication).

Hamilton Park Elementary School is part of RISD; school district and municipal units do not coincide. The RISD covers an area of high residential, shopping center, and office building growth; electronics, insurance, and regional distribution figure prominently. Professionals in these occupations, more conservative than medicine, law, teaching, and journalism, are less conservative than some of the established "bible-belt" businessmen. Old time Texans, long-term Dallasites, and newcomers now mingle. Increased ethnic group heterogeneity is evident in the range of produce sold in the grocery stores for Italians, Greeks, Vietnamese, Koreans, and Indians, in addition to the Czechs, Germans, Polish, Mexicans, and blacks who have been in the area for some time.

Creation of a Black Community

The court-ordered integration of the formerly segregated black Hamilton Park School evoked strong hostility on the part of many

29

community residents. The history of blacks in Dallas, similar to their history elsewhere in the United States, helps explain why. Blacks were forced to live in segregated places, often with some self-governance. When whites realized the value of areas inhabited by blacks for roads, airports, and white residences or when black areas spread too close, whites pushed them out. Homes were bombed and water wells were contaminated, as revealed in the following letter in a 1948 issue of the *Dallas News:*

> We are located near Forest Lane and Coit Road. We work in the nearby city of Dallas. This settlement was once [in the mid-1930s] located near Forest Lane and Hillcrest. We had a school with concrete basement and water well. Our church was located on Forest Lane and Hillcrest. Whites began building nearby. They promised us, if we would move our church and school to a new location, we would not be bothered any more. We agreed. Today, our school has been partly wrecked and our children are drinking water from an old tin tank. . . . Now we are told that we are in the path of the Central Boulevard and we must move onward. What we want to know is, when and where will we be secure. It is so cruel to wreck our homes when the boulevard can go east of us. There is no room in the city for us. It is not right to wreck our homes when we have no place to go.[2]

Within three months of Warren Leslie's May 3, 1948 *News* report, "Disappearing Act: Central Work to Doom Tiny Negro Settlement," the one-story houses vanished. The city had given warning of the impending move the previous year and then gave blacks little compensation for their acreage, ignoring the cost of land improvement. Although the boulevard left the schoolhouse and one of the churches untouched, residents' relocation on the other side of Coit Road was distant from electric lights, telephones, and transportation. Furthermore, the ground was low and in a flood area. The black optometrist Dr. J. O. Chisum charged that his people were being put out of their homes "by people to whom money is god." The push continues, with mixed success. The black Mt. Pisgah Missionary Baptist Church, built in 1888 in what was then isolated farmland by exslaves, became surrounded by costly, white, single-dwelling residences; expensive town houses; and upper-income apartments. White developers wanted the church property at 1400 Preston Road, a prestigious address, and the city planned to widen and extend Spring Valley Road, a street that intersects Preston Road, to accommodate development. Ten feet of land would be necessary to save the church, which had a membership of about 250 in 1977. However, a large white-owned corporation that purchased land adjacent to the church did not want its own land used for road rerouting. When Spring Valley Road was widened in 1980, it created so much congestion and came so close to the church that entry and exit were difficult in view of a simultaneous explosion of the church membership (it reached approximately 1,000 by 1987). Consequently, in 1982, the church leased its property to a smaller congregation and relocated on 11611 Webb Chapel Road in a building situated in a predominantly white neighborhood, by buying out yet another congregation.

During the 1950s, there was an economic boom in Dallas. Population increased, but housing opportunities did not expand. The two defense plants, Chance Vought and Temco, which became LTV (Ling, Temco, Vought), contributed to new employment. The black population also grew because of new job and salary opportunities. Agricultural mechanization sent many East Texans to the city, and soldiers stationed in the South chose to settle in Dallas and use the skills they had acquired while in the service. As in the past, men and women from Louisiana, the Carolinas, Kentucky, Tennessee, Oklahoma, Alabama, and elsewhere moved to the city in pursuit of bread, work, freedom, and dignity. Blacks could not live in Grand Prairie where there was employment but they were confined to two areas: West Dallas was one small pocket, the other where most of the blacks lived was South Dallas, an area bounded by Harwood to the West, Fair Park to the East, Grand Avenue to the North, and Hatcher and Warren to the South.

With a natural population growth compounded by the wartime baby boom and rural-urban migration, an aneurism developed in South Dallas. The black population in Dallas increased from about 50,000 in 1940 to 80,000 in 1950. Among these 30,000 people were about 8,000 families in need of housing. Approximately 21,000 families crowded into 14,000 dwelling units. Blacks began to move north toward Peabody. In 1951 there was a concentrated outburst of violence. It began with three bombings on a Sunday night in 1951 of black-owned property in a heretofore predominantly white area, part of nine unsolved explosions within a year. A home was bombed just before builders had completed it. In February of the previous year, a $6,000 home recently purchased by a black in a white section just beyond a large black section was bombed. A total of eleven bombings executed without warning as well as mysterious fires rocked homes in Dallas within an eighteen-month period, leaving destruction in an eight-square-mile black neighborhood once occupied by white residents.

The conflict was heated. Police, bemoaning the lack of cooperation in the bombing investigation, suggested that white residents in the neighborhoods where the blasts occurred might be involved (some Dallas old-timers believed the bombs were made in white churches) or that blacks might be encouraging violence to keep trouble stirred up; the police also considered the possibility of maniacs seeking to overthrow the

31

government. A. Maceo Smith, regional race relations administrator for the FHA and a civic leader in the 1950s, believed the bombing and fire incidents were part of a conspiracy.

Texas Rangers entered the case. Numerous committees and the Dallas City Council met to consider the problem. Because law enforcement agencies could not find perpetrators, the city council, as well as a builder of a bomb-damaged FHA-approved house for blacks, called on the FBI to intervene. Lacking jurisdiction, it declined.

Rev. E. C. Estell, president of the Dallas Council of Negro Organizations, called for a special grand jury. The black community, he argued, should not get the impression it was being abandoned to a group of criminals.

A sixteen-member grand jury, specially appointed to deal with this terrorist case, included presidents of major utility companies, civic workers, business leaders, managing editors of key newspapers, and three blacks. Among the arsonists identified was a labor union leader. White blue-collar resentment had emerged during the use of blacks on plantations, which pushed out working-class whites, often of Scottish and Irish descent and labeled "white trash." The grand jury placed thirteen indictments against ten men and told the ringleaders to stop their violence. The major indictment charged lay and religious community groups, through misguided leadership, for acting, perhaps unwittingly, in ways that resulted in shameful destruction.

Two obstacles stood in the way of coping with the lack of decent and adequate housing—the root cause of the trouble. Segregation limited housing sites, and limited incomes precluded purchasing standard housing. Twenty percent of the black families were estimated to be able to afford to rent or buy standard dwellings if given the opportunity to obtain mortgages. (At the time, a myth existed that blacks were unreliable. When blacks paid back their loans, shattering the myths, new vistas opened up.) In 1951, 900 public housing units accommodated 3,954 individuals, of which 1,922 were minors. The Dallas Housing Authority had on file applications from about 7,000 black families for two housing projects, Roseland Homes and Frazier Courts. A private builder said he had on file 2,000 applications in excess of available apartments.

Families, consequently, were forced to double up on living accommodations. For example, about fifty people lived in nine shacks built less than three feet apart. They used one outdoor dry toilet and one outdoor hydrant for drinking water, bathing water, and laundry water. The entire area was a swamp of standing water and mud.

Blacks and whites alike recognized the critical housing shortage for blacks. Many proposals for housing programs were presented to the Dallas City Council; within a two-year period, there were nine. White citizens opposed six, and only one proposal overcame objections. The possibility of forced sales and losses to expand existing black sites created distress and tension. White protest groups cried out loudly; they had "war plans" and "alert committees" and were able to block both private enterprise projects and public housing.

Dallas businessmen recognized the need for a peaceful labor pool to feed current and projected industrial and small-business needs. Private builders were eager to supply fully the housing needs for the blacks. The Dallas City Council had warned them if they could not do it, the council would supply public housing.

In 1951 the committees on black housing of the Dallas Chamber of Commerce and Dallas Citizens Council recommended a housing program with three key characteristics: (1) The program should be undertaken within the corporate limits of the City of Dallas so that government regulatory services could be provided in such a manner as to ensure that future construction would not develop into slum areas; (2) the housing should be segregated; however, the South could not practice segregation unless it gave the blacks someplace in which to be segregated; and (3) the program should have a number of black residential sections in various parts of the city that would provide accessibility to work, schools, churches, transportation, parks, and shopping facilities.

Jerome K. Crossman, attorney, corporation executive, and Chamber of Commerce president, put forth a proposal as chairman of the housing committee of the Dallas Citizens Interracial Association, Inc., a fifteen-member organization chartered by the state in 1951 as a nonprofit corporation. With representatives from forty civil groups and two hundred invited groups asked to serve in advisory capacity, this "benevolent, charitable, and educational" organization was mandated to survey housing needs and seek a solution. The Crossman plan called for forming a nonprofit organization that would obtain loans from interested businessmen in order to buy a large tract of land for a planned black community with houses, school, park, churches, and a shopping center. The land would be resold to builders or prospective homeowners for development. The plan was for middle- and higher-income families, since the Dallas Housing Authority was building several thousand public housing units for very low-income black families in South Dallas, Oak Cliff, and West Dallas. Low-interest debenture sales to businesses and individuals were to be used to finance the purchase of housing sites. As the homes were sold on the proposed black sites, the money was to be invested in more sites.

The initial project of the Dallas Citizens Interracial Association was a 500-home black residential section called Hamilton Park after Dr. Richard T. Hamilton, a Dallas physician, YMCA worker in the black community, and first manager of the Dallas Negro Chamber of Commerce. The association purchased a sprawling, hilly seventy-three-acre site and paid for the extension of water and sanitary lines. The city annexed the site at $1,000 per acre. Demarcated physically by natural boundaries, the Hamilton Park community area, at the southeast corner of the City of Richardson just north of Forest Lane, and 1,500 feet east of Central Expressway, was provided with Schroeder as the only entrance and exit road. Perhaps the single access was for security reasons so the community could be protected from the kind of harassment blacks experienced in earlier years. If trouble should break out in the community, it could be contained.

The Hamilton Park project climaxed more than three years of work to obtain adequate housing for middle-income blacks. At the opening ceremonies on May 2, 1954, there were fifty one-story frame dwellings with car ports and graveled roofs. Priority was given to families being displaced as a result of the Love Field Expansion. Eventually, there were two- and three-bedroom frame and three-bedroom brick houses built under FHA and GI loans. These residential units ranged from $7,000 to $8,950, with $650 to $900 down, and $45 to $50 in monthly payment. Space was set aside for a shopping center, school, and several churches.

In 1966 Hamilton Park had 750 dwelling homes and a population of 3,500. The shopping area, Hamilton Park Village Center, included two grocery stores, one drugstore, two dry cleaners, one laundry, one snackshop, two service stations, one barber and beauty shop, and one auto supply store.

The community had social organizations, such as the Hamiltonite Charity and Social Club, the Hamiltonian Charity and Social Club, the Hamiltonette Charity and Social Club, and the Gold Cup Garden Club. The Hamilton Park Church of Christ was established in 1957; First Baptist Church, in 1954 and Hamilton Park Methodist Church, in 1957. Two months after constructing the first houses in Hamilton Park in 1954, a civil league had been organized. It actively petitioned for paved allies, streetlights, adequate law enforcement, park facilities, a recreational program, proper mail delivery and bus service, stopping the adjacent Texas Instruments plant from using the area as a dumping ground and rezoning for apartments. The league urged community members to be active and exercise their franchise.

The Segregated School

In 1961 Hamilton Park School administrators undertook an appraisal of the school in order to "check our present status for the purpose of measuring and establishing the amount of progress we have made . . . and try to speculate on our chance for endurance in the future." Their efforts resulted in the 1962 accreditation of Hamilton Park High School by the Southern Association of Schools and Colleges.

In May 1965 several concerned parents complained to the high school principal that students were not making proper use of leisure time. Several mothers said that their children were not learning anything and never had homework. (The principal reported that about one-third of the pupils simply did not do their homework!) A second community study project was initiated in September 1965. Some Hamilton Park residents levelled harsh criticism at the school program, staff, and policies. Principal E. V. Goss viewed this as a "reflection of their genuine concern and interest in our community. It is also the 'growing pains' of a progressing people. . . . who want to make sure that this generation has 'more' than we had and is getting what is long overdue them."[3]

Hamilton Park adults were predominantly forty-five years old and younger. In 1966 approximately 28 percent of all high school students' fathers had college degrees; 22 percent had an education above the eighth-grade level; 32 percent of the mothers had completed high school; and 14 percent had college training. Some skilled and semi-skilled people were employed at Collins Radio, Texas Instruments, in downtown and village department stores; Hamilton Park also had its public school teachers, postal workers, doctors, nurses, barbers, and beauticians.

The black administration of the all-black school recognized problems that persist today: "Deprivation and dependency, crime and delinquency, sickness, unemployment, discontent, and other youth problems brought on by both working parents. The widespread lack of adult supervision because of parental working hours provide a direct and inescapable challenge . . . to the Hamilton Park program of education."[4] More than 90 percent of both parents in black families worked long hours.

The second study of Hamilton Park's segregated black school found that two-thirds of the students were "a little below average in intelligence and needed special education or some remedial school reading and mathematics programs." Over one hundred youths of average or above-average intelligence were working as much as two grades below grade level.

J. O. Griffin, who joined Hamilton Park School in 1957, became vice-principal in 1965 (and coprincipal of the desegregated HPES at its inception in 1975), chaired an enrichment center set up after the second study of Hamilton Park School. The center's objectives were to provide compensatory education, enrichment for average students, study method instruction, and a cooperative supervised home assignment program for children whose parents worked.

In 1978 many Hamilton Park parents had high aspirations for their children, whom they provided with the material things they had not had. These parents wanted their children to be able to avoid what they had experienced: walking to school through mud, rain, and cold; eating lunch among flies and gnats; drawing water from a well; seeking shade under a tree to find relief from the hot Texas sun. Older people remember "sweating as they picked cotton, pulled corn, baled hay, made sorghum, cane syrup and meal, milked the cows, farmed," said Mr. Gus Fields, a long-time resident of the area, sixty-three years old at the time of my field work, school district employee since 1949, and member of Mt. Pisgah Baptist Church. Formerly a bus driver, he had transported black students many miles from their homes to all-black schools.

"Some Hamilton Park residents believe," Mr. Fields observed, "that prosperity has made it hard for people. The children are lazy, complain about the heat, don't realize what life is all about. They don't know the value of work and working well." He recalled a poem, learned in the third or fourth grade, that had guided him:

> If a task is once begun,
> Never leave it 'til it's done
> Do the labor, great or small
> Do it well or not at all
> Do it well or not at all.

"That's been my motto," he said. "They'd done fire me if not." Mr. Fields remembers his paternal grandfather, who was a slave on the Caruth farm. Mr. Fields, who has worked at Hamilton Park School since its inception, had a daughter who completed her education the year it became HPES. Reflecting on his five children who achieved what he had not had the opportunity to obtain—college, white-collar and professional careers—he asserted,

> Attention, it's got to start before they get to school. If a teacher gets the Attention, something happens. Some kids go'n get it; some not go'n get it. You cripple a child if you give 'em something they don' deserve. Some parents don't try; their kids are like them. It's in the blood. I knew this kid's mom, his daddy. His mother's contrary; the child come up like that. Sometime people have to bump their head [learn by their mistakes].

School Desegregation and Out of the Protected Nest

When the desegregation issue came to the fore in 1970, some Hamilton Park residents perceived this as a case of their being pushed around again and losing local control rather than as something that would benefit them.[5] The issue was one of basic liberties and control of the most basic social environment, the neighborhood school. The paradoxical imposition of federal government controls to equalize educational opportunity was confusing and emotionally charged. Hamilton Park, a black island isolated by a district boundary, railroad, industrial park, and freeway, experienced anxieties; mixing had led to violence in the past.

When the large, modern, well-built, red brick Hamilton Park School opened in 1955, it served students in grades 1 to 12 in the separate or dual system of public education. Until 1952, when Richardson Junior/ Senior High School opened, white students attended the Greenville Avenue School. (As recently as 1946, the RISD population was about 1 percent of its current size, that is, about 350 students.) Black students had attended a school on Coit Road near Forest Lane on a site that is now the Olla Podrida Shopping Center. Black high school students from Richardson, Dallas, and Addison were bused all the way to Booker T. Washington High School in downtown Dallas. The first white teacher was hired for Hamilton Park School in 1969.

In 1975, however, the school was desegregated—half the student body was white, and 20 of the 24 teachers were now white: Hamilton Park with its 762 families, well-kept, landscaped homes, clean streets, and renovations as families grew in size or acquired additional income was once again a focal point of attention. However, since the passage of antidiscrimination laws, many of the middle-class blacks had moved out and renters and the unemployed had replaced employed homeowners. Crime had increased according to a long-time resident whom I saw rushing home one day before Christmas to check on her belongings. The police confirmed her report. The area's residents, with an average yearly income of about $9,000, were surrounded by middle- and upper-income predominantly white residential areas. Only the adjacent—and more expensive—Stultz Road area could be said to be residentially integrated.

A five-year U.S. Justice Department effort to desegregate Hamilton Park culminated in 1975.[6] Prior to the court case, in June 1965, RISD adopted a desegregation plan based on geographic attendance zones. Two months later, the U.S. Department of Health, Education, and Welfare approved the plan. Students were to attend neighborhood elementary schools near their homes with no restrictions as to race. Elementary schools would "feed" nearby junior and senior high schools.

Parents from Hamilton Park had requested that a greater variety of courses be made available to their high school students. In September 1969, the high school portion of Hamilton Park had been closed, and students had begun attending Richardson and Lake Highlands high schools. With capacity to hold one thousand students, Hamilton Park School now had extra space that was converted for other RISD uses.

In July 1970, RISD was one of thirty-seven Texas school districts requested to meet with officials of the Justice Department and the Department of Health, Education, and Welfare concerning the one or more identifiable, all-black schools that each district had. Federal authorities did not make specific recommendations to RISD but asserted that the Justice Department should file a federal suit in order to have the courts settle the matter.

The U.S. government filed a suit in August 1970 in the district court in Dallas. Judge William M. Taylor heard the case and in 1971 ordered the junior high portion of Hamilton Park School closed and students reassigned and bused to three other predominantly white junior high schools (Northwood, Forest Meadow, and Richardson) and the faculty reassigned so that every school would reflect the districtwide racial balance of 3 percent black, 97 percent white. Transfers from racially homogeneous schools were to be permitted. The court at this time ruled that the all-black HPES was a "constitutional" neighborhood school.

Judge Taylor requested that a Richardson biracial committee be formed in 1970. The purpose of the committee, comprised of two high school juniors, two seniors, and six adults, was to function as an advisory group for the school board and court.

In May 1974, federal attorneys filed a motion seeking to expand the desegregation order to include the elementary school. Judge Taylor denied the motion on August 3, ruling that RISD was in compliance with its earlier court order. He argued that pairing or clustering predominantly white schools with Hamilton Park would not accomplish effective or stable desegregation. On April 20, 1975, the U.S. Fifth Court of Appeals in New Orleans reversed Judge Taylor's 1971 order permitting a black HPES, supporting instead the Justice Department's demand to desegregate the school. This court action caught RISD by surprise and without a plan. Superintendent J. J. Pearce stated the widely held sentiment: "You have the great fathers in Washington who sit and tell you what to do down here." Since RISD did not apply for or receive any federal money in order to avoid federal intervention, it was not surprising that the school officials disliked the order.

The RISD School Board of Trustees voted unanimously to appeal the decision. In October 1975, the Supreme Court affirmed the circuit court's order requiring desegregation. The Justice Department attorneys sought to pair the all-black HPES with the predominantly white Stultz Elementary School. By July 1975, ten controversial plans for desegregation were presented. Four came from the school district (three involved pairing; one was the Pacesetter Plan). The Hamilton Park Civic League proposed three plans. Another plan came from a parent in the Dobie School area, and two plans came from the Justice Department.

Pairing and clustering were opposed vociferously. The PTA president of one of the schools under consideration said about 400 people signed a petition objecting to the fact that residents of the two school areas were not involved in the planning. She said the Dobie School area had about 3,000 apartments and 217 homes: Families would rather move than bus! Dobie already had a 10.83 percent black student body. Stultz was 20 percent black in 1974 (26.2 percent in 1976); its surrounding community had become integrated naturally through residential patterns. Many people thought it was only a matter of time before whites moved out of the area. Other whites, however, believed the area would stabilize. (They did not accept the myth of property values decreasing with black in-migration—this devaluation occurs when residents panic and sell cheaply.)

Some black parents expressed irritation with RISD's claim that there was no forced busing. "Our junior and senior high students are bused across town to the white schools. They must think the black children are nothing." Some blacks thought the sacrifice should be shared by both blacks and whites and preferred to have children bused into Hamilton Park, not out.

Judge Taylor conditionally accepted the RISD Pacesetter Plan for HPES. This plan was originally proposed by a Richardson resident, Steve Potter, a social worker for the Southwestern Medical School Department of Pediatrics. His idea of a magnet school that would attract white students the way a magnet attracts iron filings came from reading about such schools in Boston:[7] Given a program of superior quality, parents would vie to send their children to the school. He sent his former neighbor, Deputy Superintendent John Roberts, a letter about the magnet concept as a possible plan for Hamilton Park. Because the school is centrally located in RISD, no student would have more than a thirty-minute bus ride. Some white leaders thought the black community was middle class, that is, property owners, and therefore social values of blacks and whites would be similar. The Justice Department objected to the Pacesetter Plan on the grounds that it was not fully developed and left too many questions unanswered.

Judge Taylor's condition for the Pacesetter Plan in his July 15, 1975 decision was that by August 1 of that year, 250 white volunteer students had to sign up for the school year beginning on August 20. An added stipulation was that a fifty-fifty white to black ratio in student enrollment must be maintained at each grade level, which it was at the time of my study.

The Pacesetter program was desegregation by incentive. The key word was "attract." Attracting students from all over the district through the compelling factor of educational excellence would, many people hoped, provide a workable substitute for ineffective integration through forced busing, pairing, or clustering. The Texas legislature provided funds to improve the Hamilton Park facility and assist the school in providing special programs.

Incentives to attract white volunteers included the following: 84 percent of the teachers would have experience and master's degrees rather than 41 percent, as was generally the case in the district. Pacesetter teachers would have demonstrated interest in individualizing instruction; the professional to pupil ratio would be fourteen to one rather than eighteen to one; and the teacher to pupil ratio would be sixteen to one rather than twenty to one. A key attraction for many people in rapidly growing RISD was average classroom size: Pacesetter would have a twenty-student maximum. The average classroom size elsewhere was twenty-six, and several classes had thirty-five pupils. Pacesetter would have coprincipals rather than a building principal with both instructional and noninstructional responsibilities. There would be two teaching assistants per grade level and other special aides to bring the total number of assistants to twenty-seven; other schools had far fewer aides.

In 1977 Pacesetter was unique in having a black counselor handling upper grades and a white counselor handling lower grades, a full-time educational diagnostician, nurse, discipline room teacher, and a public relations person. Pacesetter had four rather than three special education teachers for children academically below grade level according to national standardized tests.

Pacesetter's individualized instruction and accelerated programs were the drawing card for many whites with children above their chronological age in academic skills who found the traditional RISD step-level, repetitive, slow-paced classroom instruction boring. Children who came from schools outside Texas where programmed, individualized learning was part of the education of the total child were especially dissatisfied. The RISD teachers tended to drill and give bright children more of the same work if they understood and completed the assignments before other children. Enriched exercises at the child's chronological age level that were offered in some schools failed to alleviate the problem. Individualized instruction was in fact provided for only slow learners.

Curriculum content was supposed to be the same at Pacesetter as elsewhere, although the school was touted as providing enrichment with computer-assisted instruction.

Pacesetter was given special teachers in art, physical education, music, and Spanish to serve grades one to six. In other schools, homeroom teachers gave instruction in all subjects and foreign language training was not available. As in other schools, there would be a full-time speech therapist and librarian. In addition, Pacesetter would have a library assistant and an audiovisual materials coordinator.

Since the Hamilton Park school was formerly designed for grades K to twelve, Pacesetter facilities were clearly superior, with a spacious gym, 750-seat auditorium, music room, art barn, large lunchroom–cafeteria, library, media center, a regulation track, grass areas for two regulation-size ball fields, swings, and a merry-go-round assigned to the upper grades. In another area allocated to the lower grades, there was a blacktop area with climbing ladder, slide, and swing equipment as well as a grass ball field. At this school, further improvements were made. Wide hallways in parts of the school were carpeted to accommodate expanded learning environments with work tables, chairs, and computer terminals; a student services center housed offices for a counselor, educational diagnostician, part-time psychologist, assistant, and a secretary. A study lab permitted children and teachers to use study carrels, listen to recordings, and view films.

Another feature to attract volunteers to Pacesetter was the Extended Day Program, cocurricular activities beginning at 7:00 A.M. and ending at 6:00 P.M. to challenge and care for children, especially those of working parents. Between 3:30 and 5 P.M., there were classes in astronomy at the planetarium, gymnastics, private piano, class piano, chess, computer workshop, arts and crafts, drama, intramural athletics, bowling, and dancing. Most classes were free. Children could also remain in a library–television room until 6:00 P.M. About twenty adults, including some regular teachers, were on the Extended Day staff.

The RISD launched a crash publicity program to recruit Pacesetter volunteers before the judge's two-week deadline. It was probably the first time in history that a school district ran what it called a "fourteen-day special." A mass mailing of 16,000 letters to families explained the educational and cultural advantages of Pacesetter, and this was followed by a door-to-door delivery of flyers. Then there was a series of nine briefing sessions for parents and children to learn about the unique program. Richardson Independent School District established a Pacesetter information center and five Pacesetter hot line telephones. Sixty

41

principals and counselors cut short by two weeks their summer vacations to be hurried through a briefing by administration officials. About three hundred RISD PTA officers received the same briefing.

Roberts, the plan's quarterback, feared that children would not want to leave schools reputed to be of high quality. In RISD homebuilders promote new developments with signs advertising their location in "quality education" RISD. Roberts appealed to teachers to enroll their children in Hamilton Park. Although recruitment began slowly—only three children enrolled during the first day applications became available—by the deadline, 304 had signed up, and there was a waiting list. The appropriate ratio was met in each grade except the first; grade six received the lowest number of applications. However, ratios quickly reached the mandated proportion and waiting lists grew.

Pacesetter Students and Their Backgrounds

Hamilton Park Elementary School opened in August 1975 with nationwide scrutiny. In addition to local and state newspaper coverage, there were reports in Tennessee and Florida newspapers, the *Christian Science Monitor, Newsweek,* and *Time.* Local and national television covered Pacesetter. It was touted as a stellar example of how desegregation could work without forced busing and the trauma and frustration associated with it. Reporters lauded children making a personal sacrifice for a social goal, riding a bus six miles instead of walking four blocks.

In 1975 RISD was a thirty-nine-square-mile school district encompassing the rapidly growing City of Richardson as well as a northern strip of Dallas. Children living more than two miles from their schools were bused. The district served 35,000 students, of whom 10 percent were minority members. Its instructional staff included 1,922 teachers, 98 more than the previous year. In 1974 only 3 percent of RISD was black (1,069 out of 32,319 students). In 1975 71 percent of the black elementary-school-age children attended Hamilton Park; the rest attended predominantly white schools.

The white volunteers, Texas newcomers, and old-timers, were interested in the superior education Pacesetter promised, participating in a historical ground breaker for the area, or opportunity for children to learn to get along with different groups of people. In HPES's first year, 64 percent of the volunteers said they chose the school because of its quality of education, and 25 percent mentioned the school's multicultural composition as the reason for its choice.[8] Out of necessity, some volunteers opted for the school because of its Extended Day Program (only about 20 percent of the volunteer families had single parents). In some cases, the children rather than their parents chose to participate. Of course, many white people mistrusted the experimental program or had ingrained prejudices that made them hesitate to send their children to HPES.

Because the HPES neighborhood blacks had priority in meeting the limited black quota of 50 percent per classroom, blacks who did not live in the Hamilton Park community but wanted to send their children to HPES because of its alleged superior educational program were unable to do so. Some middle-class blacks used friends' or relatives' addresses in Hamilton Park to bypass the residency requirement.

Formal acceptance of the Pacesetter Plan came on August 13, 1975, the day that teacher orientation and inservice began. Meanwhile, the district had created a school staff, begun to refurbish unused rooms (fifteen had been in use the previous year and now forty were needed), and initiated equipment and supply requests for reactivated classrooms. At the August open house, teachers emphasized individuality and the need for everyone to work together rather than group characteristics.

After the first year, Roberts reported that only 12 percent of the students elected not to continue at HPES. At that time, thirty-five students at each grade level were on the waiting list to attend the magnet school.

Judge Taylor required monthly reports on student enrollment. In May 1976, he issued the supplementary order that HPES was to have the same male to female ratio and educational character as the rest of the district. He would not permit HPES to be a school solely for gifted or slow students. In order for HPES to maintain its ethnic balance in each classroom, Taylor allowed new students moving into the HPES attendance area after the inception of Pacesetter to be assigned to the nearby Stults Road Elementary School.

Tension was high the first year of Pacesetter's existence and persisted the second year, according to some black adults. By the third year, however, tension seemed to have subsided. An aide said the black community did not welcome desegregation. Many black and white parents, as well as other school personnel, substantiated this view. Blacks continued to complain that "they took our school away and all our good teachers." In 1977 there were two black teachers out of a total of forty, and one black teaching assistant out of twenty. Some black community residents felt their school was being invaded; they did not recognize the improvements the school was making, including providing for the large number of black children who required remedial work in basic skills.[9] Blacks elsewhere in the United States were also bitter about the loss of their schools and alma maters.[10] Desegregation meant the loss of "black

43

turf," the territorial divisions whites had created, as well as a symbol of unity, identity, and beloved black teachers and leaders who held prestigious positions in the school and community.

Some black HPES parents told their children to stay away from the whites, volunteer children, and teachers who also volunteered to teach at HPES: "Don't let the teachers [most were white] touch you!" Thus black parents' hostility may have led some of their children to have a chip on their shoulders. Those parents who felt they could not protect their children became alienated.

Neighborhood youngsters continued to view the school possessively as their turf, and translating this perspective into behavior created friction. Some black girls would brush imaginary specks off their shoulders and shake their bodies away from white teachers as if the teachers were spewing dirt. A black girl threatened a white girl, "You gonna sing this way, you in soul country now." Many youngsters were self-conscious and somewhat afraid. Mixing was new and scary. "Why do I have to be in a situation where some of them don't like me?" was a concern of adults and children, who feared potential embarrassment and rebuff and anticipated communication and interactional problems.

In anticipation of potential difficulties, these words appeared on a wall poster in the office of Phyllis Owen, one of the two principals at HPES:

> Don't walk in front of me
> I may not follow.
> Don't walk behind me
> I may not lead.
> Walk beside me
> And be my friend.

Acting with federal sanction, the school had—despite all the difficulties—been successful in implementing an innovative approach to desegregation according to the RISD-contracted first-year evaluation. The evaluators, Drs. Estes and Skipper, used a number of instruments to tap several dimensions of program effectiveness: student academic achievement, student emotional comfort, consumer satisfaction for students and parents, and teacher satisfaction. The evaluation design involved a pretest (fall 1975) and posttest (spring 1976) comparison of HPES with an ethnically similar school that had become naturally desegregated. Educators generally assume that naturally desegregated neighborhood schools constitute the most effective desegregation plan; however, HPES was shown to be as effective as the school with which it was compared.

Achievement at HPES reflected a national trend. A larger percent-age of whites tested higher in almost all areas than their black peers; this disparity tended to increase with age. Average scores for white students at HPES tended to be two grade levels above chronological age, whereas black students' scores tended to be two or more grade levels below. Several factors, to be discussed in the following chapters, may account for this. Suffice it for now to note the factors that appeared in the evaluation study. Fewer white families had two parents at work; thus white parents were likely to provide their children with activities that reinforced the school's programs. At HPES, whites' income and educa-tional levels were above the national average. Half earned in excess of $20,000 a year and were college graduates. Approximately two-thirds of the white fathers held professional or managerial positions or were craftsmen. In contrast, the average income in the Hamilton Park com-munity was about $9,000 a year, and one-third of the black fathers were laborers; another third occupied professional or managerial positions or were craftsmen. About 7 percent were unemployed; the others' occupa-tions were unknown. The community had some college graduates. White mothers who worked tended to be somewhat higher on the socioeconomic scale than their black counterparts. More whites (70 per-cent) lived with their natural mother and father, whereas more blacks (60 percent) lived with a single parent or in a nonparent arrangement.

Although there is a common belief that desegregation is best begun in the early years, in terms of students' emotional comfort, evaluators found that for grades one to three, white students' self-concept of their intellectual status, popularity, and happiness declined. For blacks, there was an increase from pretest to posttest in popularity and total self-concept scores. The reason for the decline in white self-concept may lie in the fact that students in this age group had relatively rigid notions about what constituted correct behavior.

By nursery school age, children have clear conceptions of honor, prestige, and status as power.[11] Children in the early elementary grades, however, have not developed tolerance nor explanations for alternative norms;[12] nor have they acquired competency in flexible role-taking, putting themselves in another's situation. Because older children have learned these skills, they can rationalize rule deviations from their own norms. White children and the few middle-class blacks at HPES con-fronted low-income black children who deviated from what was consid-ered acceptable behavior by middle-class standards.[13] Thus exposure to black children's behavior that white children thought was wrong prob-ably challenged the white youngsters' self-concepts.

Teachers at HPES perceived more problems after working with

45

students for a year than at the beginning of the experiment with its initial exciting media coverage fanfare. Excuses initially made for children not becoming adjusted ceased to be acceptable to teachers. Teachers found black males to be overly aggressive. (By the third year of the Pacesetter effort and adjustment period, parents also became concerned about various school-linked problems.) Most white students reported greater friction in their classrooms at the end than at the beginning of the year. Black student dissatisfaction with school increased. Unfulfilled expectations of the impact of the magnet school on their lives may have accounted for student, parent, and teacher disappointment.

School Culture

Part of the difficulty was the different cultures that came together in HPES. Public schools, usually controlled by the white middle class, are stages on which many tensions and conflicts in American society are acted out. Schools teach ideal values, not all of which mesh with reality. What is taught and what occurs in some children's lives diverge, and this divergence undermines the educational system's credibility. The school sustains some attitudes generated in the home, reinforces some, deemphasizes others, and makes its own contribution with varying degrees of success. As schools perpetuate traditions, they sometimes inadvertently cause new problems. Some critics have charged the schools with pacifying and assimilating minorities into dominant American culture, state, and city traditions and thereby destroying minority heritage and dignity. While the distortion of history through neglect or falsification is gradually being remedied, in pursuing a particular view of education schools have rarely made use of the cultural heritage of most white or black ethnic groups.

Visitors to HPES noticed a warm and friendly atmosphere: Most children appeared to be happy, and a bustling activity pervaded the school. The facility was contemporary with clean, unlittered halls and many windows for good lighting. Children's work adorned many classroom and hall walls. Some classrooms had organized learning centers. In others, work groups sprawled on the floor or spilled into the halls, which had work areas for special projects and individualized interest groups. There was much touching and embracing in an atmosphere of informality. Students from other RISD schools said that there was less peer pressure in HPES to conform to one style of dress or hairdo. Classroom groups moved quietly and in an apparently orderly line from one activity to another—for example, from homeroom to reading, math, music, art, physical education, and back to homeroom for social studies and science. Counselors and Spanish-language teachers moved their audiovisual equipment in and out of the homerooms they visited. The head custodian was always on hand to help the teachers.

One sensed the school's philosophy: Begin where you are and grow; education for the total child. The goal was not just intellectual growth but emotional, social, aesthetic, creative, and physical development. HPES represented dominant American culture, Texan influences, and innovation in RISD. The school continually evaluated children's strengths and weaknesses in an attempt to meet their needs. Teachers praised children for progress no matter where they began; thus the school encouraged youngsters to experience self-satisfaction and a feeling of accomplishment. Because HPES recognized that the child is part of a family, it provided free "parenting" courses, where counselors met with interested parents, mostly white, to help them understand and develop their children's potential.

The classroom structure at HPES was usually organized within set periods of time in an orderly manner, with uniformity and regularity. Times were set aside for academic subjects, eating, drinking, and restroom breaks. Parents who had recently moved to the area believed orderliness, obedience, and conformity were emphasized more than in their children's former schools. They observed that youngsters had to sit still for longer periods of time and were supposed to focus their energy on specific assigned work involving books, pencil and paper to the exclusion of such body movements as squirming, or playing or other activities.

Most HPES teachers were earnest, idealistic, and dedicated. They viewed working with different groups and individuals as a challenge. By seeking relevant materials, experimenting with new projects, and establishing good relationships with their charges, teachers tried to increase students' interest in academic material.

Administrators and teachers commonly showed concern for student differences. They celebrated Jewish as well as Christian holidays and invited parents representing different nationalities and ethnic groups to visit the classroom and share their values, beliefs, and customs. Black heritage received continuing recognition in many classrooms.

Sometimes, however, faculty members, victims of the naïveté of training programs, were unaware of the impact of cultural and class differences on children in their race relations at school and in their academic work. There were some children who did not share the school's cultural patterns and therefore needed to learn and practice these at the same time that they acquired (at home, in the neighborhood, and among peers) the rules governing behavior in their own culture. And children who shared the school's culture had to learn the other cultural patterns in order to get along. Sometimes the "deviating" children became new models; at other times, they were labeled as inferior.

Most students liked their teachers and viewed them as warm, helpful, and fair. In fact, teachers were at the top of the list of what children liked best about HPES. Children respected teachers who met them on their own terms. Many Hamilton Park children appreciated those who helped them with their work, explained it, and did not give homework. A sixth-grade black girl said, "You get to pick what you want to do. The teachers don't tell [you] what to say. They don't try to boss you around, and if somebody hit you, they'll try to help you work it out." A second-grade girl thought HPES had "a bunch of nice teachers. My teacher always passes out candy if we get good marks." A white fourth-grade boy said, "I like best that everybody gets to do something. And even if they are good at something, they get to do it. And if they're not good at it, the teacher will help them with it." Children said a "mean" teacher "yells at you," "fusses at you," or "gives too much work."

Children took pride in HPES, especially in track and Extended Day activities. Appreciation for HPES appeared strongly in the contributions in *The Bobcat Beat,* the sixth-grade's literary booklet. The school had field trips and such activities as workshops, a talent show, art show, science fair, visiting poet, kite day, dance performance, theatrical play, Drum and Bugle Corps concert, balloonist, fire safety show, "sharing fair" with booths to suggest how children can develop their own unique potential, and fifth-grade musical performance.

During a second-grade recess, I observed a black boy and a white boy leave the school building together with their hands linked; a black girl and white girl also exited holding hands. On the playground, a soccer game began with four white boys and eight black boys. When the game was well underway, more children had joined: six white boys, fourteen black boys. On the merry-go-round, eight black girls and one white boy were playing. Soon there were three white girls, four black girls, three white girls, and three black girls seated in that arrangement. A black girl and white girl paired up on the seesaw. Children had interracial friendships.

Parents received newsletters from each grade informing them of events. There were the *First in Line, Two Scoops, Third Dimension, Quarter Notes, Focus on Fifth,* and *Sixth Sense* newsletters in addition to the schoolwide *Bobcat Pacer, PTA Newsletter,* and *RISD Views.* Some teachers sent home announcements of their own individual classroom activities.

In 1977 two mothers, Sharon Tipping and Minnie Champ, organized Volunteers in Pacesetter (VIP). More than one hundred adults' skills were matched with teacher requests for help in classrooms, the media center, student computer work, the Extended Day Program, and school office. Other parents worked at home preparing materials for school use.

HPES appeared calm on the surface, yet I discovered an undercurrent of questioning among black and white parents about the Pacesetter experiment. Many informal groups met and chatted about things that disturbed them, but they did not usually bring these to the attention of individuals who were in a position to solve them. Few parents participated in the PTA, and of those who did, there were more whites than blacks. Some blacks felt uncomfortable because they were less well educated than the volunteer parents; others had a sense of futility about making suggestions or other contributions.

One of the principals explained the ethos of not actively working within a structure to improve it: Some people who had power by virtue of inherited wealth and land were threatened by those with ability and discouraged the notion of changing the status quo. A Texan who was president of a local university said, "If you don't like the local school, put your child in private school!" But not everyone could afford to do this. Furthermore, some people believed in supporting the public educational system.

Anxious to have problems brought out into the open so that constructive change could occur, a Texas-born white woman, Judy Nassif, who lived in an integrated neighborhood and knew members of separate black and white informal groups, was critical in bringing white and black parents together along with HPES administrators to talk. Nassif volunteered her home as a meeting place for the group, which called itself Parents for Improving Pacesetter (PIP). This 1977 parent initiative perpetuated the tradition of school criticism that began in the 1960s when the school was segregated and served grades K to 12. The small group identified some problems and concluded that all parents in the school should participate if they so desired.

Nassif prepared a questionnaire in accord with suggestions from parents and administrators. Accompanied by cover letters for students and parents, the school sent the questionnaire home with students. Youngsters were asked to share their problems and feelings with their parents or guardians, who would then fill out the form, which included space to comment on busing, curriculum, communication, discipline, ability grouping in math and reading, the Extended Day Program, field trips and assemblies, homework, neighborhood and volunteer student relations, school policies, special education counseling programs, diagnostic testing, student safety, teachers and principals, and other categories for opinions, complaints, and suggestions. Parents were asked to give their names and areas of interest if they wanted to work with parents, faculty, and administrators to solve particular problems. Even before the questionnaires were returned, some of the problems that parents identified and shared with the principals were solved—evidence of an administration dedicated to continued growth and improvement.

What perceptions were shared? What perceptions varied? What were the areas of potential friction? Answers to these questions came from comments by parents, teachers, administrators, and children; researcher observations; and historical documents.

Black Culture, White Culture

Differences between black and white Americans exist because of the historical separation of the races as well as their respective cultural origins, opportunities, and the tendency for whites to be economically better off than blacks. Whether appreciated or considered dangerous,[14] there are differences in both values and their expression and communication.

Being culturally different from the dominant group in society is often a liability incurring severe social and economic penalties. This awareness underlies blacks' and other minority groups' protestations that they are no different from anyone else. On the other hand, the assertion that everyone is the same provides the rationale for ignoring historical conditions and perpetuating the status quo.

If some of the differences are evaluated negatively by the dominant culture, does discussing them hurt the minority's civil rights cause? Among some scholars (especially anthropologists, sociologists, and folklorists) and civil rights activists, there is a taboo against discussing such differences and a "knee-jerk siding with the deviant, the minority, the underdog."[15] The assumption is that minorities have been victimized by the dominant society and negative stereotypes must be reversed. On the other hand, a black lawyer, Derrick Bell, who argued desegregation cases, later became dean of the University of Oregon Law School, and recently joined the Harvard University Law School faculty, compared integration ideology to a religion and the twentieth-century equivalent of the Christian Crusades. Failure to question the implications of ideology and action, to recognize realities, and to offer positive criticism have led, worst of all, he says, to most minority children remaining in schools that are mainly separate and predictably unequal.[16]

50

There is no such phenomenon as *the* black culture or *the* white culture. Generalizations about any aspect of American culture are risky. Wide variations abound within groups. A racial or class cultural designation can become a false and damaging stereotype behind which an individual is lost. Whites who attended HPES were not typical Texans. Many had come to Texas expecting to find the kind of education they had had elsewhere in the United States. Some Texan whites disliked the crowding in their neighborhood schools as a result of residential growth. Some white parents made a public statement of commitment to integration by sending their children to the school. Several HPES children said they wanted to meet different kinds of people.

How does black culture compare with white culture at HPES? Blacks are often regarded as a homogeneous, unified group because of their common experiences as an oppressed minority with African roots. But as surveys point out, there is much diversity among them.[17] Eddie Bernice Johnson, former Texas state representative from Dallas and more recently principal regional officer of the U.S. Department of Health, Education, and Welfare, said, "The middle- and upper-class blacks are just as alienated from the poor blacks as are the whites. We must educate our brothers and sisters."[18] Indeed, with laws against segregation, many middle- and upper-class blacks have moved out of the Hamilton Park community into integrated neighborhoods and separated themselves from poor blacks.

Class differences are present among blacks partly for the same reasons as among whites, and partly due to the heritage of plantation slave life. Blacks, however, did not always inherit the social status of their parents in the same way that whites benefited from the resources their families had accumulated. Because they have less financial underpinning and more prejudices to confront, blacks may be more vulnerable to disaster and loss of resources. However, blacks and whites at similar income levels do tend to develop similar patterns of behavior or life styles.[19]

Whatever the social class, having black skin usually has its effect on individual living in a predominantly white society with a history of black slavery, discrimination, different jobs for blacks and whites, and hiring practices and seniority systems that preserve past racial distinctions in face of the dismantling of formal segregation.

Consequences of oppressive experience vary. Even the African heritage brought to the United States varied: While some blacks came from kingdoms with slavery, others came from egalitarian societies. And therein women, men, boys, girls, the old, young, and those initiated into special societies were treated differently; each had distinctive rights and responsibilities.[20] However, the effect of the African socioeconomic heritage in the United States is little known. In America, masters gave house slaves, including female servants whom they sexually exploited, preferential treatment over field slaves. Artisans and craftsmen were in between. Some blacks achieved freedom. Some, especially light-skinned individuals who worked exclusively with whites, established tightly-knit families and achieved the values, affluence, and culture of many white middle- and upper-class people. They strove to obtain education and disassociate themselves from unskilled, illiterate blacks.

Those blacks who escaped the stigma of inferiority during the 1890s were invariably individuals with a middle-class background. They also escaped poor public schools and attended private schools.[21] Most of the top black leaders in the United States come from families who have been going to college longer than whites.[22] In recent times, this black middle class (along with other enterprising blacks) has grown from about 5 to 25 percent of the black population.[23]

The black middle class had provided models for the poor. Black neighborhoods in the past tended to be more heterogeneous in class, taste, religiosity, education, color, and life style than their white counterparts, because blacks were not free to move where they wished.[24]

Social status in a black community differs from that in other communities:

> A member of the Negro middle class [bourgeoisie or "bougies"] may both idealize and reject the masses of working-class Negroes. A working-class Negro may at the same time be proud of the skill and poise of Negro leaders and resent and suspect them because of their education and achievement. . . . The present unrealities and distortions of ghetto life make it difficult to differentiate between empty flamboyance and valid achievement. . . . Those who have been deeply damaged by the ghetto seem unable to trust their own feelings. They cannot afford the psychic luxury of depth of emotion . . . The same person might move from indifference to adoration to condemnation of a fellow Negro within a single conversation without his or her audience's seeming to be conscious of any inconsistency.[25]

The long-time existence of conflict and ambiguity in black culture is suggested in these lyrics from a song John Lomax reported in the *Nation*, August 9, 1917:

> Niggers gettin' mo' like white fo'ks,
> Mo' like white fo'ks eve'y day.
> Niggers learnin' Greek an' Latin,
> Niggers wearin' silk an' satin,
> Niggers gettin' mo' like white fo'ks every day (p. 144).

These lines could present the positive side of improving social conditions, or they could be lower-class black satire and anger directed at those blacks who were trying to become culturally white and this includes acquiring academic education.[26] The 1960s black-power and black-is-beautiful movements rejected aping white men and women and recognized the natural characteristics and cultures of black peoples as inherently attractive. Having white ancestry had been a status symbol prior to 1960; afterward, whites were considered to have corrupted a black lineage.

As is the case in many ethnic groups, there are class differences in child upbringing that create divisiveness. Middle-class black parents' teaching differs in some ways from lower-class black parents' teaching. The middle class usually emphasizes verbal negotiation and academic success over physical "street" prowess. In several Dallas high schools, blacks whose parents have high-income jobs, residential property, and take expensive vacations form friendship groups that exclude blacks whose parents have low-income jobs, reside in housing projects, and do not take vacations. Individuals from less advantageous backgrounds may rise and become part of the prestigious group if they have some special redeeming quality, such as athletic prowess, academic success, humor, or musical talent.

Although Hamilton Park was originally a community of employed homeowners, in 1976 some people rented or were unemployed.[27] Their children did not have telephones, adequate clothing, or money to purchase many of the things offered at school (for example, milk, lunches, pictures, pendants, books, schoolbags, tickets for magic shows presented during school, and so forth). With the passage of antidiscrimination laws, the black middle class has gained many new residential options. Middle-class children who remained in HPES were exposed to more children of different backgrounds than their white or black middle-class counterparts from homogeneous neighborhoods.[28]

Following the rationale that HPES was supposed to remain a neighborhood school and keep a racial balance, Judge Taylor did not permit middle-class blacks who lived in predominantly white neighborhoods and whose experience had been primarily with middle-class children to attend HPES. Whether those blacks from Hamilton Park who move to a nearby higher socioeconomic neighborhood will be allowed to continue at HPES is uncertain.

With the exception of racial discrimination, from which black youngsters may have been sheltered, middle-income black and white children have similar experiences. I have already mentioned the black child who had associated with middle-class blacks and whites telling his mother when he attended HPES that he did not want to play with blacks because "they don't play nice." The remnants of slavery affect low-income black children more because the middle class eschews those remnants as they take on the middle-class culture reflected by the majority of whites in the United States. The few middle-income black youngsters in the school were not difficult to identify. Teachers pointed them out, children mentioned their parents' activities, and parents commented to other parents. Several middle-class black parents described to me the identity conflict their youngsters experienced at HPES, where the majority of the black children came from low-income families. These blacks taunted middle-class blacks with being white because they spoke standard English, earned good grades like whites in the school, and had white friends.

Blacks are often compared to other ethnic groups that have made great socioeconomic progress after starting with little in the United States. However, blacks under slavery were unique in having come involuntarily, with few options, and they were reduced to a state of total dependency. Their creative responses to force, coercion, and oppression determined their survival. The white sentiment that blacks were categorically inferior helped justify discrimination against blacks. Some blacks submitted, others, through primarily covert acts of sabotage and subversion of work, control techniques of "suicide, self-mutilation, infanticide, too, and equipment abuse, livestock misuse, slowdowns, running away, and revolt" ameliorated their difficult working conditions.[29] The survival technique for many blacks involved banding together against white authority. Powerless to do much about the rules of society, they felt no obligation to uphold them. The artistic and folklore realms of language, music, dance, gossip, and tales reveal a stream of rebelliousness. Historically, the fantasy life expressed in folklore and religious belief in the hereafter provided solace and support.

Results of past black–white interaction have been black self-hatred, shame, lack of aspirations, low self-esteem, suppressed aggression and rage, dependency, subserviency, and a vulnerability to alcoholism, drug addiction, and compulsive gambling.[30]

Conditions have changed for many blacks, but the legacy remains. Suspicion is the result of a persistent pattern of conflict. A perennial concern was with dominance and individual strength. Contemporary responses evoked by turbulent and accelerating change are more assertive than in the past. The black-power and black-is-beautiful movements manifest themselves in the kind of dramatic presentations Imamu Baraka and Ed Bullin produce. These movements are also characterized by the organized, radical, and revolutionary ethos in some segments of black America; the Black Panther party is the most noteworthy example. Now some blacks argue openly for their children's civil rights and urge the youngsters to assert themselves.

All black behavior does not result from environmental deprivation or cultural stripping. More than a defensive reaction to racial oppression, black culture preserves African and Afro-American cultural traditions that stress the importance of the extended family and cooperative efforts, acceptance of the body without shame, and aesthetic style.

I have suggested some of the reasons black culture differs from white culture at HPES. Today many blacks have greater options than in the past, and some blacks share white middle-class culture. Black children in the Hamilton Park community have not directly experienced the discrimination their ancestors knew. Relatively free from the social controls and self-discipline their parents possessed, most of the youngsters did not have the restraints of a granny or an aunt at home to supervise them while their parents were working. Nor did they have the constraints of conservative religion and acceptance of the inevitability of white supremacy.[31] Some of the children live in the isolation of suburban neighborhoods found throughout dominant American society. However, Hamilton Park neighborhood children learn distrust of whites from comments made by individuals in their environment or television programs and school texts that report the past. Consequently, these black youngsters often interpret their interactions with white adults and students at HPES within this framework. Some incidents reinforce prior learning; other incidents cast doubt.

The history of the development of Hamilton Park, replete with the terror of mysterious fires and bombings and segregation, was still vivid in some residents' memories at the time of my study. The U.S. court-ordered desegregation led to whites taking control of the local black school from the blacks. Amid such controversy, a magnet school evolved to meet the legal mandate for equal educational opportunity and to provide advantages for blacks and whites. Although the school was generally successful, some problems existed. Friction between cultural styles appeared to be the source.

NOTES

1. This history of Dallas and the Pacesetter school neighborhood is based on reports in the *Dallas Morning News* (5-3-48, 7-20-48, 1-13-50, 2-11-50, 6-29-51, 7-13-51, 7-14-51, 7-16-51, 7-18-51, 7-19-51, 7-20-51, 11-2-51, 3-16-52, 3-27-52, 4-23-54, 5-2-54, 7-11-75, 7-16-75, 7-18-75, 7-23-75, 7-24-75, 7-27-75, 7-29-75, 10-7-75); *Dallas Times Herald* (10-3-39, 4-30-48, 4-24-50, 2-15-50,

2-26-50, 6-29-51, 7-6-51, 8-15-51, 7-6-51, 7-22-51, 8-10-51, 8-15-51, 9-23-51, 10-1-51, 11-1-51, 4-25-52, 4-28-54, 5-2-54, 5-3-54, 5-24-54, 10-24-74, 4-23-75, 5-4-75, 7-21-75, 7-22-75, 7-23-75, 7-24-75, 8-10-75, 8-14-75, 8-21-75, 10-9-75, 5-12-76, 1-20-77); *Richardson Daily News* (4-23-75, 4-24-75, 4-29-75, 4-30-75, 6-4-75, 6-17-75, 7-9-75, 7-11-75, 7-17-75, 7-20-75, 7-21-75, 7-23-75, 7-24-75, 7-25-75, 7-27-75, 7-29-75, 7-31-75, 8-1-75, 8-3-75, 8-4-75, 8-6-75, 8-10-75, 8-14-75, 8-15-75, 8-24-75, 8-25-75, 8-26-75, 8-28-75, 10-17-75, 9-11-75, 9-16-75, 9-17-75, 9-18-75, 9-24-75, 10-1-75, 10-2-75, 10-7-75, 10-8-75, 10-9-75, 10-12-75, 10-19-75); *Richardson Times* (7-9-75); and from Dallas residents. Special assistance with the history of Hamilton Park developments came from Aletta Scuka, library associate, history and social sciences division, Dallas Public Library; Irving Statman, deputy director, Department of Housing and Urban Development, Dallas; and George W. "Gus" Fields, Pacesetter school employee.

The oppression of blacks is generally described in such works as Myrdal (1944); Kardiner and Ovesey (1951); Clark (1965); Grier and Cobbs (1968); Taubb (1970); Meier and Rudwick (1976); Franklin (1978); Pettigrew (1975); Levine (1977); Weinberg (1977) and Wilson (1980).

2. John Grant, Route 7, Dallas, *Dallas Morning News*, April 20, 1948.
3. Goss et al. 1966.
4. Ibid.
5. Cf. Eddy 1975.
6. Richardson Independent District v. United States, 512 F. 2d 896 (5th cir. 1975), cert. denied, 423 U.S. 837 (1975).
7. See Dentler and Scott 1981 for a description.
8. Estes and Skipper 1976.
9. See, for example, Eddy 1975:168; Wax 1980:26.
10. The magnet school had expanded during the 1970s to include over 1,000 schools in more than 130 of the largest urban school districts. In their survey of 715 school districts and 45 magnet schools, Blank et al. (1983) found magnet schools often provide high quality education and have a positive impact on desegregation.
11. Corsaro 1979.
12. Piaget 1932; Sutton-Smith 1977.
13. A number of researchers have found among black children what Rodman (1963) called the "value stretch."
14. Patterson (1978a) believes the ethnic revival, with its support of "so-called liberals and minority activists" is reactionary, socially explosive, and a retreat from the ideal of equality. Ethnic revival obfuscates the real issues, such as poverty and unemployment; furthermore, the dogma of separate but equal resurfaces.
15. Kando 1983.
16. Bell 1980:viii.
17. Raspberry 1978.
18. Segrest 1978.
19. Kronus 1971.
20. Cf. Hanna 1988a.
21. Weinberg 1977:55.
22. Sowell 1980.
23. Kronus 1971; Pettigrew 1971.
24. Cf. Warren 1975, Taueber and Taueber 1965:132, and Powdermaker 1939:13.

25. Clark 1965:196.
26. Levine 1977; *The Nation*, August 9, 1917, p. 144.
27. However, in 1976 Dallas had a better unemployment record for minority youth, particularly blacks, than many other cities, especially in the northeast. Nationwide the unemployment picture was about what it was for the entire nation in the depths of the Great Depression (Herbers 1979). The jobless rate for nonwhite youths was 35.3 percent (Flint 1979). The 1976 breakdown (U.S. Bureau of Labor Statistics) follows:

	Dallas-Fort Worth	New York City
	(%)	(%)
Overall unemployment	4.6	10.4
Black and other minority	7.1	12.6
White teen	15.2	22.1
Black and other teen	27.0	47.0

28. Cf. Scanzioni 1977:284.
29. Phillips 1971:157.
30. Ibid., 163.
31. Pettigrew 1971.

3

CULTURAL DISSONANCE: COLOR AND CLASS

HAMILTON Park community and its educational institutions were both unique and a reflection of the underlying history of black–white relations in the United States. Because black people are disproportionately represented among the poor, they are affected by the consequences of class as well as race.[1] A preoccupation with race and racial conflict may obscure fundamental problems that derive from the intersection of race with class, which coincide in HPES. In this chapter, I examine some specific issues of diversity: academic achievement, classroom disruption, individual versus cooperative work, expressive role validation, and expressions of anger and friendship.

Academic Achievement

Faculty and students tend to expect whites to do better academically than blacks, and such expectations may affect behavior. Teachers tend to be both female and middle class. A teacher relatively free of prejudice toward blacks may react to class-associated differences in her own orientations and those of her pupils' toward learning, work, and discipline. Teachers tend to reward passivity and docility—qualities that are not rewarded in the adult world.

Academic achievement is associated with higher social class, family stability, and an individual's ability to exercise self-control and autonomy. At HPES, the academic achievement patterns of neighborhood and volunteer children generally supported findings from elsewhere in the United States.[2] With few exceptions, blacks were two grade levels behind in the early grades, and the difference increased over time for many students. Even in an art exercise, several art therapists described the

58

unidentified work of HPES black second-graders to be that of children two years younger than their actual chronological age.

On the one hand, many blacks aspire to academic success. Sometimes difficulties vitiate their aspirations, for example, the lack of concrete plans, little belief in their ability to control their environment, and peer influences.[3] On the other hand, especially since the 1960s, there has been a strong distaste among blacks nationwide for becoming "white," in particular among blue-collar workers. Some Pentecostal churches have negative attitudes toward education, considering it trivial and of little value because this world is only temporary.[4]

This ambiguity manifested itself in HPES classroom performance, where some black children considered academic book learning white because in the past, the white master kept knowledge of how to read from black slaves. A sixth-grade black boy at HPES remarked, "Fags [homosexuals] book it!" And as another student replied, to my query, How does the child who does the best school work act?

> Like a fag. Like a real sissy. You know, people on a middle level, you know, like in vocabulary, people get mad at me 'cause I, you know, see I try to, you know, and my vocabulary is pretty good, so I try to use it around various people, you know. They kinda give me a high sign, you know, not to do that. They just jealous, 'cause in art, you know, the other day we was makin' sentences out of "graphic," and then I made a big sentence out of that, you know, using other vocabulary words than that one. And then they got real mad, you know, 'cause I got more points then they did with that one sentence; and they say it's not fair for me to, you know, get that up (91 bb 6th).[5]

Because this boy "pumps one hundred pounds of iron," as he put it, and is a good fighter, he can assume the burden of excelling academically: proving that he is "all right, not a sissy."[6] Boys generally exhibit traits of aggressiveness and independence that the school does not reward, although society does. The behavior demanded by schools is more "feminine" than "masculine." Consequently, groups that place a high value on masculinity have little enthusiasm for schooling and its associations.

When I asked how the neatest, smartest, most admirable child acted, a sixth-grade black girl said, "They don't have no high goals and a lot of learning—but they nice and everything" (24). Researchers found that "intellectual achievement is regarded as elevating oneself to a higher plane and removing oneself from the black brotherhood."[8] Being bookish is a renegade action and subject to peer chiding, harassment, or ostracism. Pejorative labels are heaped on the deserter.

Loss of career opportunities through poor academic performance is not a deterrent to failure because of perceived limited options. Low-income blacks rarely see evidence of education's contribution to socio-economic success. Individuals engaged in what dominant culture deems illegal activities are often models of financial reward. A churchman in Hamilton Park said, "What can we say when we try to motivate black children to follow a path less successfully charted in their experience or that of their immediate family and neighbors?"

Historically, in their competition with mainstreamers for occupational positions, promotion, and wages, many blacks lost whether or not they had education. This has been a disincentive for many lower-class blacks who do not consider the potential rewards of schoolwork. Compared historically with whites, blacks could not expect academic efforts actually to be rewarded.

Most HPES parents shared the same educational goals for their children.[10] However, black parents often had little free time, and perhaps few of the needed skills, to encourage schoolwork and supervise their offspring. They expressed the same concerns and complaints when the school was segregated and blacks administered the all-black school. Some parents conveyed their mistrust of the white-run school system and their doubt concerning the value of education. A child's failure was often blamed on the system, school, or a "racist" teacher. Furthermore, peer pressures against spending time on schoolwork impeded academic success. One member of the Washington, D.C. Board of Education, Linda Cropp, said that as a former teacher, she saw, as I did at HPES, good students "intimidated if they tried to excel."[11] Peer pressure[12] *not* to work hard is widespread; many adults, however, are unaware of the salience of the children's world—a critical interface between home, school, and society.

A few Hamilton Park neighborhood children who lived with a succession of guardians, some in different parts of the country, typify the case for some black low-income children who adapt to survival without adult security or instrumental aid.[13] Since socioeconomic circumstances caused their parents to be unreliable in helping them materially and psychologically, they develop a mistrust of adults. In building defenses against adult tenderness, dependency, and disappointment, children turn to their peers for support needs.

Street and school serve as places for peers to meet and participate in activities, many of which run counter to school objectives and expectations.[14] Competence in reading and competence in classroom politics may be inversely related.[15] Some reading disabilities reflected "situationally induced inattention patterns" in which peer group activity drew students away from their assigned curricular tasks.

Several HPES children commented that tough bullies can get what they want with their muscles, so they do not have to study to get rewards. Poor academic achievers can excel with physical power and thereby rationalize their lack of study habits or ability. Although middle-class black parents usually emphasize educational achievement, their children's lower-class peers are not supportive.

Research among white populations indicated high academic achievement is not necessary for financial gain: grade point average in school and achieved adult socioeconomic status later in life are not closely related except that there is a minimum standard necessary to reach high socioeconomic status.

Language presents some children with a barrier to academic mastery. The Standard English Dialect (SED) and its accompanying body language differ from what is called Black English Vernacular (BEV), whose features include a number of variations in phonology and grammar[16] as well as words and phrases considered vulgar or profane in SED. All school texts and teachers require SED usage and understanding. Speech habits also have accompanying social patterns.

Language reflects a child's experience, and that experience is the foundation on which growth develops. Black adults in some rural areas do not engage in dialogue with their young children nor expand the speech of children as middle-class adults do to fill in children's incomplete sentences. These blacks correct children's behavior, not their language use.[17] When black children know their codes differ from Standard English verbal and body language and are devalued for that reason, they may feel a sense of inferiority and communicative insecurity—verbal and nonverbal.

Apparently when people learn two different language systems, they tend to have only partial interconnections between them.[18] Thus blacks operating in a dual system of SED and BEV have a higher cognitive load than individuals operating in a single system in which there are few translations necessary. Many children had not learned code switching.[19] As early as 1919 in the relatively isolated Sea Island, blacks were noted to have the ability to alter their vocabulary and syntax depending on whether they were speaking to strangers or their own people. Many white Texans learn to do the same thing, according to Barbara Burnham, a native Texan and former social science editor at the University of Texas Press.

Because nonverbal styles may affect teacher–student rapport, which

61

in turn may bear on academic achievement, nonverbal code switching may be appropriate. For example, a white middle-class listener usually gazes steadily at a speaker, whereas an Afro-American does not. Consequently, white teachers may assume blacks are not paying attention when in fact they may regard the expected behavior as a sign of disrespect.[20]

Classroom Disruption: Discipline and Dancing Insubordination

There were black low-income and middle-income differences in classroom behavior that were related to differences in academic achievement. The antisocial behavior of students is frequently "an expression of their incompetence in the role of student and its adjunct roles in the school and wider social environment."[21] A student may set in motion psychological forces to eliminate a poor self-image;[22] delinquent behavior or withdrawal are expressions of such forces. Some children may start out determined to succeed academically and behaviorally. Setbacks due to discouragement with their own performance, adults, or peers may erode these youngsters' commitment to academic work.

When some whites and blacks earned the teacher's reward for good schoolwork, some blacks who did not reversed the role of superior by playing to a peer audience for recognition. Aggression, with its high intensity, sudden movement, close approach, and unpredictability evoked immediate attention and created arousal, anxiety, fear, or pain.

Fights started when children tried to "get someone" for the amusement of a group: "When they hit 'em hard when they be playin' with 'em. Sometimes to get your enemies in trouble so they can laugh" (107 bb 2nd).

As in Harlem, "Fighting excited and stimulated the children, but it also frightened many of them. . . . Many children remained hyperalert to changes in the environment that might be threatening to them. . . . A feeling of tension . . . often loomed ominously over many classrooms."[23]

One HPES student remarked: "Lot of people in sixth grade lose their temper; most, well what I say about it—15 percent. At the beginning of the school year, it was a lot of fighting" (91 bb 6th). A fourth-grade student gave her perception of classroom disruption, confusion about it, and its extension into her neighborhood:

If I tell the teacher, then they'll keep on bugging me, and I wouldn't want that. So I don't tell the teacher, and the next day, they don't do anything about it. I tell them to stop, but if they don't, I tell the teacher and my

62

mother. Like last year, they did it to me all last year: They called me names, and they hit me whenever I didn't do anything. They did that to almost everyone in the class. They said they were just kidding. But I told them it didn't seem like they were kidding because "When you hit me it hurts. It doesn't seem like you're kidding then." Then I tol' my mom and my teacher. Then they talked about it, and then the teacher talked to the children, and they said they didn't do anything. This girl named Cheril and Terry and mostly Cheril does it. Last year at the end of the year, they stopped it. I realize they were just playing and kidding and everything. Sometimes they do it to each other. Like, say, they're wearing these clothes that the other person thinks is weird, and the other person says, "Those clothes are weird," and starts bugging them and everything. Also some people do that on our street [in the residentially integrated Stultz area] like one of them steals my bike. See, sometimes their mother and father aren't there. They're at work, and they're about to come home, and that's when he does it, when they're not there. This other boy named Tony one time stole a minibike from this man's garage . . . Sometimes I say something that makes them mad—they are mad already at something, and I say something and I laugh, not at them, I'm just laughing: They come over and hit me, and I try to explain to them I was not laughing at them, that I was laughing at something else. They won't listen. They just come over there and hit me and then go back to their seats (64 wg 4th).

Several HPES teachers commented, "In other schools, the end of the week is the most chaotic time. But not at HPES where many of the neighborhood children lack a home structure that is similar to the school's." Teachers said it took "several days at the beginning of each week to reinstill the structure."

All children misbehave occasionally. However, children's and teachers' comments and classroom and other school area observations revealed that most of the classroom disruptions were the result of a *few* black children countering school norms. If a teacher were not firmly in control, these children wandered around the classroom when they were supposed to be seated, spoke to their neighbors, and copied others' work when they were instructed to do their own. These children sometimes yelled or "chunked" books and pencils across the room. Walking to the pencil sharpener to repair a deliberately broken pencil, a child would tease or harass another student along the way. Blowing pins through straws at others was one fourth-grade game that they started. Another was breaking up crayons, covering them with silver foil, and shooting them with a rubber band slingshot. Tripping children going about their business also occupied classroom time; pushing and shoving individuals in and out of the lines formed to move a class from one activity to another was common. Expressing sullen compliance, open contempt, or complete disinterest; and talking back to the teacher or dancing insubordination (performing a dance sequence at an inappropriate time and place) were yet other tactics.

Minority cultures may create verbal and nonverbal communication codes that "protect the thoughts and actions of group members from the gaze and negative sanctions of the dominant society."[24] Having learned that spoken words can be held against them as self-incriminating evidence, children use body language for self-assertion and defiance: saving face before one's self and peers.

By disrupting classroom routines and academic performances, these children communicated through humor or aggression that they did not esteem the evaluation processes of the school. They defined both the situation and their own performance in it as matters to be taken lightly and irrelevant as a judgment of their worth or capabilities.[25]

Similar values, styles, and behavior found among low-income black school children also occur in working-class white neighborhood schools in Boston,[26] Parkersburg, West Virginia,[27] and the United Kingdom.[28] In twelve London high schools studied over a three-year period, schools with a high proportion of academically less-able children who experienced the effects of scholastic failure on feelings of personal worth tended to have an antischool counterculture with its own reward system.[29]

At HPES, teachers referred disruptive children to what the administration called the discipline room and sixth-graders nicknamed the jail cell or pen. It is a place where children could, teachers and students said, cool off or calm down, quietly finish their work without peer distraction, or discuss a problem. By looking at referral records covering a four-week period, I was able to identify children whom teachers thought were disruptive elements in their classes: Three-fourths were black, and three-fourths were boys. There were no white female disciplinary problems.

The HPES parents differed in their view of how the school should handle misbehavior. Teachers and coprincipals said that some black parents became impatient with the school and claimed it was shirking responsibility if it did not "whup" (paddle) the child with "the licks he or she deserves."[30] These parents expected what they experienced in school; they learned to read and write, and those who misbehaved received physical punishment. Thus they condemned such activities as counseling, field trips, and assemblies that help educate the total child. This view is common to many minority and lower-class individuals.[31]

Some black children who were firmly and authoritatively controlled at home found the HPES permissive policies of individual choice and responsibility disturbing. Such children are afraid because of what they are allowed to get away with; they become anxious, says a black psychiatrist.[32] One youngster was aware of the black–white difference in obedience to parents and the family's control systems. He thought black and white children should be disciplined differently, "'cause the black children are more gooder than the white children. The boys and girls mind their mommies and daddies" (42 bb 2d).

Some HPES teachers condoned black children's misbehavior because they thought these children were unfamiliar with the school rules. Such children disturbed others in the classroom and lagged in learning dominant culture standards. Other teachers feared disciplining black children who they knew would challenge their authority or charge racism. Reluctant to confront misbehaving students for fear of their own safety, some teachers were leary of handling difficult problems that might involve a child's parents or older siblings and their friends. (In the National Institute of Education 1978 study, 28 percent of big-city teachers reported such fear.) Disciplining compliant white children, they felt, was worth their effort because it was likely to achieve the results they desired.

In one year, there were about three spankings, and a few children were sent home. Parents who had to leave work because of children who misbehaved became irate and let their youngsters know it. Indeed, many times teachers and principals were reluctant to call certain parents because the staff knew that these adults would severely punish their offspring after the school had already punished them. In such cases, the school explored ways of correcting the problems before contacting these parents.

Some teachers felt that the school's inconsistency in its disciplinary measures encouraged children to risk misbehaving. One day, a child struck a teacher and was lectured for it; another day, a youngster did the same thing and received a three-day suspension. The youngsters acted out their inability or disinterest in competing academically by performing for peers and gaining a following if they got away with misbehaving. Some black pupils blamed whites for "picking on" them for one reason or other.

Surprisingly, and contrary to the National Institute of Education study of principals' perceptions of where violence occurred, children at HPES reported that usually fighting took place in the classroom or in the halls:

> That's where we have violence most. Sometimes the teachers aren't in our classroom. A lot of people fight in our classroom. That's where I'm gettin' all this stuff. And so when they go out in the hall or they're dismissed from

something, and we're the only class that is dismissed, then a few people will go out in the hall and fight. Ms. X can be down in the lounge and the office, and all the other poor teachers will be in their classrooms and not even know what's going on (77 wg 4th).

From the sixth grade came this report:

Some people just can't handle themselves. Like some people in class just wanna be the best person, and they've got to have everybody listen to 'em and do what they want. It's just some people—they're always fighting [black children were identified by name]. Like when the teacher isn't really looking, when the teacher's out of the room, or something like that. That's usually when it happens. Sometimes, like our room knows when it happens in our class. Usually there's not too much in our class, but there's one thing about kids always running around the room and stuff like that, not doing what they're supposed to be doing—like other people trying to work, and they're running around the room throwing stuff at each other. They usually start out pushing at each other, yelling; friendly. It starts with talking and then it gets louder and then they start fighting. Like if they don't fight, like all the kids gather around.

Individual versus Cooperative Work

Cultural diversity appeared in HPES children's manner of work and created dissonance. We know that peer influences on children are strong—they begin earlier and are more intense for low-income blacks. The school usually required children to do their own work, especially on tests. Black children learn early in life to assume family responsibilities. Work is cooperative, a group's own concern, and not talked about. The kind of work a person does is not considered the basis for judging individual worth as it is in dominant American culture.[33] Black children left alone must fend for themselves; in concert with other children, they gain strength. Cooperative behavior, individuals interacting with peer groups or other audiences in work, play, or aggression, is part of the black cultural pattern found in many parts of Africa and the United States. During the slave era, black children raised each other, for the most part. Planters consigned the care of young slaves to elderly black women who supervised primarily the older ones attending their juniors.[34] Even the play of slave children was more cooperative and group centered than that of white children.[35]

"If a cultural-racial group is denied power by the larger society, a cooperative solidarity develops within the group."[36] Black children's dance games manifest this pattern. In southern black Baptist churches there is group vocal response to prayers, sermons, and testimonies. The computer teacher in the HPES Extended Day Program noted that black children picked up the team concept in computer games faster than white children. Dissonance, however, occurred when some white children perceived a few black children's transferal of the family cooperative pattern to the school setting as "all black kids cheat."

Cultural diversity exists in the pattern of "work leader." In many black families, there is little verbal interaction between generations, so that children informally teach each other.[37] The nature of the task determines who is the teacher and who is the student; roles are interchangeable and depend on demonstrated abilities. In contrast, the flow of instruction in dominant American culture is from the adult teacher to the student and the role of the teacher is irreversible.

Expressive Role Validation: On-Stage Soul

When a new child enters school or after a long vacation recess, there is an introductory phase when youngsters negotiate interpersonal relationships and participants probe for common experience. Children seek clues in order to know how to act and what to expect. Styles of self-expression differ between lower-class blacks and middle-class black and white youngsters. Children's social interactions can be understood from a dramaturgical perspective.[38] In general, compared to whites, blacks are more "onstage" than "offstage" in projecting their identities. Using verbal and nonverbal language, they are more theatrical. The low-income black's concern with drama, style, soul, and jockeying for leadership is characterized by higher energy, faster response, and less restrained overt emotion than in that of the middle class. Furthermore, black children often possess some knowledge about life and behave in some ways that white adults expect only among adolescents. Lower-class blacks sometimes use more tone and passion in their communication; they exhibit a kind of behavior that other cultures often regard as threatening and unduly assertive.[39] Middle-class black and white children who have been at HPES awhile are more sensitive to gradations and meanings than newcomers and therefore better able to cope.

A number of scholars[40] have documented the value blacks place on speech, song, dance, athletics, and drum forms that have great potential for assertive expression. Historically among blacks, especially the working class, dance has been an aspect of black personal identity, cultural integrity, and a boundary marker to distinguish one's ingroup from the outgroup. "Dance becomes a litmus test . . . Proper Afro-American dance demands the demonstration of certain postures and gestures held in esteem in black culture. . . . Inability to dance indicates that one's cultural base is not black, that one has taken on another cultural identity."[41] Afro-Americans feel a "deep-seated bitterness" when they directly witness the violation of attributes they recognize as culturally theirs." Relevant to HPES is the observation that "dance is the arena in which black confronts white and wins. It is the province over which black rule has prevailed relatively unchallenged. When whites attempt to 'dance black,' they pose what is perceived in the black mind as a challenge to that rule."[42]

With a realism and candor uncharacteristic of white children's songs, the songs of blacks accumulate word images to create a feeling of perceived power and independence. Black children throughout history have spontaneously organized dances (called cheers, ring plays, or line plays) that combined stylized body movement and song. Using the spatial form of children's dances of probably British origin, learned from white Americans, Afro-Americans meshed the African movement style of loose, flexible torso, extending and flexing knees with a certain ease, shuffling steps, and pelvic swings and thrusts to create syncretistic dances called ring and line plays.[43] Children dance to pass time, assert fellowship, have fun, and work through problems in a world they do not control.

At HPES, it was difficult to miss the distinctive, energetic black motor activity. Most black children carried themselves differently: More swagger, looseness, swing, hand rapping, "appropriate" dress, "right talk," and sparring characterized their activities. The polyrhythmic walk of many blacks exuded dynamism as parts of the torso moved counter to each other; hips shifted or rotated sideways while the upper torso was held relatively upright. Some children shimmied their shoulders and rippled their spines. Boys often walked with a springiness, the heel only momentarily placed on the ground. Several times, I saw five boys exit single file from a second-grade classroom and each perform sequentially three steps of the Charleston dance where flexed knees opened and closed while the hands simultaneously opened and crossed. When children were asked to line up, black boys more commonly than white boys would swing on a nearby pole or sprawl on a nearby table.

An adult put it this way: "Rather than simply walk, we *move:* the swaying swagger of the hips and the bouncing, bobbing, head–shoulder motion associated with *bopping* are derived from a strong, rhythmic mode of walking."[44] Note that this pattern is not innate: Africans who experience early education in British or American settings often move "like whites."

Clothing can accent body movement.

"Clothes . . . are not simply worn to cover the body; they are designed by the wearer to affect a magical attitude . . . It's all about power: When one hits the turbulence of the streets, one must know before passing the door of the house that one's magic is complete."[45] Verbal aggression among HPES black children included criticizing someone's dress.

In a second-grade classroom early in the semester, I observed the following physical activity during a forty-minute period that began with the white teacher conducting a game in which someone thinks of an animal and the other children try to guess what it is:

Two black boys in the back of the room jumped over chairs that they used as horses. Keith jumped over the back of his chair to the seat, then jumped up and down on it. Chris tried to imitate this feat but was less agile; Otis also tried. Keith performed his skillful feat three times. Then the spelling lesson began. A white girl seated between Keith and Chris called out: "I want to move! Keith wants to cut my hair!" The spelling lesson continued. Keith jumped from his seat over the desk to the floor. He ate some of his lunch, walked around, went over to the wall to play with the clock. Chris walked around the room and then played with some blocks. Keith and Chris then drummed on tabletops. Turning his chair upside down, Keith sat on it. Spinning his chair around in a circle, he used the legs like a submachine gun. Chris hit Aron, a white boy, who pushed a black girl. Keith hit Chris on the back twice. A black girl called out, "Dummy! dummy!" A black boy pulled a black girl's leg while she sat in her seat. Otis took off his shoes. A black girl was speaking loudly. In response to the teacher's question, "Would you like to go out?" she got up from her chair and walked into the aisle where she stood, feet apart and knees bent. She brought her knees together and apart four times while crossing her hands together and apart in unison with the knees in a Charleston step. Then she scurried back to her assigned seat and sat down. Moments later, she skipped to the door, opened it, picked up a book outside, then ran back to her place. Then she got up on her chair seat and performed what is called an arabesque in ballet: Standing on the ball of one foot, she raised the other leg back as high as she could, one arm held diagonally up and forward, the other diagonally down. From this position, she laughingly lost her balance and fell to the floor. The teacher picked her up and carried her out of the classroom. A black boy seated in the front row hit a black girl, then pushed and grabbed her; she screamed. Another child yelled, "Shut up y'all!" Michael was using a piece of paper as a musical instrument.

69

Part of the black expressive style involves testing one's performance. The person on stage calls and receives a response, a counterstatement to a statement, a reaction to an action. For instance, a person might answer "no shit" with "look out" or "amen" with "I hear you."[46] When a black child speaks to a child who does not engage in the response process, the black child interprets this as lack of involvement; thus, the child may repeatedly ask, "you lis'enin' to me? You hear me?"

White Anglo cultures tend to be more low key expressively; Latin and Mediterranean expressiveness is closer to that of many blacks. Regional differences also exist: White Anglo New Yorkers tend to be louder and more assertive than Southerners. Individuals who are part of corporations or governmental institutions comply with norms of etiquette requiring checked impulses and stylized self-assertion.[47] Discussion rather than argument, understatement rather than exhibitionism characterize the valued interactional patterns among whites. The behavioral consequence of different values, and therefore different socialization processes, is that in contrast to whites, blacks learn to manage more intense feeling, expressed in social exchanges, without becoming overwhelmed.[48] Part of the problem in social relations, then, is that middle-class whites and blacks, who have learned to repress impulses, have less tolerance for emotionally heated encounters than do lower-class blacks. Of course, blacks and whites are equally able to mask feelings.

A group's expressive style often influences the development of social status in the broader society and consequently intergroup relations. Several groups can operate within a single classroom. Children's performances within their peer group determine the structure of their activities, which are often very different from the structure of their activities with adults.[49]

Children have diverse ways of validating their roles and status. In the school, a student performs well academically in writing or orally. Black culture emphasizes immediate verbal and nonverbal expressive performance. Such roles as friend, the strongest child, or the authority are constantly established and reestablished on the basis of performance. Similarly, the egalitarian Igbo of Nigeria say, "No one knows the womb that bears the chief"; performance determines leadership, not birth.

Many black children continually test—explore—how a person responds to different challenges. They defer to people in positions of authority on the basis of their demonstrated performances in these positions.[50] A teacher's or student monitor's power to direct others derives not from a position, but leadership attributes of strength, forcefulness, intelligence, persuasiveness, and generosity. In contrast, white children generally show teachers respect because they hold the position of teacher, which was earned through credentials and experience. These contrasting black and white orientations created cultural dissonance in the school setting.

Many low-income blacks believe that rules should emerge from the requirements of an activity. While children trained in the dominant culture respond to a teacher because of the position the teacher occupies—one of authority, many black children test a teacher. It is not that they lack rules or are unpredictable; rather, "blacks see similar events, separated in time and space, and involving different individuals as unique and independent of each other and thereby requiring their own set of rules and regulations."[51]

From their middle-class vantage, black and white school personnel describe lower-class blacks as more physical, more restless. Much of their activity involves carrying out learned interactional processes that sanction cooperative efforts and expressive role validation. Interpersonal relations are continually being tested and renegotiated.[53] Middle-class children engage in such activity but not to the same extent and with the same dramatic effect. Although the black style may indicate a healthy pattern of adapting to change and opportunity, passivity may mean depression or accepting the status quo.[53]

Desegregated blacks sometimes have to show that they are no longer in slavery nor unhappy about restricted opportunity. Just as the newly rich may feel compelled to display recently acquired wealth, black children often go out of their way to show that they are no longer submissive as a group to whites. At HPES, a black child would tell a white one, "I'll make you my slave." Slavery is not too distant: The school custodian's grandfather was a slave, and many children watched the television program on African heritage, *Roots*.

Part of expressive role validation is the emphasis on the body. Although we do not know how Africans during the slave era perceived the body, it is interesting that many Africans today view the body in motion, especially in dancing, as indicative of an individual's personality, work capability, creativity, and innovation.[54] They foster a mind–body integration, that is, simultaneously using one's intellect and senses. The significance of the Afro-American body in motion also has roots in the slave auction block where a muscular, healthy-looking physique predicted the individual's capability for work. The antebellum period continued to support the importance of the body for heavy manual labor jobs available to blacks. When sports opened up to blacks in the 1940s, they achieved socioeconomic success through athletics—boxing, baseball, and basketball. Over time, dominant white America communicated to

71

blacks that their physical prowess was great; blacks believe it and behave accordingly.

Some Americans associate the body with weakness and sin, even the devil incarnate, while extolling the mind. Not only did the puritan tradition reject corporeality in favor of the promised eternal life of spiritual bliss, but the growth of technology and white-collar work upstaged the importance of the body.[55]

A psychiatrist argues that black victims of racism have become estranged from the body by contagion. Devaluation of the body is further exacerbated by having black skin and other physical features that are dissonant with the white body aesthetic—one unobtainable for blacks. "The black body became the repository of and target for all bad objects in the collective psyche of the West—the stereotype for everything from dirt to evil."[56] While white children have good and bad poles in the body, black children must contend with a body that has been devalued in totality.[57]

On the other hand, Martin Luther King, Jr. suggested the importance of the body and the body in motion as a result of the psychological consequences of segregation:

> The absence of freedom imposes restraints on my deliberations as to what I shall do, where I shall live or the kind of task I shall pursue. I am robbed of the basic quality of manness. When I cannot choose what I shall do or where I shall live, it means in fact that someone or some system has already made these decisions for me, and I am reduced to an animal. The only resemblance I have to a man is my motor responses and functions. I cannot adequately assume responsibility as a person because I have been made the victim of a decision in which I played no part.[58]

Touch, another form of physical expression used to gain attention, was initiated sooner and was more common among black than white children at HPES. Skin, is the oldest and most sensitive of our organs.[59] It is the first medium of communication. Touching may be aggressive, affectionate, comforting, or exploratory. There are also status and class differences in touching: the higher the class, the less frequent; the lower the class, the more.[60] What Edward Hall calls the space bubble is the area surrounding the person within which an individual feels comfortable so long as no one enters it. North American Anglo males are less accessible to touch than females, who receive more touching than men and have a smaller personal space, so people can come closer to them before they consider their space invaded.[61] Boys learn not to seek tactile contact except in limited acceptable activities, such as football, for tactile contact connotes sexual intimacy. White children's hair had a fascination for black children. They liked to see "the fluff fly" as one black boy put it. In a HPES counseling session on action and interaction, a black boy brushed a white boy's hair with his hand. The white boy interpreted the touching gesture as aggressive, as an incursion into his privacy: "He messed up my hair." The black boy said he was saying hi!

Touching patterns may have caused some white students to leave HPES after the fifth grade, when more children left than at any other-time during the school's first two years. Although some parents said their children's departure was to enable them to become integrated into the neighborhood friendship network before going to junior high, other parents commented that their girls would come home crying. Youngsters are often especially sensitive to touching at the time of pubescent body changes and heightened self-consciousness. There were no fifth-grade transfers at the end of HPES's third year. Perhaps children or faculty learned how to deflect the touching.

Anger: Styles of Ventilation

The sequence of activities and method of ventilating anger contrib-ute to a dramatic expressive style that creates dissonance between low-income and middle-class youngsters. Hostile responses to situations can be reflective and passive or extraverted and active. At HPES, when middle-class children were becoming especially upset, they were likely to signal this with words or tears. They often directed anger inward, with-drew, or displaced aggression. "Black children explode faster," com-mented one teacher. They were more likely to externalize anger. The black coprincipal said, "We are more expressive; we hit in play. Black children are faster to hit, get the argument over with, and get on with the playing." In disputes, the nonverbal, such as hitting and pushing, emphasizes commands.[62]

Lower-class blacks are socialized to more aggression than the middle class,[63] and they bring this learning to school. At home among adults, these black children are usually not allowed free rein. Instead, they are told to obey and tend to be swiftly slapped if they err. Accustomed to being hit by family adults, youngsters often viewed hitting as a sign of affection.[64] "When you hit a kid, he feels you care about him."[65]

Because adults in the Hamilton Park community are often not at home but cannot afford a sitter, and because "baby-sitting" relatives do not live with the family as commonly as they used to, youngsters learn early to be independent.

In contrast, middle-class children tend to acquire an "emotional

73

tidiness."[66] Even the unruliness—nasty games, the play that seems involuntarily brutish—is curiously formal, even restrained. Even in therapy, these children's violence in the midst of a game was almost a caricature of violence: safe, camouflaged, and quarantined. Because of Anglo whites' general emotional control, many blacks find them cool and aloof.

There appears to be a difference between dominant culture and a black culture over "the rights of the asserter versus the rights of the asserted on":

> For mainstreamers it hurts more to hear something unfavorable than it hurts them not to say it—therefore, they rather suppress their own assertion of feeling in deference to the feelings of those receivers who might be hurt by their expression, whereas for blacks it hurts more not to say something, that is, to suppress the feelings underlying assertion, than to hear something unfavorable—therefore, they choose rather to speak what they feel to others in expectations that others will reciprocate.[67]

Perhaps the distinction is between overt and covert aggression. At HPES, a black parent said, "Because blacks are more open about it [aggression], they are more likely to get caught." None of the children interviewed, however, mentioned this to me.

The HPES children passively or aggressively signaled an unwelcome intrusion of their space. Passive signs included rocking, leg swinging, tapping, looking up, or moving away; the message was "go away, you do not exist." Middle-class children tended to respond this way or to verbalize their displeasure. A white girl in the fourth grade (1) said, "I get a mad look on my face and then I go sit down and think about it." A black girl (6) said, "You sul" (sulk). However, many blacks responded by pushing, hitting, or kicking.

A general assumption is that cognitive and social abilities are differentially structured according to age and sex. The same type of interaction at one age will be perceived, processed, and reacted to differently than at a later level of development. Yet male and female children in grades 2, 4, and 6 all recognized differences between whites and blacks in handling anger. Whites learn conventions and manners that protect the sensibilities of others, and these are maintained as a means of expressing respect.

"How can you tell if a child is angry?" I asked. "Sometimes they slug you" (2 bb 6th). "Look at them, the eyes, they turn green," said a second-grade black boy (15). "Sometime they puff up, and most girls, they roll they eyes at you, get all hunched up" (24 bg 6th). A fourth-grader (44 bb) remarked, "Usually when a boy gets mad, his lip start sticking out, and I start to laugh." Another said, "I laugh because it's funny. It's their face that makes them funny. They be making faces" (5 bg). This response to an angry child often provokes a fight. "He hit, rolls his eyes, and squints. Girls say some kind ugly words. I roll my eyes, and I stomp my feet" said a second-grader (88 bb). "Blacks go, 'who's a nigger?' 'come mon nigger—you askin' for it nigger.' POW!" reported a white second-grade boy. "I can tell if a child is angry by the way he looks—mad and mean—they balls his fist—they push people around."

I observed a girl do exactly what she told me in an interview:

> I go beat 'em up. If they hurt me, I beat 'em up. I start to almost cry, but then I go beat up the person and tell the teacher. If she don't do nothin' about it, I go beat 'em up. If someone meddle my friend, I go and tell 'em, "If you pick on my friend one more time, I'm gonna kick your hinny," and if they do that, I sneak up behind 'em, and my foot come up there and then they start beatin' up me, and I start beatin' on them, and then we go to the office. I keep goin' till I get a whuppin'. If I get a whuppin', I don't do it anymore if it hurts (102 bg 2d).

A second-grader complained:

> When they get mad at you and you do somethin' wrong to 'em, they get mad and start fighting. I didn't do nothin' to 'em today, and he just said he was gonna beat me up after school. Ryan just said that. He just said, "I oughta tear your name tag off and beat you up after school" (99 bb).

Body bluff occurs in expressions of anger: "He makes a fist and says, 'I'm going to get you.' He lifts me up by the shirt. K would not play. He's the nastiest. He told me to grab his shirt and say, 'the law can't help you now.' I did. He pulled his dick out" (120 wb 4th).

The suggestion that children be disciplined differently on the basis of color reveals differences in expressing anger.

> Black children should be treated *hard,* and white children should be kind of little hard, but not too hard, because white people only go like, "You better do that or I'm gonna do something to you" in a little voice. But black people hit 'em, but white people don't always (105 wb 2d).

I observed both black and white children fighting at HPES. However, when I asked a fourth-grade black boy if neighborhood and volunteer children who were both behaving incorrectly should be treated the same or differently, he replied:

> Maybe if they did the same thing. But one probably wasn't trying to hurt 'em that bad and the other ones try to hurt 'em real bad. They [whites] try to

hurt, most of 'em try to hurt, but I don't think they try to hurt as bad as neighborhood kids do.

"Is it because they can't or because they don't want to?"

They don't want to. 'Cause I seen a lot of people do it. When we be walkin' home, and there be's a fight, they fight real bad, like somebody, they was staying by the apartments over there, and they had a person that had stabbed one person, and one of 'em had hit 'im with a brick.

"How old were they," I asked? "No, not that old, eleven. They did go to Pacesetter school before when I was about in third" (92 bb 4th). A sixth grader explained:

Like most the black kids act like they're gonna beat 'em up or something. Here, a white person just talks about you sometimes. They talk about what they've done to one another, and then sometimes they get back friends. In sixth grade now, it seems like black kids want to beat up white kids when they want to be friends with them. When they're angry at them, then they'll beat up on 'em, and then they'll, the white kids, try to talk 'em out of it, say they didn't do it. Sometimes most of the white people didn't do it. But then, well, sometimes, they talk their way out of it or they try to face up to them, and the teacher comes along and breaks it up (93 bg).

Friendship, Initiation, Continuation, and Termination

How children initiated, sustained, and terminated friendship differed at HPES by income group and created dissonance. There are several levels of friendship:[68] Level one: Friends are those with whom one comes in frequent contact and plays, such as neighbors and school mates. Sharing food, toys, and other valued resources sustains the friendship. Establishing and terminating friendships may occur quickly and easily without long-term bases. Level two: Friends are those who help each other spontaneously or when one of them expresses a need. Reciprocal trust is a key element of friendship. Level three: Friends are those in whom one can confide, share interests, and find psychological support. Friendship is affirmed over time.

Many of the black children had been attending HPES since preschool; for some, this meant seven years. By forcing blacks to band together, segregation reinforced the usual basis for friendship—that of frequent contact. Thus white-imposed segregation during which blacks were forced to stay together has had ramifications. When children had the option of sitting together, in the classroom or at lunch, they chose to sit with their friends, individuals with whom they had established relationships. Often a group of blacks sat with one white, or a group of whites sat with one black. Those black children who were newcomers to the Hamilton Park community and had no relatives there generally found themselves loners, as did the volunteer children. Youngsters in the neighborhood who were different and excluded from its group were the ones more likely to mix with the volunteer whites. One girl, for example, had lived in Mexico and traveled elsewhere in the United States and had no relatives in the Hamilton Park community. She said,

> The way other kids act toward each other makes it harder for one person to go here. I feel like that should be changed so that everybody would be equal to one another, and there won't be racial discrimination against one. Well, okay, like, if you are new here, and you're another color, if you are Spanish, then it makes it harder for you to get along with the black and white children cause they sometimes won't talk or play with you. When I first came here, it happened to me. Then after the second year was over, it started getting, it was easier to get along because we had known each other for about a year then. Well, I am fully black, but it just seemed like I was from somewhere else that they treated me like that. Like from outer space (93 bg 6th).

Most of the white children who attended HPES came to the school as loners; that is, they came from all over RISD and did not have established social networks that accompanied them to HPES. They lacked the strong friendship groups that provide mutual protection and whose games of cooperative orderliness serve to counter the disorder of the environment. However, HPES volunteers were not, like most blacks, part of narrow friendship groups whose pressures toward conformity often thwarted individual academic aspirations.

Groups tend to have dominant individuals on whom attention focuses visually and around whom social cohesion occurs. The ethological literature suggests that persistent attention paid by subordinates toward more dominant members has adaptive functions because it allows the group to coalesce rapidly during periods of common danger.[69] Learning to recognize the dominant individuals and relate to them in a nonviolent manner through the use of gestures and other social signals decreases likelihood of being physically harmed.

Among white middle-class children, one who is strong and athletic has characteristics that enable that child to have many friends. A youngster said: "The best fighter always has friends . . . 'cause if a kid beats on you, you can ask Don to beat him up."[70]

Because young children are phenomenological, they respond to individuals as leaders in part on the basis of size. Children without the advantage of size can prove their toughness by leading in contests. Judging from the names mentioned in interviews, most youngsters agreed on who was the toughest. This quality was especially important for leadership in black neighborhood groups. Thus two children might fight to establish rank before they became friends.

The initial phase of communication in exploring friendship is often the most significant. Greetings may suggest politeness, establish one's presence and identity, deny threat, suggest a preliminary petition, evoke attention, reduce uncertainty, or establish respect or solidarity. A child's saying, "Hi, what's your name?" or hanging around another child in order to participate in the other child's play initiates a sequence, which if uninterrupted may proceed to cooperative play, reciprocal sharing of goods or services, following and/or leading, and self-validation. Because there are rules for positive social relationships, the response to "Hi" must fall within a range of what is anticipated or conceived. Other responses would be considered strange or unacceptable. A punch, for example, in response to a white middle-class child's "Hi" would be considered an unfriendly rather than a friendly act.

Blacks make friends differently, according to a white sixth-grade boy: "Cool. They smile; they talk sort of funny, you know, like 'whatch yuh doin' boy?'" (16). A common greeting among blacks is a slap or punch, whereas words are more common among whites. A white teacher broke up a "fight" between two black boys. The mother of one, a teaching assistant in HPES, expressed surprise, for she knew the friendship between the boys and the friendliness of the act. A fourth-grade black girl's comments suggest the greater range of expression among blacks:

> Some kids say what's your name, and then they say, Would you like to play with me, and then another says Will you be my friend? Some are just bashful. Some kids just come around you and just look at you. I say, "Do you want to play?" And I play with them, and then we just be good friends. And sometimes we have fights and come back friends (18 bg).

A sixth-grade black girl said: "Some kids—okay, I'm talking about different races now—go up and hit you, hey man, this stuff and all that. Yeah, they just hit you. They don't know how to act. I used to, didn't know that, and [in] the third grade I was just like that" (67 bg).

"Why do they pick fights if they want to make friends?" I asked. "So you can try to fuss at them, try to get along, so you can get closer to them," replied a classmate (8 bg 6th). A white fourth-grade boy finally figured it out: "They pick on you to make you recognize them" (120). A black boy who likes him offers him money as well. He calls him before school to ask him "silly things like, are you wearing underpants today?"

Verbal and nonverbal taunting and teasing caused a new white girl who was a tomboy at her former school to fear blacks at HPES. She was popular among blacks, according to the teacher, but she did not perceive their approach as friendly. When she cried, they zeroed in. Although she had adjusted to blacks, she socialized with whites. Making friends is difficult for newcomers anywhere. Cultural differences compound the problem: "Sometimes they act mean; they sorta hit you and sometimes they're nice." "How do you know whether they are being mean or being friendly?" I asked. "Sometimes the teachers said that, and sometimes I sort of wonder. Some people say they might be friendly, the word might get around" (106 wg 6th).

A black child who is friendly to a middle-class youngster and then strikes out with less restraint than is found among the middle class, puzzles the target child who tends to give clues to anger and to negotiate rules. The comparative passivity puzzles many blacks, who interpret this behavior as weakness.

Cultural Duality

Children attending HPES left a neighborhood play group and entered a multicultural world: the school culture and the two cultures of children.[79] Middle-class youngsters, as varied as they were, were closer to the culture the school espoused. The neighborhood black children entering HPES generally moved with a local play group and close community of friends and relatives. These children faced a world of school culture in some ways different from that of the home environment. Reflecting dominant white culture, the school culture is not unfamiliar, however, for the mass medium of television brings it into black homes.[72]

Both white and black children found contradictory patterns, values, and attitudes at HPES.[73] Each group had to understand the social competence of the other, how to know what to do with whom and when. Blacks experienced greater discrepancies, for the roles of student in school and member of a neighborhood peer group were rife with contradictions. Middle-class blacks were taunted about whether they were black or white.

Through its formal and hidden curricula,[74] we assume the school has some impact. The dual agenda of adult academic concerns and children's work tasks, on the one hand, and children's social survival, on the other, provide experiences that create expectations for performance and social relations in adult life. Much of what concerns children is irrelevant to teachers.

By manipulating school rules, expressing themselves openly, and keeping some nonapproved behavior under cover, children send messages to each other about self-dignity and power relations. Formal education conveyed by teachers, however, depends on effective communication and cognizance of mutually agreed-on as well as different values and standards of behavior. Awareness of multicultural communication patterns in social interaction is necessary to correct crossed, missed, or improperly interpreted messages. Unsatisfactory social relations between students and teachers and among students often block achieving educational and socioeconomic goals.

Table 3.I summarizes this chapter's exploration of the cultural duality at HPES and elsewhere that sometimes creates friction. Note that the categorizations are ideal. In everyday life, individuals may adopt different behavior styles according to their knowledge, inclination, and the situation.

Table 3.1

CULTURAL DUALITY IN SCHOOL

MODAL MAINSTREAM WHITE CULTURE AND MIDDLE-CLASS BLACK CULTURE	MODAL LOW-INCOME BLACK CULTURE
School, Work, and Authority	
Academic achievement emphasized	Less academic achievement orientation and classroom disruption
Standard English	Black vernacular English
Emphasis on self-responsibility and autonomy	Command and control orientation
Individualistic orientation; consulting with peers is cheating	Cooperative work orientation; consulting with peers solves problems
Work is the basis of person's individual worth	Personal performance style is basis of individual worth
Learning is generally through intergenerational communication	Learning is generally through peer communication after the infancy stage
Adult soliciting and giving information occur in a range of emotional situations	Adult soliciting and giving information occur more often in tense situations associated with an accusation of wrongdoing
Mind–body separation in school and work	Mind–body integration in expressive performance using verbal and kinesthetic means

80

Table 3.1 (continued)

CULTURAL DUALITY IN SCHOOL

MODAL MAINSTREAM WHITE CULTURE AND MIDDLE-CLASS BLACK CULTURE	MODAL LOW-INCOME BLACK CULTURE
Performance success measured by a cold sign, for example, a grade	Performance success measured by extent to which a child stimulates others to provide encouraging responses
Audience participation is passive, receptive	Audience participation is active in school, church, theatre, street
Performance for recognition by authority	Performance is for peer verbal and kinesic recognition and support; positive valuation accrues to recognizably black things
Teacher–student roles are distinct	Teacher–student roles often reverse according to demonstrated abilities
Acceptance of authority on the basis of status, role (for example, teacher)	Acceptance of authority through personal role validation—testing expressive performance of strength, intelligence, and persuasiveness

Trust and Stability

Acceptance of middle-class mainstream dominated system	Suspicion and distrust of whites and their institutions; learned ways of expressing respect to adults may inhibit the kind of communication teachers want
Predetermined rules applicable to all situations irrespective of time of occurrence	Negotiated rules for each situation; similar events viewed as separated in time and space if individuals involved are different
Whether a nonhappening is a result of design or impotence is crucial for white middle-class America; failure may be due to personal malice, be willful neglect, or restrictions put on a person because the institutional position does not allow certain actions	What counts is whether something happens or does not; failure is seen as operating selectively, for example, due to discrimination
Friendship initiation and maintenance is gentle	Friendship initiation and maintenance has aggressive dimensions as well

Space, Gaze, Image

Body distance, stillness	Body closeness, movement[a]
More other-directed gaze during listening than speaking[b]	Less other-directed gaze during listening
Greet at closer distances	Greet at further distances[c]

Table 3.1 *(continued)*

CULTURAL DUALITY IN SCHOOL

MODAL MAINSTREAM WHITE CULTURE AND MIDDLE-CLASS BLACK CULTURE	MODAL LOW-INCOME BLACK CULTURE
Prefer more space between speaker (twenty-six to twenty-eight inches)[d]	Prefer less space between speakers (twenty-one to twenty-four inches)
Prefer to manipulate the image of others in using film, make a film about the distant, exotic	Prefer to manipulate themselves as image, be in a film, make a film about behavior close to home

Conflict

Minimize antagonisms to encapsulate them in scenes so that bad feelings are not carried away from a confrontation	View oppositions as constant contrarieties that may affect a larger sense of cultural affirmation of community through dramatizing opposing forces

[a] Heinig 1975.
[b] LaFrance and Mayo 1976.
[c] Willis 1966; Baxter 1970. Scherer 1974 found interpersonal distances a function of class.
[d] Connolly 1973.

NOTES

1. Berger (1978:11) put the race/class issue this way:

> An argument can indeed be made that the fixation on race . . . as a root cause of inequity in American society actually serves to obfuscate (Marx would say "mystify") the underlying realities of class, class interest, and class struggle. It is class, not race . . . that has shaped the American stratification system most fundamentally.

See Wilson 1980.

An indication of the decreasing importance of race may be the change in white attitudes toward blacks. The former have become more tolerant between 1968 and 1978. A Gallup Poll (1978) found that the proportion of whites who says it approves of interracial marriages increased from 20 to 36 percent. Nonwhites were twice as likely as whites to express approval of interracial marriages (*Newsweek* 1979).

2. The average scores of black and white students in the College Board Scholastic Aptitude Tests reveal a gap between the two groups, with blacks 14.5 points below whites (Feinberg 1979).

3. See Harrington 1973; Hall and Jefferson 1976; Bradley and Bradley 1977:402.

4. Cf. Levine 1977:245; Kronus 1971; and Williams 1974:112–13, 169.

5. The first number in the parenthesis refers to the individual interviewed. The symbols for black and white are *b* and *w*, respectively. Sex is indicated by *g* for girl, *b* for boy. Grade levels are indicated by 2d, 4th, or 6th. The names of

children that appear in the text are fictitious in order to protect the youngsters' privacy.

6. Raspberry 1979a; cf. Noblit and Collins 1978:26.
7. Ray Warner in Raspberry 1979a.
8. Grier and Cobbs 1968:144.
9. See Ogbu 1974 and Metz 1978:253. For Americans, Bowles and Gintis (1976) generally argue that education was never a potent force for economic equality. From an educational gap between blacks and whites of 3.3 years or 38 percent of the median white education in 1940 to a reduced educational gap of 18 percent, this narrowing of the educational difference would have achieved black/white income equality had blacks received the same benefits from education as whites (Reich 1973).

The Wingate School experience suggests the relationship between academic performance, school policy, and employment. Hentoff (1979) reported that a principal transformed a chaotic high school by individualizing programs, stressing reading in all subjects, discouraging teachers from treating students as losers, providing realistic vocational training, *and* providing after-school and summer jobs through a nearly $1 million federally funded Cooperative Education Program. A San Diego school pays children to attend (Barringer 1980).

Larkin's (1979) comparison of white middle-class affluent suburban youth in the 1950s, 1960s, and 1970s provides an important perspective in considering the plight of youth in America generally.

10. Cf. Gerard and Miller 1975.
11. Quoted in Valente 1980; see Latimer 1986.
12. A peer group is made up of individuals who have a psychological relationship to each other; share common goals, motives, and norms; and interact with each other. Bradley and Bradley (1977) point out that the literature on peer group influence does not usually take into account the multiplicity of peer groups operating within a single classroom.
13. Silverstein and Krate 1975:118.
14. These behaviors are the common adaptive responses of many working-class populations to their historical, political, and economic situations. See, for example, Sennett and Cobb (1973) and Willis (1977).

Willis (1977:126) points out that the white working-class youth's counterschool culture is skeptical of rewards for conformism and obedience that the school seeks to exact as well as the long-term values of education in a tight job market. The boys are unwilling to sacrifice the immediate gratification of their creative, self-made oppositional style in school, which involves imposing their own frameworks and meanings, exercising their abilities, and seeking enjoyment even where most controlled by the school. Willis concludes, "In contradictory and unintended ways, the counterschool culture actually achieves for education one of its main though misrecognised objectives—the directions of a proportion of working kids 'voluntarily' to skilled, semiskilled, and unskilled manual work" (1977:178).

In contrast with middle-class parents, stable, blue-collar working-class parents in industrial societies believe the most important thing their children should learn is to obey (Scanzioni 1977:290). Some low-income black parents now urge their children not to be pushed around by white authority figures, and this attitude sometimes manifests itself in children's attitude toward their teachers' instructions in academic areas.

15. McDermott 1974.
16. Labov 1972; Mitchell-Kernan 1971.
17. Ward 1971.
18. Hall and Freedle 1975:151.
19. Bernstein 1972.
20. See Hanna 1984 for a state of the art overview of black–white communication.
21. Gold and Mann 1977.
22. Hare (1978) suggests that low-income children have more numerous sources of self-esteem. Furthermore, their need for achievement may be collective rather than individual (Ramirez and Price-Williams 1976). See also Powell (1973); Rosenberg and Simmons (1972); and Wolf (1981:141–142) on minority children who have developed positive concepts of themselves, sometimes more positive than majority students have of themselves.
23. Silverstein and Krate 1975:118.
24. Rich 1987:148.
25. Cf. Metz 1978:105; National Institute of Education 1978.
26. Sennett and Cobb 1973.
27. Cosnow 1979; see Roebuck and Neff 1980.
28. Willis 1977; Rutter et al. 1979.
29. Ibid.
30. Ruchkin (1977:239) found that although corporal punishment was officially prohibited in some Maryland schools, it was nonetheless administered by black adults to black youngsters in response to direct or implied parental request.
31. Harrington 1975.
32. Harrison-Ross and Wyden 1973:182.
33. Gay and Abrahams 1973:335.
34. Genovese 1974:508.
35. Wiggins 1980:29.
36. Sedlacek and Brooks 1976:20.
37. On the basis of their cross-cultural study, Weisner and Gallimore found that nonparental caretaking is either the norm or a significant form of caretaking in most societies. They note that "while child caretaking may not foster individual differentiation, it may prepare well for societies in which personal achievement and independence are not common options" (1977:178–79).
38. Goffman 1959.
39. Kochman 1981.
40. For example, Kochman 1971, 1977, 1981; Abrahams and Szwed 1975; Pasteur and Toldson 1982.
41. Hazzard-Gordon 1983a:24, 1983b.
42. Ibid.
43. Jones and Hawes 1972:67–68.
44. Harrison-Ross and Wyden 1973:73.
45. Ibid., 33.
46. See Smitherman 1977:106–7 for further illustrations.
47. Alihan 1970.
48. Kochman 1981.
49. Bernstein 1975:31.
50. Kochman (1971:6) distinguishes between attributes of a person (at-

84

tributive orientation) versus prerogatives of the office (extensional orientation). Gay and Abrahams (1973) use the terms expressive versus instrumental.

51.   Gay and Abrahams 1973:336.

52.   Silverstein and Krate (1975) found that many members of Harlem street peer groups continually sought acceptance and anchorage with the dominants. Experiencing frequent frustration, they withdrew for interim periods into detached sullen isolation.

53.   Recent studies have suggested that the reason some poor people seem unable to modify their condition is the result of depression. Middle- and upper-class whites often receive immediate attention for their stress and mental health breakdown. The repetitive and futile exercises of job hunting and coping with inflation lead some poor people to become depressed and do nothing (cf. Lerner 1972).

54.   Hanna 1988b.

55.   Hanna 1983b.

56.   Manganyi 1977:76.

57.   Ibid., 79.

58.   King, Jr. 1967:99. Takaki (1979) argues that the fusion of protestant asceticism, republican theory, bourgeois acquisitiveness, and modern capitalism in the United States created a hierarchy of values. Work, frugality, self-control of passion and sensual appetite predominated. Self-control meant controlling the body and further, controlling people who primarily engaged in physical labor.

59.   Montagu 1986.

60.   Henley 1977:74–123.

61.   LaFrance and Mayo 1978a:156, 163, 167.

62.   Goodwin 1982.

63.   Coles 1967:597; see chapter 4.

64.   Silverstein and Krate 1975; Foster 1974.

65.   Rosenfeld 1971:18.

66.   Coles 1967:592; Hochschild 1979.

67.   Kochman 1977:57.

68.   Damon 1977.

69.   Chance and Larsen 1976.

70.   Damon 1977:161.

71.   Similar patterns were found in Los Angeles (Gustaitis 1979).

72.   Gilliam (1978) reports that "an estimated 12.2 percent of all nonwhite households watch daytime dramas compared to 7.7 percent of all white households."

73.   Cf. Mitchell-Kernan 1972:29.

74.   Several researchers (for example, Eddy 1965, 1975; Leacock 1969; Rist 1970; Sieber 1978; LeCompte 1978) speak of the special function of schooling, which prepares youngsters for the work world through an implicit rather than explicit curriculum stressing authority, time, work, and order. Hurn (1978:192) speaks of what is "*implied* by the organization of the classroom and the rewards and punishments schools employ to regulate student behavior." I use the term more broadly to include children's styles of social relations, which are also important in determining behavior.

4

MEDDLIN': IT WOULD HURT YOU TOO

WE all know about Tom Sawyer, Huckleberry Finn, and the Little Rascals: Aggressive play with contests between individuals or groups is universal.[1] Indeed rowdy, unruly play is the product of biological heritage, culture, creativity, and capability. Bullying, intimidating, fighting, pranks, and defiance of authority exist in every school. Reasons for aggression are the same in many cases. Behavior generally considered playful occurring between two students of the same race might be considered aggressive by adults if it occurs crossracially. Small towns usually have a single school mixed socioeconomically where students are tracked, separated into groups within or in different classrooms, according to academic ability and performance. Aggression occurs and is accepted as part of school life. Now, however, with central-city desegregation, color and social classes overlap within a historical context of slavery, emancipation, and changing concepts of equal opportunity.

How do children view their lives at school? How do they define the situations in which they find themselves? These perceptions affect their attitudes and behavior, which, in turn, have implications for future school policy and societal differentiation. Children are necessarily dependent biologically and economically. However, they are also the active subjects of their own choices—which increase with maturation—as well as the objects of parental and school efforts.

Although *there were far more pleasant* than unpleasant encounters at HPES, adversive interactions (for targets of aggression who were harmed or feared they would be harmed) are the subject of this chapter because aggressive experiences in desegregated settings with low-income youngsters are new and dramatic for many middle-class children. Displays of aggression in any school setting create a climate that impedes

86

children from reaching their potential, especially low-income young-sters' academic achievement and later socioeconomic advancement.

I did not ask HPES youngsters about fighting; they mentioned it in response to several open-ended questions. Aggression came to the fore because it was on children's minds and before their eyes. Sometimes it touched them.

Let me underscore once again that children generally engage in some physical aggression in family, neighborhood, and school situations. However, in my interviews with black, white, female, male, second-, fourth-, and sixth-graders, the overriding difference between black (lower-class) and white (middle-class) children was the more positive value that blacks placed on fighting and their greater, more intense, and more varied participation in *meddlin'*—"If somebody just be messin' with you, just to try and aggravate you, just hit ya and do it with words" (112 bg 6th). Most middle-class adults have not experienced such language and behavior; their school lives took place in a different historical era when there was more respect for authority and less personal freedom of expression.

"Most the black kids act like they're gonna beat you up; here a white person talks about you sometimes," said a black child. A girl said, "The whites look scarylike. They don't pick on each other much, you know. Whites have patience; they're not very tough" (119 bg 6th). Another black girl said, "Fighting is okay if you win and don't do it often. You can lose friends." A sixth-grade black boy remarked, "Fightin' toughens you for life" (116). Another black sixth-grader reported: "Blacks try to hurt more in a fight; whites try to hurt less" (91).[2]

Some parents and commentators outside the school claimed that white children engaged in meddlin' as much as black children but white styles were more subtle and therefore less visible to adults. A further claim was that some children misinterpret harmless meddlin' as threat-ening. These arguments may be true. Yet both black and white children spoke more about black children meddlin'.

> I think the neighborhood children do it more. At my other school, I mean you just go up and tell somebody to quit, and they'd normally quit. Here the neighborhood kids are a little bit tougher than the volunteer kids. I guess their parents, maybe, are rougher on 'em or whatever. I know at our school everybody was just about the same. I mean nobody was too much stronger. If some, they had to have their way; if you just pushed back, they'd normally stop. Here you have a fight. I guess they've been in fights before a lots. I think it's their parents, the way they see their point of view: You have to be tough to live. I think the toughest one is the one who backs off (69 wb 6th).

Children's reports and my observations suggested that although generally more physical, black low-income children's styles of aggravating others encompassed a broad range of behavior. With the exception of three white second-grade boys from broken homes, I did not observe angry, impulsive white meddlin' on the playground or in classrooms.

The HPES was not atypical: In Harlem, youngsters engage in physical abuse and ridicule "to an extent unheard of in most middle-class communities."[3] Similarly, in five desegregated schools that would be ranked among the better institutions in their respective areas, the level and kinds of aggression differed for black and white.[4]

The National Institute for Education (NIE) study of the frequency and seriousness of crime in elementary and secondary schools, required from the Department of Health, Education, and Welfare as part of the Ninety-third Congress Education Amendments of 1974 (Public Law 93-380), found that risks of serious attack and robbery (five or more incidents reported a month) are twice as high in predominantly minority schools (less than 40 percent non-Hispanic white) than in predominantly white schools (more than 70 percent white).[5] However, it is not race per se but amount of crime in the attendance area of the school that seems to be the critical factor in the rate of violence. The study found no relationship between the number of students bused for desegregation purposes and school violence. There seemed to be agreement among many respondents in the nationwide survey that there was a core of disruptive students who were responsible for the aggression. They were students who had difficulty academically, were often in trouble in the community, and came from broken homes.

In another study, when eighty black and white sixth-grade males were shown a variety of ambiguously aggressive behaviors performed by black and white stimulus figures, all boys rated the behaviors as more mean and threatening when the perpetrator was black.[6]

Other research found that low-income black youngsters caused Asian refugee families who had formerly lived in Washington, D.C., unhappiness about the public schools: "Too much fighting at school in that place. Gangs of tough blacks . . . Always afraid in bathroom and playground. Here there are no black gangs. Here, Americans. Here my children not afraid to go to school, and I not afraid for them." The Lao translator and family members appeared "uneasy after reporting that they did not like the black students in their former community. They explained that they did not like the "constant fighting and blacks did the fighting."[7]

Although most children are fascinated by dramatic events, no white boy or girl whom I interviewed at HPES expressed a positive attitude toward fighting. When I asked, "If you could change one thing about HPES, what would you change?" or "What don't you like about Pacesetter?" a common answer was the fighting. Similarly, when asked, "What do you think is bad behavior in the classroom?" the most frequent answers were fighting and meddlin' when the teacher leaves the room. When asked, "What do you think is bad behavior on the playground?" most children replied "Fighting!" Two white boys thought it was all right to fight if someone else started it. One black girl was positive; four thought it was self-defense. Five black boys volunteered a positive judgment about fighting; seven, a qualified positive answer. For example,

> I think fighting is bad but not bad bad. That's the rules. The grown-ups don't want nobody get hurt or nothin'. The kids don't care. Sometimes I think we should get frustration out of our systems—but not with the wrong person. I think that a person that bothers you the most should be the target. After a fight, the students keep sayin', "Aw, he won, I know he won; you just got beat up" or somethin' like that (115 bb 6th).

Many children suggest their mothers do not like fighting "unless someone starts it or deserves it":

> I don't like to fight unless they start the whole thing 'cause my mother told me if anyone starts a fight with you, knock them off their feet if you can. I've gotten in one fight, no two, no three, since I've been going to this school [second year], and I didn't get in trouble in any of them. I was sorta working, and this girl comes along and hits me on the head with her books. I tell her to quit it, and she whacks me on the head. She sits down, and I knock her out of her chair, and that starts the whole battle. The second fight was when I was walking to school and this boy, *D*, he starts bothering me. You know, see, he stutters, and I stuttered right back at him. And he got real mad, and he hit me, and then that started another fight. And another fight was when *DW*, he came up and hit me on the nose, and if the teacher didn't come along, he would have been hanging out the window, 'cause he was real close to the window, and I was going to knock him out the window. He was getting on my nerves, bothering me all the time. Everyday he's bothering me, and he's tempting me again this year (19 bb, 6th).

Sixty-one percent of the whites volunteered a negative attitude toward fighting in contrast to 43 percent of the blacks. Girls were more negative about fighting than boys. Sixth-grade boys and girls differed more than children in other grades, and sixth-grade black and white boys differed most. There is little evidence of negative attitudes among black boys. See Table 4.1 for a breakdown by grade level, race, and sex.

Although boys were expected to be more aggressive than girls, and black boys were demonstrably more so than white boys, there were also black girls who were fighters and even bested the boys. The HPES evidence comes from student identification of aggressive peers, teacher and parent perception, and my observations.

When I asked children if they were *afraid* of anyone at school, they most often mentioned the names of black children or referred to blacks who engaged in meddlin'. Rarely was a white or middle-class child mentioned. Fifty-two (43 percent) black and white children said they feared black children. One black and two white second-grade boys (2 percent) were afraid of three white male classmates (see Table 4.2). Children's perceptions of blacks' aggression challenge the claim that a disproportionate number of black children in desegregated schools are disciplined because of racism.[8]

"Are you afraid of anyone at school?" I asked a child who had attended HPES for three years. "It's really a bunch of kids at school, not just one person. Usually it's a group that forms like if one person's mad at you, his friends group up with him" (78 wg 6th).

White boys are the most fearful.[9] In American culture, physical competition is more appropriate for males. One white boy at HPES said, "I think I shouldn't be part of the school. They'd make fun of me if I went back [to Lake Highlands where the sixth-grader had been], they'd call me half-nigger" (79).

Supporting the children's perception of the occurrence of fighting are the most frequent types of misconduct for which teachers referred students to the discipline room over a four-week period. Fighting or physically abusing another child (for example, pushing, hitting, poking with a pencil) ranked highest along with generally uncooperative behavior. Three-fourths of the referrals were black, and three-fourths were boys; see Table 4.3.

Bullies, Bullied, Funny People, and the Protected

Every school has its bullies and aggression. In Stockholm and Solna, Sweden, over a three-year period, individual children were harrassed by another child, a small group, or a whole class.[10] Approximately 5 percent of the boys could be judged to be pronounced whipping-boys. The whipping-boy–bully problems were strongly related to stable interpersonal relations among the boys. The whipping-boy victims were physically weaker and more anxious, insecure, and nervous than bullies and well-adjusted boys. Bullies had aggressive personality patterns—strong aggressive tendencies, weak aggression inhibitions, and a generally

Table 4.1

CHILDREN WHO VOLUNTEERED A NEGATIVE OPINION ABOUT FIGHTING

GRADE	NUMBER	PERCENT
2	19/40	47
4	20/40	50
6	24/40	60
RACE		
Black	26/60	73
White	37/60	61
SEX		
Boys	23/60	38
Girls	40/60	66

CATEGORIES GENERATED BY ATTRIBUTES OF GRADE, RACE, AND SEX

		Grade		
		2	4	6
Black	Boy	30%	30%	10%
	Girl	60%	60%	70%
White	Boy	40%	40%	80%
	Girl	60%	70%	80%

Sample n = 120
Cell n = 10

91

Table 4.2

UNEQUIVOCAL FEAR OF SOME CHILDREN AT SCHOOL

		GRADE 2		GRADE 4		GRADE 6		
		B	0	B	2	B	0	Sample = 120
		wb	1	wb	0	wb	0	Sample per grade/ sex/race category = 10
	Boy	bb	0	bb	2	bb	1	Percent = % within category who are
		bg	0	bg	0	bg	0	fearful
BLACK		10% afraid		40% afraid		10% afraid		*Feared*
		B	0	B	2	B	3	B = blacks as a group
		wb	0	wb	0	wb	0	wb = white boy
	Girl	bb	3	bb	2	bb	1	bb = black boy
		bg	0	bg	1	bg	1	bg = black girl (a child may fear more than one of the above)
		30% afraid		50% afraid		50% afraid		
		B	1	B	3	B	0	*Fearful*
		wb	2	wb	0	wb	0	Grade (n = 40)
	Boy	bb	3	bb	7	bb	3	2d 33%
		bg	0	bg	1	bg	1	4th 60%
						everyone	1	6th 47%
WHITE		60% afraid		100% afraid		40% afraid		
		B	0	B	1	B	4	
		wb	0	wb	0	wb	0	
	Girl	bb	3	bb	3	bb	3	
		bg	2	bg	2	bg	2	
		30% afraid		50% afraid		90% afraid		

Table 4.3

REFERRAL TO DISCIPLINE ROOM AT HPES[a]

	Race		Grade			Sex	
	Black	White	2	4	6	Male	Female
	(N = 120)		(N = 118)			(N = 119)	
N	91	21	63	22	33	90	19
%	75	25	53	18	27	75	25

[a]*November 18 to December 14, about four weeks.* Most frequent type of misconduct (teacher report): fighting or physical abuse: 21 cases; generally uncooperative: 14 cases; vocal abuse of teacher: 9 cases; noisy: 8 cases; physical restlessness: 8 cases.

positive attitude toward violence. These boys tended to come from homes that were rejecting or indifferent toward children and did not place consistent demands on them for nonaggressive behavior. Imitating the bully, some children, especially if frustrated and the bully's aggressive behavior seemed justified, ganged up on another child. Seeing an aggressor easily overpower a weak opponent can arouse expectations of a successful outcome in similar aggression with the same opponent, especially for boys with low status among their peers who want to increase their ranking. Furthermore, when several youngsters join an aggressive act, the individual feeling of personal responsibility is likely to decrease.

Not only does every school have its instances of aggression, but much play aggression occurs between boys and girls as part of preadolescent courtship. At HPES, incidents occurred in classrooms, in the lunch line, on the playground, and in the restroom. Some children said the classroom permitted more opportunity for meddlin' another child than the playground. In the classroom, there was usually only one teacher to watch; on the playground there were several. Sometimes children made arrangements to fight outside the school.

Youngsters did not want school authorities to catch them fighting. Sometimes a tough "on parole" for such misbehavior was bullied and could not defend himself in school:

Most of the time at school they won't mess with you; at home they do—outside they can meddle you more. Well, like yesterday, one of my friends, like three girls jumped on him and beat him up, and he didn't like that. He didn't beat them up 'cause he'd get expelled (2 bb 6th).

Who were the primary targets of children's meddlin'? They were peers of the same or different sex and the same or different race, teachers, or school property. Aggressors and targets were individuals or groups. When I asked if there were anyone whom she was afraid of at school, a second-grade black girl said, "The boys; I scared of boys. They're mean. They hit girls. They hit girls in the stomach" (56). She mentioned the names of several black boys. Boys tend to be more physically aggressive: "Boys fight badder; girls are more sensitive; they cry," a second-grade black boy told me (37). However, a few girls did get into physical fights and some even beat up the boys. There were children whom youngsters and adults recognized as bullies, the bullied, the funny people who disengaged aggressors with humor, and the protected children who sought adult protection or peers to "take up for them." Patron-client and alliance behaviors occurred among children.

Although blacks harrassed both whites and blacks, children's fights were most often intraracial, indeed, blacks often mentioned that they were afraid of other blacks: They had seen, heard, or experienced aggression. Some blacks find it easier to become angry with other blacks than with racist whites. Reverend Jesse Jackson guesses that "it's because blacks fear white retaliation that they are more quick to fight the victim instead of the victimizer, the bound instead of the binder, and the conditioned instead of the conditioner."[11] Comparative statistics among different groups in American society show that blacks are most often victims of black violence. In a desegregated middle school, black boys were observed hitting or punching nine times as often as white boys and boxing twice as often. Only four out of ten observed fights were interracial.[12] The NIE study on violence and vandalism in schools found that the majority of attacks on, and robberies of, students at school involve victims and offenders of the same race. Victims and victimizers in real fights are likely to be black; furthermore, they tend to be youngsters who are in trouble at school or home.

At HPES, one-on-one fights were most common between two tough children who challenged each other. Although I noticed such fights attracted others who merely encircled the contestants and cheered them on, I also saw encounters in which each contestant's friends would take up the battle and participate.

This kind of incident often caught my eye at HPES: Standing in line to enter the school building, Ivan, a black boy, pinched the buttock of a white boy who stood in front of him. The child responded by pushing Ivan with his elbow. Thereon Ivan's black friend, standing in front of the white boy, hit him.

Most people fight over silly things. If somebody's hittin' on somebody, then they start hittin' them. Mostly the neighborhood kids stick up for each other

94

'cause they've been together since first or second grade. The kids in my neighborhood usually don't get in fights as much. I don't know why, it's weird. Maybe they [HP blacks] resent the volunteer children coming into their school (104 wg 6th).

There was resentment. Recall the history of the Hamilton Park community built in response to white terrorism; blacks were bused to segregated schools. Then, when the black community finally had its own neighborhood school, it was taken away. Some people viewed this as being pushed around as in the past.

HPES blacks and whites shared the notion that whites did not engage in fighting at school because they were weaker, afraid to "take on" blacks. A fourth-grade black boy said, "Whites fight less at school. They probably do it at home" (21).

Some children cannot compete with equals, thus a few youngsters pick on a child who is unequal in some way, for example a newcomer or someone small, timid, afraid to stand up to an aggressor,[13] excessively fat or thin, or wearing unusual clothes.[14] Such behavior may also express an intolerance of deviance. For example, in one of the second-grade classrooms, an exceptionally bright, timid, self-conscious child was the butt of aggression (parent's report). Black girls tormented her with "you smell," "you're ugly." Furthermore, the child had a slight speech impediment, which exacerbated the problem, for she feared being laughed at if she asserted herself verbally. Two other bright white girls, "goody-goodies," customarily defended her.

In order to avoid getting into trouble herself, Allison, a bright black girl from a broken home, induced Tina, a less-bright, large black girl (repeating second grade) to misbehave. Tina harrassed three well-behaved, academically successful white girls (Jane, Louise, and Jo). One day Tina, who sat next to Jane and "drove her crazy," chased Jane to a secluded part of the playground and forcibly tried to pull down her pants. Allison also did her own mischief: She threw a learning-disabled child into a trash can; when she wanted another child's desk moved, she threw it down; and when she became angry during a Spanish lesson, her scissors somehow struck the teacher's arm, requiring several stitches.

In addition to the physically handicapped, children identified as "big shots, braggarts, bookworms, or putting on airs" are targets of aggression for youngsters everywhere. Many blacks are especially sensitive to immodesty. There is a duality of thought: impotent resignation to conditions of abuse and powerlessness on one hand and a growing sense of being able to control one's future on the other. Blacks espoused Christian humility; it was dangerous for them to forget their situation. Black folklore has tales that present a caveat against undue pride and self-assertiveness.[15] Female pride and egocentricity are not appreciated, and male assertiveness is subject to challenge.

All HPES bullies tried to avoid encounters with other bullies, strong athletes, and those with tough patrons; they knew "not to mess with 'um" unless they were prepared for a showdown. Those who deliberately or inadvertently challenged someone to call their bluff invited aggression.

> I tell my friend, "If someone meddles you, come tell me." And one time, my friend named Marily, someone was meddlin' her named J, and she came up and tell me. And I say, "J, you better stop messin' with her or else you get hurt." And then he left her alone, 'cause I can beat him up (45 bg 4th).

There are four general constraints on aggression: (1) an adult presence, (2) an activity ends and children move to different places, (3) fear of painful retaliation (compare chapter 5 on alliance behavior), and (4) knowledge that authority figures will learn of the aggression and penalize it. Moreover, children use "strong-suit tactics"[16] in school life, that is, drawing on one's strengths. Those with academic skills may capitalize on them and help aggressors in exchange for kindness. One child will use size and physical prowess, another will use a vocabulary and "a way with words." These kinds of responses are further discussed in chapters 6 and 7.

Besides individual and cooperative styles of meddlin' that have been described, there are verbal and nonverbal forms of aggressive behavior. Whites view the use of angry words as the beginning of a fight, whereas blacks do not.[17] However, this distinction did not appear at HPES. Black and white children used verbal insults, taunts, or boasts directed at an adversary as a prelude to fighting—a provocation. Blacks used words to incite an opponent to fight. A black boy said fights started this way: "They say, 'shut up mother fucker' and then comes the fight" (44-4th). A second-grade black boy remarked, "When you run up to somebody and say, 'I don't like that' and you push them out of the way— that'll cause a fight" (14). When I asked if he were afraid of other children at school, a white boy said: "*Yes*. A lot of black people in my class, because they're real mean to me. They say stupid words at me—*shit* and all that stuff. When somebody starts pickin' on you and sayin' stupid words and then a big fight comes" (105 wb 2d).

Blacks conventionally consider movement as the sign that someone intends to fight:

> If two guys are talkin' loud and then one or the other starts to reduce the distance between them, that's a sign because it's important to get in the first blow. Or if a guy puts his hand in his pocket and that's not a part of his

normal stance, then you watch for that—he might be reaching for a knife. But if they're just talkin'—doesn't matter how loud it gets—then you got nothin' to worry about.[18]

A person who anticipates physical blows tries to get in the first one. I watched children use verbal, nonverbal, or combinations of these expressions sequentially or simultaneously.

Verbal Aggression

There were at least six kinds of verbal aggression.

(1) Calling people *insulting names* or using descriptive words viewed as hostile was a style of meddlin' someone. Most name calling refers to: physical peculiarities of a child or the child's relations; pun or parody of a child's own name, usually with a body reference; or names based on behavioral traits, usually with body reference. Descriptive epithets sometimes become nicknames a child accepts and does not regard as baiting.

At HPES, an aggressor would single out a child's most vulnerable spot. Heavy children were called "watermelon stomach," "tank tummy," "ol' fat thing," "fat mama," "ugly," or by animal names, such as "pig" or "horse." "Shrimpo and "shorty" were epithets hurled at short individuals, thin children "legs," "toothpick," and "skinny bones". "Four eyes" referred to a child with glasses, cowardly youngsters were called "mis' soup—just chicken," "fraidy cat," or "fag" or "punk." A black, heavy, sensitive girl, the butt of "ol' fat chicken," complained that her peers always "chose those skinny bones not me."

Contrary to some research findings[19] names based on mental traits of the "dummy" type were very offensive at HPES, especially among slow learners, most of whom were blacks. Many HPES black and white children did not recognize anyone as dumb, they believed anyone could be smart by trying or getting help. Some slow learners, to the school's credit, verbalized a positive self-concept: "Nobody's dumb!" "We don't got no dumbest in our class!" And yet, in a group of four sixth-grade black male nonreaders, one member would not participate in oral reading attempts because he was ridiculed by the three more advanced nonreaders who called him dummy. When he worked individually with a perceptive special education teacher, he learned to read. A fourth-grade girl said, "It's the bullies who's the ones who are the dumbest; all they ever think about is fighting and never pay attention to their work." Dumb children are viewed as using nasty language:

This black girl says she's going to beat their "umph" out. You know. She says what that "umph" is. It's a nasty word you know. I'm going to kick your——
—out. [I asked the boy to write it and he wrote *butt.*] I don't mean to be nasty, but they'll say the word ass a lot of times. How about burning it? [word written on piece of paper] (16 wb 6th).

Children attach importance to spoken words as a source of control—words have the power to evoke shame, fear, anger, and fights. Words are the teacher's primary vehicle for controlling children, "managing classrooms." Because blacks were not inducted into the literature world of their white slave masters, the African oral tradition of songs, tales, and skillful oratory took root and flourished in the United States, and hence they feel the power of spoken words with particular sensitivity.

Another child's talking about a black child's mama was incendiary. *Your mama* or *mudder* became a substitute for the insulting and fight-provoking *mother-fucker* when the principal disciplined anyone using the latter phrase. In fact, the art teachers stopped white children from talking about their own mothers' work at the school lest black children misunderstand and become angry.

Some black children made anti-Semitic statements: During class, a second-grade black girl kept saying to a white Jewish boy, "All Jews are cheats and liars." One of the special resource teachers said the blacks hate the Jews because the Jews are smart and succeed academically. Jews have been at the forefront of the civil rights movement and are concerned with good education and are heavily represented in magnet schools, such as HPES. Some blacks' negative attitudes toward Jews come from the history of Jews as scapegoats, and the blacks project their own feelings.[20] It may also be that black culture absorbed a white Protestant fundamentalist culture that saw Jews as killers of Jesus and a people who have never accepted the truth of Christian teachings.[21]

Verbal abuse meant to amuse onlookers and participants may become aggressive play or at other times be transformed into fighting. Verbal aggression, as typically found in middle-class interaction, may save a person from physical aggression.[22] This kind of abuse teaches participants how to keep their temper or take the consequences; it sharpens the ability to control emotion and anger when an authority figure assaults someone's dignity, but he or she cannot safely respond. Frequently, a participant reaches his or her breaking point and goes after the tormentor with physical force.

(2) "Putting them down is making them *feel sorry* that they ever came in this world or something like that. And teasing them is just playing with

them," said a sixth-grade black boy (17). "How do you know the difference?" I asked.

> Well, it's kind of hard. Let me see, oh, they'll probably say, I got this and you don't; I got six model cars and you don't. That would be someone putting down. I know a boy named Greg who can put people down. Like he got a rich godmother; he'll brag all about her. I only told him once, and I never mention this to him. See, I'm kin to Natalie Cole.

Another way of putting someone down is singling out something new in a child's life: "That's an ugly, stupid-looking dress you have on today." "I hate the way your hair is today." "I call them some names, like if their breath stink" (5 bg 4th). Laughing about someone's father being arrested is another type of aggressive put down.

> If I knew something and you know that they didn't want me to tell, I'd do that; like if they been and got arrested. "You got arrested?" And I'd kinda say it real loud so everybody could hear it and start laughin' at that particular person, and, you know, sometimes they go on, so then I quit; you know, like I'd stop teasin' 'em (91 bb 6th).

Sounds are as important as the verbal and visual meanings that are communicated. Speech tones along with other kinds of sounds are excellent attention-getting devices; they move people to feeling and action. Intonational countering is the specific use of stress and pitch in pronouncing words in the black style to register sarcastic belief or contradiction about what somebody has just said.[23] The speaker can mean the opposite of *yeah* and *un-huh*. Some HPES children also make "farting" noises to punctuate their verbal assertions or put someone down; children's folklorists have noted such "fartlore" elsewhere.

Laughter can mute the effect of an uncomfortable situation by releasing suppressed feelings and/or exacerbating them. Children often laughed at a schoolmate who was taken to task by a teacher. They sometimes also laughed, mimicked, or sassed a teacher in a defiant "put down."

(3) Another style of aggression involves using *profanity* or crude and irreverent language common to working-class men,[24] and English words deemed foul to refer to parts and functions of the body traditionally considered most unclean. Those related to sex bear the historical Christian view of sex as depraved. Abusive profanity also serves other functions, especially to express frustration or discontent and as a catharsis.[25] Because it is impulsive, strong emotion, often forbidden and anti-

establishment, profanity may generate prestige among peers or divert attention from other issues.

At HPES, youngsters from the Hamilton Park neighborhood were more likely to hear profanity at home and on the street. They used profanity more frequently than middle-class children, although the former were careful not to use such language when authority figures were present. The black male principal punished students for profanity when the desegregated institution began.

The use of crude language by those excluded from broader societal decision-making bodies is a means of identifying with power. The use of sexual references sometimes reflects the insecurity an individual feels in relation to his or her own sexual and social identity. Childhood is a time of rapid growth and establishing self-identity as a person apart from family and in relation to others. As I pointed out in chapter 1, identity is shaped by others' perceptions of the self as well as the self creating identity by contrasting it with the qualities or positions of another. Although gender bears on relationships between men and women, gender may provide a symbolic basis for ranking individuals in society. Thus maleness and heterosexuality may be associated with power and dominance in contrast to female qualities of weakness and submission.[26] For example, male chemical factory workers, who labored and showered together in close quarters, verbalized their fear of homosexuality under such provocative conditions (and loss of freedom) through abusive and joking crude language, and thereby asserted the value of heterosexuality, autonomy, and dominance.[27]

The middle and upper classes, generally removed from using the body in physical labor, are accustomed to crude language in literature rather than in speech. In contrast, a black secretary from a working-class background became embarrassed about typing a transcript using profane language, whereas hearing such discourse was not a source of discomfort. Many middle-class youngsters who thought black ghetto talk was part of "cool lingo" used profanity among themselves.

(4) *Talking about someone* was the phrase children used to refer to two kinds of hearsay that upset a person. Rumor dwells on topical content that has an unsubstantiated basis; gossip deals with the personal affairs of an individual.[28] Hearsay is an oppositional tactic to denigrate or maliciously raise misgivings about a person. The instigator often used this to form alliances. Those who participated did so out of mischief or for titillation and entertainment. The hearsay process created drama and was not only a means of passing time but helped maintain fluidity in communication and social network patterns. Tensions fueled the communication.

Children also engaged in what is called ribbin' and signifying in literature on black culture, although I did not hear these terms at HPES. *Ribbin'* is when an agitator creates a story about a person and tells that individual a third person started it; *signifying* refers to behavior that also involved telling tales to goad someone directly, using eyes, hands, and innumerable gestures and expressions. It is a way of making fun of someone to stir up a fight.

(5) *Lying* to get someone in trouble was another form of verbal meddlin', as well as a source of amusement. A black boy who lied about his classmates said: "When my friend gets in trouble, I laugh; but when a girl in trouble, I say, 'you got in trouble.' And when the boy gets mad, his lip starts sticking out and it looks like a funny face, and I start to laugh" (44 4th).

(6) Verbal *intimidation* was a frequent aggressive style at HPES: "Listen to me [give me . . .] or I'll beat you up [blow your head off!] Knock out your guts! Kick you' hinney]." "Hey boy, you git over here!" A second-grade boy told his teacher, "Wait Ms. ———. I'll blow your head off if you don't!" Because of difficult situations, some blacks developed a control language.[29] "Sit down!" "Shut up!" "Be nice." Some children used this language and backed their commands and taunts with physical force if necessary. "A bully says somebody shut up, and they talk back— he go back there and hit him and they don't hit back 'cause they scared," reported a black boy (44 4th).

Some black children felt that since whites had come to their neighborhood and school, black children should be the rulers (79 wb 6th). During an indoor recess, a black girl told a white girl who wanted to play a record of her choice, "You in soul country now; you listen to soul music!" The tone used suggested repercussions if the child did not comply. "You be my slave," as mentioned earlier, was a common black command; not everyone was receptive to this. A white sixth-grade boy explained, "Because they've been here for six years and I've only been here for three years, 'cause I'm an original Pacesetter, and let's see—I think I should have the same rights as they should 'cause I'm here for the learning just like they are" (31).

(7) *Not speaking* to a child was another aggressive strategy. A group of black girls ganged up on Bridget: "Like this girl named Bridget she did somethin'—make a lot of girls mad and so not (*sic*) the whole sixth grade is speakin' to her." "What did she do?" I asked. The response was:

I can't tell you [laugh]. At home, had to do about a boy. It was about this boy. There was some boys in it who are mad at her, too, and she went and told

101

her cousin somethin', and her cousin came out there fussin' at a whole bunch of people, and we had just come from a soul party. We was walkin', and we met a lot of our friends and stuff. And she went and told her cousin a certain thing. She told her cousin that, see this certain person she goes with, Gerome, he quit her. And so she told her cousin that we were sayin' a lot of things about her, and that's why we quit her and stuff. And her cousin came out and tried to jump on us and all that stuff (109 bb 6th).

Nonverbal Aggression

In addition to attacks with words, youngsters used their bodies in at least five ways.

(1) *Body bluster*—posing and moving in a menacing way to make oneself threatening—was a common style of meddlin'. One could give the eye, roll the eyes, make the eyes smaller and beady, wrinkle the face, "frown up" with tense lips extended forward, the head and chin also thrust forward, "puff up," stick out the lip or jaw and make a fist. Girls sent hostile body messages by turning away with tilted head or twitching nose or posing in a fixed stance with one hip extended and both hands on the hips. The shoulder shrug, swaggering walk, limp stance saying, "I'm not paying attention," and dancing where such behavior is inappropriate, expressed defiance and insubordination.

The appearance of the eye region changes in relation to changes of mouth shape. Since the pouch under the eye is not under voluntary control, the meaning of a smile, for example, is closely affected by signals from the eye region.[30]

Rolling the eyes is a predominantly black-female visual gesture communicating hostility, displeasure, impudence, or general rejection of the person toward whom it is directed. An initial glare, not an eye-to-eye stare, precedes the eyeballs moving to the side away from the target of aggression, toward the opposite side, and upward in an arc to the other side.[31] The eye invades the person's space and "rummages up, down, and about another's preserve,"[32] to proclaim the individual's worthlessness, especially when the eyes are finally turned away. Without necessarily doing or saying anything to a person who "gives the eye," a victim may merely rub an aggressor the wrong way in dress, looks, or behavior. For example, a white girl who rolled her eyes at some black girls really angered them.

Part of body bluster includes arranging one's appearance. A signal of maleness or dominance in the peer pecking order is size, height, and enlarged outline (other than the stomach region). Some HPES black

102

boys let their hair grow into large Afros to increase their size. One bully wore a tank T-shirt to reveal his muscles. In restrooms, I was told, some boys used genitalia as weapons wielded in a competitive display of penis size. High-heeled shoes, whistles, and pocket knives were also part of body bluster.

A child acting tough, strong, and in charge is implicitly asking those around to believe in the image created before them. People observing is a fundamental biological act. Performers may or may not be taken in by their own act. If they can convince others that they possess attributes they appear to have and the others respond to their demands, pretended power may become a reality. Parents are continually confronted with stages as their children develop. Human survival requires intuition and canniness about other human beings: sizing them up, learning what they are likely to do, and what can be done to control their behavior.

"To run a game" is the term in the literature about black culture that describes acting in a physical way to achieve something, to put someone down. Chris, a special education student, was big for his age and well coordinated. In contests for a ball in any game, I saw him get the ball he went after. If his opponent got the ball first, he pushed him aside and would kick his "booty" (buttocks) besides. If the attacked child retorted with verbal insults, for example, calling him dumbo, he would receive a violent rebuttal. When a child reported Chris for hitting him, Chris said he had hit the child because the youngster called him dumbo. Prior developments in the incident were neither told nor solicited, and Chris continued "to run a game." Chris needed only to body bluster after children experienced or heard about his assertiveness.

(2) Another style of meddlin' consisted of *abusing possessions* of other children, for example, taking girls' purses and stealing (food, supplies, clothing, toys, and so on). Some children pushed others' pencils to make them mess up their papers, or scribbled on someone else's paper.

(3) A common form of nonverbal meddlin' was to *create a situation to get a child into trouble.* A black youngster said that one tactic was to make faces behind the teacher's back so that a child facing the teacher laughed and was then accused of being disrespectful. Another ruse that I observed several times involved children pushing others off their seats. The youngsters who are then "out of place" get berated for not being properly seated.

(4) *Physical assault* is the most aggressive component of an aversive style. It included a number of different behaviors: unwanted touching;

kicking; tripping; with a fist "beating on" or "hittin' on" someone's face, arms, back, or buttocks; choking; fingers snapping against someone's body; pulling or cutting hair; blowing pins out of straws; throwing rocks, dead or live crickets or other objects; and pushing (out of swings, off a seat so that the victim is reprimanded for being on the floor instead of in the seat); or misusing the toilet. Angry children have even drawn students' and teachers' blood.

Children reported that personal space was invaded in the restroom. In the process of eliminating waste products, individuals necessarily lose the protection of clothing. Nakedness connotes exposure and submission; however, some children were merely curious about the color pigmentation of the other race's genitals.

There seemed to be a fascination with "booty," "hinney," "ass," or "butt" kicking or pinching. It was common for a black boy to grab the buttock of a white boy and move him aside. Children are most commonly spanked by adults on the buttocks, a place that can be "whipped" without serious damage. Furthermore, there is a rural southern "cane patch" or "burrhead" pattern where older black women "don't talk to 'um—they move 'um physically."

> For this reverse area of the body, with its aggressive and libidinal focus in the sphincters and buttocks, cannot be seen by the child, and yet it can be dominated by the will of others. The "behind" is the small being's dark continent, an area of the body which can be magically dominated and effectively invaded by those who would attack one's power of autonomy and who would designate as evil those products of the bowels which were felt to be all right when they were being passed.[33]

(5) Another style of aggression involved *attacking the school*. Children threw water bombs against the bathroom walls or wrote on them. They sometimes wet rolls of paper towels and threw them on the windows, heaters, and fans to jam them. It is hard to separate vandalism from amusement: squirting liquid soap from dispensers on the floor, letting the sink run over, and "using the bathroom all over the bathroom" (46 bb 4th), "making sissy on the floor an' skiing on it," and jumping to place one's feet on the restroom walls, desks, and table tops.

Although all children were exposed to aggressive models through the mass media, students of different grade levels, of different sexes, of different social classes, and of both races commented that blacks fight and engage in meddlin' more than whites, and that most of the time blacks victimize blacks. These perceptions agreed with researcher observations of social interactions as well as school personnel reports. Chapter 5 examines the wellsprings of meddlin'.

NOTES

1. Huizinga 1955; Aldis 1975.
2. Cf. Podhoretz 1966:382 for reflections on his childhood among black and lower-class groups—"the black boys were really tough, bad, and defiant."
3. Silverstein and Krate 1975:113.
4. Wax 1980. See chapter 1 for references to the specific studies.
5. National Institute of Education 1978:6–9, 110.
6. Sagar and Schofield 1980.
7. Blakely 1983:57.
8. Arnez 1978.
9. Schofield and Sagar 1977:132; Patchen 1982.
10. Olweus 1978:169.
11. Quoted in Poussaint 1972:30.
12. Schofield and Sagar 1977:131.
13. Cf. Wax 1980:107–8.
14. Pat Magruder, a psychiatric nurse, noted this situation in her mental health, rehabilitation therapy group in Irving, Texas. There were two schizophrenics; the other group members had better ego structures and jobs. But if one of the stronger members of the group came in angry, he or she picked on one of the weaker individuals.
15. Levine 1977:96.
16. Schofield and Sagar 1977.
17. Kochman 1981.
18. A student explanation in Kochman 1981:46.
19. Farb 1974:85.
20. Note, however, that biblical analogues hit a responsive chord in some black communities, and comparisons are made between Jews and blacks. The Old Testament reflections on the oppression, flight, and wanderings of the Jews became an inspiration for black freedom songs and sermons. The Jews were in bondage among the Egyptians and Nazis; many survived to achieve social recognition and economic security. Their traditions of crafts, trades, professions, learning, religious faith, and family life helped them to adjust and be mobile.
21. *Chronicle of Higher Education* 1986.
22. Black adolescents and adults call the competitive aggressive verbal dueling in which the contestants attempt to destroy each other with words "playing the dozens." This name was generally unknown among youngsters at HPES. Furthermore, they used less humor and wit than older blacks. This verbal aggression actually has roots among some West African groups, such as the Fanti and Ashanti of Ghana who have a tradition of one group insulting another in a ritual competitive situation. Dollard et al. 1939; Abrahams et al. 1975; Foster 1974:212–27; and Mitchell-Kernan 1975 discuss the patterns of verbal insults that have well-recognized rules.
23. Smitherman 1977.
24. Halle 1978.
25. Montagu 1942, 1967; Sullivan 1974.

105

26. Willis 1977; Hanna 1988a.
27. Halle 1978.
28. Rosnow and Fine 1976.
29. Comer and Poussaint 1975:219.
30. See Brannigan and Humphries 1972:44–47, 50–51.
31. Johnson 1976:261.
32. Rickford and Rickford 1976.
33. Erikson 1963:112.

5

WELLSPRINGS OF MEDDLIN'

WHAT are the causes at HPES and elsewhere of low-income youngsters engaging in more aggression than middle-income youngsters? Aggression, the desire or intention to harm another person, is a complex behavior mediated by many factors and part of normal nonpathological functioning. Pathological origins are sometimes possible due to brain damage, and aggression in this case can be eliminated only by treatment of the brain malfunction.[1] Nonpathological aggression may be reactive, a learned response to antecedents that cause frustration. Aggression may also have a motivational dynamic of its own: An individual may be motivated to remove some aversive, internal drive, or frustration. Another possibility is that individuals act aggressively because they anticipate reaping rewards from such behavior.[2] Observation teaches someone how to be aggressive and what the possible outcomes might be. If a child's aggression leads to obtaining such things as toys or money and satisfying such needs as making another child cry or flee, gaining status in a group and self-esteem, the likelihood of continued victimization of another child is strong.

Trends in American Society

The aggression of low-income students must be seen within the context of developments in the United States that make it more difficult for public schools generally to control student aggression.[3] First, historically American public education has increasingly separated the school from the student's family and neighborhood with larger consolidated school systems. Although HPES was in a black community and accessible to all its children, the community had felt estranged from the school

107

since desegregation and the influx of new white teachers and students from other neighborhoods. Youngsters separated from an integrated family–community–school culture tend to develop distinctive sub-cultures or countercultures in large heterogeneous schools. Designed for efficiency, the architecture of large schools precludes adult surveillance of youngsters who pursue their own interests.

Second, the children's rights movement curtailed the school's ability to control misbehavior at the same time that it prevented principals from ruling their schools autocratically and arbitrarily: "Greater democratiza-tion of schools means that unruly students get better protection against school officials, and most students get less protection from their class-mates."[4] The exodus of switch and paddle—former symbols of au-thority—left an unfilled gap. HPES authorities were certainly sensitive to the rights of children.

Third is the erosion of the high status of teachers along with the decline in respect for authority figures during the 1960s. Furthermore, best-selling books in the 1960s, like John Holt's *Why Children Fail,* James Herndon's *The Way It Spozed to Be,*[5] Jonathan Kozol's *Death at an Early Age: The Destruction of the Minds and Hearts of Negro Children in the Boston Public Schools,* and Herbert Kohl's *Thirty-Six Children,* portrayed teachers, es-pecially white middle-class teachers, as the villains of education—insen-sitive, authoritarian, and even racist.

Fourth, the pressure to keep children in school longer leads some of them to perceive themselves as prisoners and become troublemakers. And fifth, the decreased ability of the schools to obtain help with disci-pline problems from the juvenile courts encourages aggression.

Socialization to Violence: Slavery and Low-Income Patterns

In the past, blacks had to behave submissively and accept abuse from whites in order to survive. "If we [blacks] acted the dumb clown, or the 'house nigger,' whites rewarded us. Being an Uncle Tom enabled us to count on financial support for our survival."[6] Much of black self-hatred is really repressed rage at having been docile and self-effacing. "Aggres-sion leaps from wounds inflicted and ambitions spiked."[8] In addition, many blacks are socialized to violence through the history of slavery in the South and their low socioeconomic class. White dominance re-minded blacks that those who could marshal force got their way. White masters feared uprisings and perceived the necessity of controlling their black slaves; consequently, runaway and disobedient slaves were sometimes savagely punished for their transgressions. The Virginia legislature in 1669 passed a law, later overturned, giving protection to a master who in the process of disciplining his slave actually ended up killing the slave.[9] In the antebellum era, some whites whipped blacks, and this continued in the postbellum period along with brawls and nightriders, church bombings, vigilante groups, lynchings, rampaging mobs, and police dogs. With its heritage of duels, pride in military battle, and the greater proportion of poor people, the South has a consistently higher murder and assault rate than the North.[10] White America's historical repression, subjugation, and emasculation of black men contributed to the high premium many blacks place on masculinity, which is associated with toughness and winning fights. "Physical subjugation of the weak forges early in the mind of the child a link with the past."[11]

Moreover, the persisting frontier aspects of the Texas penal code and local culture support aggression as the solution to certain social conflicts. The legal system sanctions violent retaliation rather than indignation or flight from attack when an intruder infringes on people or property.[12]

A disproportionate amount of violent crime is committed by low-income people,[13] in part because those with lower incomes and less education approve of violence more than better educated individuals with higher incomes.[14] Young low-income black and southern males run the greatest risk of both committing and suffering from violence. From at least as far back as 1970, Dallas Police Department analyses revealed that most murder suspects were black and most victims were black. Of the 225 murder victims in 1977, 129 were blacks, and 96 were whites.[15] Cities with nonwhite populations have higher rates of urban crime than others.[16] The 1978 NIE school violence study found that the more crime and violence students are exposed to outside the school, the greater the problems in school. These same factors may cause violence in and out of school.

Children at HPES attested to their socialization to violence. A black second-grader explained:

> Sometimes my momma let me fight when people mess with me. She let me hit my cousin up side the head. She always stickin' out her lip and teasin'. My momma let us hit her up side the head, always with her lip stuck out. My momma think it not nice, so she let my cousin and me hit her up side the head (117 bb 2nd).

A black girl in the second grade said, "I act nice sometime; bad sometime. I like to. I'm just a wild woman like my mommy. She thinks that's good!" (38).

Although social structure and group membership may increase the likelihood of a person performing a violent act, other factors, such as personality or the immediate social situation, will determine whether the individual commits the act. American social structure has at least five bases of stratification: economic, racial, ethnic–religious, occupational, and educational. Black Americans usually rank low on all of these dimensions. Blacks are told to strive for success and monetary rewards. At the same time, through discrimination, they have been denied access to the legitimate means of achieving these goals, although the situation is now changing in many areas. Some low-income people resort to violence to achieve goods and money. Others merely develop subcultures that place a premium on using violence; prestige accrues to those who prove themselves in fighting and only cowards and individuals unworthy of respect fail to meet group expectations for its use. These groups represent mythic enclaves of independence and freedom where blacks win. "I fight on my own. My dad tells me to fight," remarked a HPES student (113 bb 6th).

Lower-class children experience inconsistent harsh physical discipline, ridicule, limited verbal communication with adults, and excitement, which may lead to a search for action, poor impulse control, psychological depression, and a continual testing of strength and attractiveness. Coupled with these factors found among the white lower class[17] is the historical background of being black in America. Adult problems envelop the child.

Racism

Because in the past, subservience was a requisite for survival and rewards, blacks denied or deflected their anger on themselves. Black mothers often cultivated the "surrendered identity" forced on blacks for generations and kept bright questioning children away from what had been a futile and dangerous competition. For survival's sake, youths were restrained to keep them "in their place as defined by an indifferent and hateful 'compact majority.'"[18] Black youths learned servitude and docility[19] at the expense of acquiring the "administrative skills and control necessary for independence and success."[20] Blacks learned to contain aggression against whites while expressing it among blacks. Other groups, regardless of race, may turn on themselves in similar situations: "The pattern of autocratic leadership and tyranny found in black churches was, in a quaint way, the sole means of sanity for black males effectively barred from participation in the political life and the play of power in their communities."[21] The church was one of the more power-ful bases for survival. Not only could blacks express their deepest an-guish, agony, and desperation, but at the same time, they could perform satisfying roles to give meaning to their existence and achieve status.

A pantheon of heroes who fought for their rights looms large in the tales blacks spin. Folk heroes of black Americans were sometimes mecha-nisms of escape or fantasies bringing relief from difficult work and reality. The Washington, D.C., riot in July 1919 exhibited the local black community's challenge to the assumption of their subordination. They protected their homes by practicing Christian virtues, but if the efficacy of practicing Christian virtue failed, they were prepared to resort to guns to impose respect. The Harlem riot of 1936, the Detroit and Harlem riots of 1943, and the riots of the 1960s shifted blacks from defense to offense and from retaliation to instigation.

Some passive black parents realized their aggressive needs through their children at HPES. They also acted out their antiwhite feelings by encouraging their children not to let any white "push them around"; what this meant was often undefined. Black children intimidating white children is now common nationwide,[22] whereas in the past, blacks had feared white gangs. With sneaking admiration, some black parents think their children's aggression may be positive—"an overreaction, a swing of the pendulum."[23]

Other black parents feel that some black children's excessive asser-tiveness has become inappropriate. The press may have exacerbated the race issue, forcing blacks to either "'overinternalize' (to become a Tom) or 'overexternalize' (to become a militant)." A modicum of aggression is conducive to achievement in American society, although in the past, the only path of advancement open to upwardly mobile blacks was a passive and conformist orientation.[25]

The changed black response to white racism is understandable. Racism is a political belief that human groups have distinctive hereditary characteristics that determine their respective cultures and behaviors. Racists believe not only that their race is superior but also that this superiority justifies domination over and discrimination against individ-uals of other races. Biological traits, such as skin color, are confused with cultural patterns associated with distinctions. As I have discussed, a far greater proportion of the black population is found in the lower class, thus color becomes confused with other social class characteristics.

A common problem is that blacks and whites experience much unintentional racism and behavior perceived as racist when none is intended. The following is an example of a white who could be seen as patronizingly racist when he tried not to be:

111

The principal, who considers himself devoid of racism because his staff has pictures of blacks on the bulletin boards, has books by black authors on reading lists in the library, and schoolwide participation in Negro History Week, but calls all his white teachers by their first names and all his black teachers by Mr., Ms., Miss, or Mrs., and their last names, and never reprimands black teachers as loudly as he reprimands white teachers.[26]

However, some blacks refer to each other by title unless they are very close friends. Thus, the principal could be sincerely trying to respect cultural differences and sensitivities; after all, whites call blacks in menial positions by their first name, whereas blacks must address the whites by title.

Because of the historical reasons described in chapter 2 and elsewhere, HPES black children feared white racism, teachers' biases, and possible rejection or inability to understand black communication and culture. A white HPES teacher was trying to show her knowledge and appreciation of black culture by asking a black student, "We really enjoy your mother's baking, but when is she going to cook chitlins for us?" The black identity appreciation backfired. The child's mother, a woman with some college education and a white-collar position, remarked indignantly and proudly that her daughter had angrily retorted: "We don't eat that trash!" Chitterlings are pig intestines originally discarded by whites and given to slaves.

When HPES counselors queried ten articulate children from the third grade and ten from the sixth, all of whom had attended the school since its inception, both blacks and whites said there was differential treatment accorded to each race. Because teachers made efforts to give special help to blacks who were generally academically behind whites, whites felt that teachers favored blacks; yet blacks felt the opposite. A black girl disliked some of the teachers who she felt slighted blacks: "Well, see, well, like some of them, they get on my nerves and talk too much. And like, most of the time I try to get help, and they never pay attention" (109 bg 6th). I did observe teachers spend extra time with blacks. I also saw teachers discipline whites for acts they ignored when blacks performed them.

The term culturally deprived refers to the divergent, disadvantaged, and/or educationally alienated. Many people consider these terms condescending. When the majority of the blacks compare themselves to whites, they become more conscious of how different and economically deprived they are. Recognizing their relative deprivation and not recognizing the uniqueness of their own cultures may lead some blacks to view all whites negatively and attack perceived frustrators.

112

Even when there is black–white harmony, there may be an underlying racism that manifests itself when conflict arises. As in interreligious and interracial marriages, in the heat of confrontations, individuals resort to slurs against the other's background. When a HPES black child complimented a white child for his physical prowess by calling him nigger or white nigger, the intensity and symbolism of racism came to the fore. Blacks sometimes use in a positive way among themselves terms considered derogatory when used by whites.

I was speaking with the white discipline room teacher when a fifth-grade black girl walked in mumbling: "She make me sick. I just ask question. You get three conduct marks. I don't care if I get ten. She *mean little white thing!* I just ask a simple question." One explanation for the girl's comments is that children used race as a way of dealing with their own insecurities and inadequacies.[27]

Racism sometimes affected innocent children at HPES and surfaced in overt confrontation. When I asked what caused fights, a youngster replied:

> The color of people. It's because, like they blame it on you, sayin' it's your fault that they were slaves and sort of take that against you from back a long time ago. And *it's not my fault,* I didn't do it. I guess it's just the color. Sometimes the whites say something about black people. It just depends on if you're mad or not mad (106 wg 6th).

The student continued:

> There are some people who are sort of prejudiced. I think it's because the white girls went with the black boys. Well sometimes the black girls got jealous, and sometimes the white girls got jealous when the black girls started going with the black boys. Now there isn't anybody in the whole sixth grade who's going with a black boy who's white. I guess it's because they said that they took over, and so the black girls, you know, they all sort of pick somebody to go with. Well, it's not like that you're in love, but it means that you're taken and nobody else can have you. . . . Everybody's always fighting in this school. Some blacks don't like the whites, and some whites don't like blacks. It's blacks versus whites. Like if they're listening to music, and the black says that's *white* music, that's when it starts off. I don't think it's white music. I just think it's music that a person likes. It doesn't matter if it's white music or black music. They fight with their fists and sometimes with names (101 wg 6th).

Misunderstanding sometimes evokes racial sensitivity:

> All right, this guy was walkin' up to the teacher, and he was trying to ask a question. This other guy was a different race. He comes up and gets his neck

113

and jerks him 'cross the floor knocking, stompin' up the chair, jumpin', actin' like somethin' from the jungle. Talkin' back to the teacher, and, uh, then he gets abducted; he's taken away. You know, like Eric and Todd, they're different races. Todd [bb] did it to Eric [wb]. Well, Todd got the misunderstandin' point. What he should have done was wait till Eric got back and asked him what did he say to Ms. Wood, for Ms. Wood to look at Todd. But you know Todd, he really deserved what he got. Todd misunderstood what Eric said. Eric was askin' a question, not complainin' about how Todd was acting over there. And Todd got the wrong perspective and went right over there, didn't ask what he was saying, didn't, you know, take any time, just went in around his neck, just out of clear daylight (92 bb 6th).

On racial sensitivity, a sixth-grade white girl said, "Blacks were slaves, they have it against you. You have to experience what it's like to be a student at Hamilton Park." "Racism forces blacks to fight for the respect that whites take for granted" (106).

"Equality" through Compensation—and the Importance of the Body

Defensive structuring, mentioned earlier, refers to a group attempting to create a feeling of self-worth and self-identity in the face of external threats to that identity. Because of oppressed minority status, some blacks seek to bolster self-esteem through channels they can readily use. In the chapter on cultural duality, I discussed the problem of black frustration in the classroom. While a school's goal is to teach certain skills and values, children's goals are to develop their self-identity and power in everyday life. Middle-class children learn the school's culture and their roots at an early age. Thrust into the dominant white culture's institution, lower-income black children often do not have the dominant American communicative, social interaction, and academic skills. Public revelation of their inadequate school work through oral recitation or other classroom activity is inevitable and often humiliating. This is the case even when youngsters reject the school and its rewards for successful school work (see chapter 3). No matter what the teacher does, most low-income black children know, as do other children in the classroom, that they do not generally perform so well academically. Usually two years behind grade level, most low-income blacks have not had the kinds of experience as middle-class black and white children, which enable the latter to know when a question or suggestion is actually a command, to ask pertinent questions, and answer questions asked of the entire classroom.

114

Of overwhelming importance to disruptive school behavior is the fact that anxious or humiliated children try to save face or divert attention from their shortcomings in classroom performance. Aggressive behavior derives from the human defense of a concept and love of self.[29] The individual is essentially a narcissistic defender who incorporates ethnocentric displays and compares the self with others.[30] The NIE study found that students who feel their school work is irrelevant and they lack control over what happens to them at school become frustrated and give up on this institution. These sentiments can erupt in violence. Sometimes individuals, in what is called displacement activity, send messages about their anger or dismay indirectly rather than direct them at the source.

Some children, socialized to violence, try to gain control and achieve self-validation by performing for approving, assertive peers. This recognition becomes the standard of competence in a kind of defensive structuring. Neighborhood peer groups often see the school environment as hostile and develop a counterschool culture reward system. By belittling formal schooling and its ethic, they deny the authorities' power to confer negative evaluations that affect an individual's self-image.

While whites as a group are dominant in intellectual performance, blacks, as a group behind grade level, often compensate by asserting themselves in physical arenas. Of course, there is individual variation: Those children who feel humiliated try to abuse and humiliate other youngsters in order to make them to cry or fight, and those humiliated try to cause the authority to lose control. Children who said they like to fight were most likely to be nominated as bullies. A black girl told me, "See, sometimes you fight 'cause you have to fight every once in awhile, 'cause you not really puttin' on a good impression on yourself you know [if you don't]" (119 bg 6th). A second-grader's comments on a situation that leads to fights suggest the ethos of saving face: "I go away when somebody's mad. I don't go away when they say, 'You crybaby!' I go back and fight 'em" (107 bb).

Although most black aggression is against blacks, some is directed at whites; such "hassling" occurred at a middle school[31] and among older adolescents and adults:

It wasn't just that you registered your protest and showed the white man that you meant business and weakened his resolve to keep up the walls of oppression. . . . There was something sweet that happened right there on the spot. You made the white man quake. You brought *fear* into his face. . . .

And now, when you got him up close and growled, this all-powerful superior animal turned out to be terrified. You could read it in his face. He had the same fear in his face as some good-doing boy who just moved onto

115

the block and is hiding behind his mama . . . while the bad dudes on the block size him up. . . .

It not only stood to bring you certain practical gains. . . . It also energized your batteries. It recharged your masculinity. You no longer had to play it cool.[32]

Most HPES children recognized fighting as having the potential to harm someone and being against the school rules; yet practical reality calls for it in some cultures. Slaves resorted to tactics that violated their African and Christian norms in order to obtain food and avoid whippings. While the slaves violated their universal ideals, they did not surrender allegiance to them. Slave trickster tales emphasize the state of perpetual war between the world's creatures and the hypocrisy and meaninglessness of their manners and rules.[33] Acts of senseless cruelty committed for no discernible motive occur in the tales. Similarly, children and adults perceive that humiliations occur for no discernible motive.

If one has few material possessions and little power in the adult world, as is the case with oppressed minorities, low-income workers, and children, the body and its use or adornment become especially important in defensive structuring and gaining a sense of equality. This is part of the ethos of expressive performance discussed in chapter 3. The use of the body has its roots in ontogenetic development; the body is the first human instrument.

Self-Fulfilling Prophecy

On the basis of general images or specific experiences, some whites interacting with blacks may expect physical communication and thus emit signals suggesting blacks behave negatively. Some blacks, in turn, may reciprocate with such behavior, thereby fulfilling the expectations of these whites;[34] that is, they "pick up the gauntlet." White children generally assume blacks are stronger and more "physical." A sixth-grade black girl said,"Everyone thinks that a black person is a blade [a fighting tough]." In a rare interracial fight at HPES, a white boy beat a black boy. Children expressed disbelief. Black children often act the role attributed to them in order to get what they want.[35]

Other Aggression Stimuli at School

Key causes of aggression include poor impulse control, sexual competition, desire to test and prove one's strength, eliciting attention, peer

116

pressure, and disagreeements about rules in a game. Children with *poor impulse control* may become angry about their own behavior or what a student or teacher has done deliberately or unintentionally. Resentment may be immediate or smolder over a long time. Black and white children both recognized that black children at HPES had poor impulse control of anger. A black girl said, "Volunteers [whites], yeah, they . . . just patient or something" (119 6th). A black boy remarked, "Lot of people in sixth grade lose their temper" referring to his black peers.

A psychiatrist[36] reports that a jealous black child became angry with a white boy because the white boy received "very good" on his writing paper and the black boy received "poor." The black child played while the white boy continued to do his work. The black boy was angry with himself and explained his reason for beating up the white boy in this way: "Well, he really did look funny at me. He was sort of showing off with that 'I told you so' look."

Many HPES children commented that if bullies are in a bad mood, they are unpredicatable; anything triggers them.

> Damone fights people. He hits them, and he doesn't mean to hit them, and then he starts a fight, and he hits him when it's not really the kids' fault. Damone always starts it—yesss. See, like Ed and Damone goin' to have a fight today after school, and he'll jump in it as usually, and then somebody is going to come out there and everybody's going to run so they don't get caught (18 bg 4th).

"Why do you think he fights so much?" I asked. "Maybe nobody hardly likes him," the girl replied. Disagreement over game rules, who got the ball, who committed a foul, or who lost the point triggers aggression. Refusing to allow a child to copy work may provoke hostility (77). Inadvertently touching a child or otherwise infringing on a person's private space or possessions triggers incidents.

Children's aggression may be directed at the teacher or educational institution for some reason, such as a rule that did not make sense to youngsters in a particular situation. Misunderstandings can escalate conflict and reduce communication and trust between student and teacher or between students. Classroom lessons that are too easy or difficult may stimulate hostility. A student's aggression toward another child or the teacher may be a message that the educational expectations and activities are incongruent with the student's self-concept and capability or interest. Some children have difficulty understanding concepts of time and the need to engage in certain behavior in only specified segments of time. A child sent to the discipline room for not accommodating to the schedule bellowed: "You wouldn't let me finish then, I won't now!"

Sexual competition is a common cause of aggression, and the race

117

issue exacerbated the competition. "Boys fighting over girls! It starts in kindergarten" (113 bb 6th). Boys and girls tease each other all the time. But a white or black boy teasing a girl a black boy considers his girl friend provokes an incident. A second-grader told me:

> I saw this morning, a white boy and a black boy was fighting. The black boy had a girl friend, and the white boy was messin' with his girl. Say, there's a girl, and this boy picks on her, and this other boy comes up and say, don't pick on her, and then the other boys says, "I have rights" (42 bb).

One of the black teacher aides at HPES reflected black female student sentiment. She said to me "One thing I can't stand is black men going with white women."[37]

Another catalyst for meddlin' is the desire *to test and prove one's strength* in comparison with other youngsters and establish the highest rank possible in a peer hierarchy or pecking order. A child may challenge another to fight: "They're just trying to prove who's tougher" (16 wb 6th) was a youngster's explanation. Since school is where the peer group resides six hours a day, five days a week, school is also where to behave in accord with aspirations for improving one's position relative to one's peers. Fighting was so much a norm for the children in Harlem that one sixth-grade boy was very annoyed when he was prevented from boxing with his friend in a classroom to determine, then and there, who could beat whom.[38]

As a volunteer parent in a desegregated school, another researcher[39] found, as I did, that when a new activity or change in routine occurred, chaos would ensue. Children would yell, run, push, and fight, jockeying for position and expressive role validation. A child may achieve self-evaluation by using others in fights as standards of competence.[40] Before a friendship can be established, many low-income black children first create an understanding of who ranks higher.

Eliciting attention (which overlaps the desire to test one's dominance) is a key stimulus for aggression. Involving the eye-catching whole body in motion, fighting arouses the basic survival emotions of fear or flight. A sixth-grader described her needs:

> I started having fights because of this thing; 'cause I had problems. Some people just love to pick on people, for attention, I guess. They get it, but not the way they'd like to have it. If a child hits you, I hit 'em back—but then I grab 'em and ask them why he do dat. Some kids try to jump on people. This is something that's happening now (67 bg).

Another girl corroborated the quest for attention as the cause of fights:

Picking on other people and especially in my grade, a lot of fights start off when other people start picking on you. And then they start picking on your parents and then just start saying things about your parents, and that's what usually gets a lot of kids mad. It was completely different at my other school. We all lived around in one neighborhood, and everyone walked to school and knew everyone else's mother and father cause everyone would go over to everyone else's house, and so they didn't really talk about them. I think they're just trying to get attention from other people (48 wg 6th).

Peer pressure in an active or reactive encounter triggers aggression. A number of children commented on how black groups gang up on others. A white boy said, "If a bully makes fun of you and you do it back, they [onlookers] say 'beat him up!'" (79 6th). A black sixth-grader said that when age mates fight, no one breaks it up. The person who tries is likely to get into a fight. "Kids like to talk about it" (85). A group eggs on a troublemaker by commenting, laughing, and crowding around (69 2b 6th). Compared with whites, blacks rely more on peer influences than school achievement in their self-evaluations.[11] A white sixth-grade girl whose friends are black said: "Well, sometimes when you really get mad, you hit 'em back and tell them you're not chicken of 'em, so they wouldn't think that you wouldn't fight back and take up for yourself" (106 wg).

A white middle-class child well known for his misbehavior at school described the peer pressure to fight:

All the boys. Black children mostly hit, more than the white children. You know what started me hitting was 'cause a black kid came up to me and hit me [a rationalization?], and then I started hitting all them, and then some other people started gettin' in the fight, and now all the black people and white people fight like I did earlier today. When the teacher's out of the room, people bother me, and I just hit 'em. But they hit me first always (105 2d).

He finds fights attractive:

If someone meddles my friend, I just watch the fight. I like to see fights, just like to sit down and watch. Like I watch my mom. One time she was throwing shoes at my dad, closing the door, havin' pillow fights. I like to see fights. At school when they start to fight, I see it. I see about every week a fight. Like a person comes up to 'em and scratches 'em, and then they start a big fight, and I'm watchin' 'em, and everybody's going *wooooo* and all that stuff. Most kids like to see who wins, who loses. They go, "Go Marlo, go Chris," and all that stuff and whoever gets hurt they call 'em a pig all day (105 2d).

119

Disagreement about rules in games causes contention. In response to the question, "Are you afraid of anyone at school?" a HPES boy said, "Not unless its like in a soccer game, like if someone says, 'No one else can come in this game,' and somebody says, 'Why don't you go in?' and I'm afraid of them 'cause I think they are going to get me for going in the game" (52 wb 4th). Another child commented on the opportunity for aggression in free play: "Well, there's two kids, they're best friends. They're always fightin' over a football—the score or who won because they're both team captains" (104 wg 6th).

"The largest proportion of violent encounters for elementary school students was in the playground or on the school athletic fields. . . . 40 percent of all such incidents," states the NIE report (1978:85). In three desegregated elementary schools in Maryland, there were more fights than in nondesegregated schools, and the fights were "mostly about balls and turns."[42]

I have described various causes of aggression, including the historical context of low-income black culture. Youngsters are usually receptive to the expressive styles of the milieu in which they grow up. Yet not all children from a low-income black background engage in meddlin' behavior at school. Certainly, there is individual variation within any group. Another explanation is that some youngsters are relatively weak and timid. Consequently, they fear attracting the attention of tougher children who may turn on them. Recall black and white children's belief that whites were weaker and the black boy's comment, "Whites fight less at school. They probably do it at home." This possibility applies to timid black children as well.

NOTES

1. Mark, a neurosurgeon, and Ervin, a psychiatrist, point out that once the brain structure has been permanently affected, violent behavior cannot be modified by manipulating educational, psychological, or social influences. For both normal and pathological individuals, the physiological effects of aggression are often moderated by personality factors, physical prowess, and social and environmental forces (1970:7).

2. Scherer et al. 1975:82ff.

3. Toby 1980.

4. Scherer et al. 1975:30.

5. Herndon (1968:82) thought that what went on in the classroom was a reaction to teachers' methods of teaching. Middle-class and lower-class reactions were not different, he argued; the latter's were only more overt and violent. While this may be true in some cases, HPES children did not view their fellow students this way.

6. Poussaint 1972:26.

7. Cf. Powdermaker 1949.
8. Grier and Cobbs 1968:3.
9. Wilson 1980:29.
10. Cf. Curtis 1975:26–27.
11. Grier and Cobbs 1968:138.
12. Lundsgaarde 1977.
13. Scherer et al. 1975:186.
14. Ibid.: 201–2; see Crain and Weisman 1972.
15. Havard 1978.
16. Jacob and Lineberry 1982.
17. Gans 1962; Miller 1958.
18. Erikson 1963:302.
19. Comer and Poussaint 1975:20.
20. Poussaint 1972:60.
21. Phillips 1971:161.
22. Black students successfully intimidating whites at the college level is called "mau mauing."
23. Harrison-Ross and Wyden 1973:179ff.
24. Crain and Weisman 1972:97.
25. Ibid., 68.
26. Foster 1974:2.
27. Cf. Comer and Poussaint 1975:229.
28. Ibid., 12.
29. Rochlin 1973.
30. Gordon 1978:90.
31. Schofield 1982:108–25.
32. Wolfe 1970:119–20.
33. Levine 1977:116ff.
34. Cf. Word et al. 1974.
35. In his study of high school blacks, Foster (1974:193) found that black youths build on white fantasies of blacks being hedonistic, aggressive "gorilla studs," or "shufflin' children" requiring help. A black youth can always "switch from the cat role to the gorilla, bogarding role, because he may feel most whites and faggots fear him."
36. Harrison-Ross and Wyden 1973:177.
37. See Taylor et al. 1974 on attitudes of army men; Mitchell-Kernan and Kernan 1975 on children's insults.
38. Silverstein and Krate 1975:118.
39. Schafft 1976:50.
40. Cf. Sutton-Smith 1971:30.
41. Epps 1975.
42. White 1977.

6

MEDDLIN' REWARDS, REINFORCEMENT, AND OTHER CONSEQUENCES

Responses to Meddlin'

IN response to meddlin', children used tactics that drew on their strengths and socialization. Coming from a litigious culture, middle-class children were usually taught to work through difficulties verbally, and many had no experience in fighting. They tended to respond to behavior that they perceived as threatening with passive "safe" strategies. These minimized the chance of overt confrontation. "I'm afraid to say much because they might be mad at me" (4 wg 6th). A white girl with many black friends said she was afraid of Alicia at times; blacks also took heed:

> Yeh. She's real pretty. She may get after somebody. She's kinda like, she had muscles, kinda like a boy. She's strong. Well, seems like when I see her, if she's gonna have a fight with somebody, then I just feel like "that could be me someday!" (93 bg 6th).

The same situation occurred in other schools.[1] Elsewhere whites also formed groups for support with special names, insignia, and modes of behavior. A few fourth-graders at HPES talked about their clubs, but they did not seem to have reached a formal state of organization.

Safe strategies for whites and blacks include accepting or ignoring the meddlin' demands, disengaging oneself with the intervention of a teacher, finding the protection of a peer friend, or diverting an aggressor with humor or negotiation, withdrawing, avoiding a meddler, or displacing the aggression. Active responses include parrying and retaliation—tit for tat, an eye for an eye. Children who have the capability, knowledge, and practice tend to be activists: "If someone meddles me, I slug 'um. This kid, he took a branch, and he started choking around my

122

neck. I just swung my arms behind my back and slapped him inside his face, and before he could recover, I just gave him a bloody nose" (16 wb 6th). Being left alone without adult support nearby sometimes results in fighting:

> Sometimes I can tell they granmammy they hit me. Ain't nothin' else to do 'cause sometimes I forget that my parents ain't home, and I be there alone, and I fight with 'em. It's okay when it's time to but not when you're just doin' it just to be havin' fun—not to be beatin' up on kids, like Eric. He always wantin' me to do stuff and I don't want to and start beatin' up on people (95 bb 4th).

Another incident illustrates the technique of passivity. Early in the semester, sixth-graders were standing in the lunch line. A black boy slapped a white boy standing next to him. He hit the child's right cheek, the left cheek, and then repeated the right–left smacking sequence twice more. The white boy, about four inches shorter, stood with his arms crossed. He said and did nothing. The response of not reacting to provocation could itself be provocative, that is, viewed as denying the existence of the aggressor, which could lead to an increase in aggravation.

In his autobiography, Dick Gregory says that he was picked on a lot, but when he learned about humor, the power of a joke, "I'd get the kids off my back, on my side."[2] This strategy often worked among HPES students.

My younger son, Aaron, usually follows the home rules of discussing difficulties instead of fighting. However, as a star goalie who played on a team with children two years older than himself, Aaron also earned high grades and was thus vulnerable to harrassment on this account. When he was kept off the soccer field, by blacks who would not let him play, I suggested a way of handling the situation. I asked Aaron who was the toughest one in his class. He said Kenneth; I then asked Aaron if Kenneth were keeping him off the field. When he said no, I asked, "Why don't you talk to Kenneth?" Aaron's eyes lit up. "Oh, Patrick (wb) and Kenneth (bb) are friends. They worked together. Any time someone bugs Patrick, he tells Kenneth, and Kenneth takes up for him." Aaron sought Kenneth's friendship and thereafter played soccer. The boys became what adults call cordial acquaintances or neighbors who help each other on occasion.

Tracing the origin of the patron–client relationship is difficult. In the South, the only black who could anticipate that a white who mistreated him or her would receive retribution was one who had strong sponsorship in the white community.

If a powerful white man regarded him as "his nigger," any other white who harmed him might incur the anger of the white sponsor. An unfortunate but valid comparison must be made: To torment one of "Mr. Charley's niggers" was like throwing rocks at his dog. Both affection for a highly regarded pet and a sense of threat to the master's status were brought into play in either case.[3]

Consequences of Meddlin'

Rewards often accrue to aggressors. They may gain family attention; establish high position in the peer hierarchy; earn respect; achieve a goal; find relief through catharsis—the restoration of a sense of power, ability, and control of the frustrated, resentful, shamed, or jealous through discharging anger; improve self-concept and esteem; or have the thrill of exploring future alternatives (being dominant rather than subordinate in society). Much wrestling, hitting, and boasting about who is the best fighter is behavior that identifies membership in a group.

Some covertly rebellious students respected black children for overtly defying adult authority. They expressed awe, disbelief, and admiration for the child's power. Obtaining control within realistic limits over one's functions, other individuals, and the environment is part of the process of maturation.

Viewing aggression as a form of play helps explain some manifestations and consequences. Play has two primary interrelated functions: (1) survival preparation for adulthood and (2) tension reduction for ongoing life experiences. These functions involve symbolism. Vivifications of some kind of real or imagined behavior occurring in other settings, play reproductions may be exaggerated—more violent, funny, creative, serendipitous.[4]

Aggressive thrill-seeking in play has the advantage of developing skills for emergencies. Self-defense against aggression is a necessity in many neighborhoods where police protection is inadequate. Children who can handle aggression—deflect it or retaliate—develop inner strength, control, adaptability, and sensitivity to multiple communication channels. Part of handling aggression is assertiveness.[5]

Attempts at mastering skills are grounded in the concept of possibility. For blacks in a school setting, fighting may be exploring the possibility of overcoming subordinate status—role reversal, gaining power in a white-dominated society.[6]

Fighting, of course, causes pain, which teaches us to avoid or better confront physical and emotional harm.[7] Individuals need time and experience to master difficult and social relations; HPES provided a training ground. Many children learned to seek places where they would be undisturbed. They learned how to scan a room and area to find friends, protectors, or proximity to the controlling, usually benevolent adult teacher. Children learned how to use brokers to mediate between themselves and an adversary. Sometimes they formed work and play alliances in order to protect themselves. They developed a sense of when to use various verbal and nonverbal patterns.

Away from HPES, white HPES children often dramatically imitated the actions of black children they feared—to empathize with the aggressors or to make them less fearsome or become more aggressive themselves. In another school,[8]

> Certain black kinesic patterns are often used by white children in front of their white peers, not as a way of making fun of the black children, but in an attempt to be "cool" without being laughed at. Finger snapping and bottom twisting accompanies a "Hey, Man! You're goin' get it!" or looking at the floor, head tilted, a white child will do a short dance just before the punch line of a joke.

White children often tried the bully tactics on other white children, especially younger siblings and imitated at home the defiance of authority and insolence they saw in blacks. According to peer learning theory in the desegregation literature, low-income blacks learn from middle- and upper-class children; in reality, many low-income children do not choose to emulate them, and reverse learning occurs. Middle-class parents become upset at what their children "pick up": aggressive and insolent behavior, improper language, and sexual knowledge.

IMPEDIMENTS TO ACADEMIC ACHIEVEMENT

Meddlin' interferred with the performance of successful school-work to the point that formal schooling took second place to the foremost challenges of the hidden curriculum. What researchers found in Harlem[9] is broadly applicable to HPES, as children's comments and experiences presented in chapters 3, 4, and 5 indicate:

> Perceptual alertness to potential danger requires so much energy and attention as to make coping with schoolwork very difficult. . . . In a classroom of children who often sought to discover others' inadequacies and expose them in stinging repartee, who were easily moved to physical aggression, paying a great deal of attention to other children rather than to books or lessons was unavoidable for many children already predisposed to defensive perceptual operations. The sorting process, which tended to group together the chil-

dren who were most likely to be concerned about their personal adequacy or safety and to behave in ways that exposed the inadequacies or threatened the safety of others, intensified the problem.

LOW MARKS FOR PACESETTER

When I asked what children liked best about HPES, appreciation of the teachers was the overriding choice, as noted earlier. Children also liked school activities and physical characteristics of the facility. Some youngsters referred to the combination of people. A sixth-grade black girl said, "I like that they integrated HPES, 'cause we got to do more stuff, and I made more friends" (115). A fourth-grade white girl re-marked, "Well, like I've never been in a school where there's been blacks and whites mixed together. I think blacks have the very same right to have a good education as whites, and I think it's kinda neat that they are in my class" (77). One white sixth-grade boy said there was less fighting at HPES than the school he had attended in Fort Worth, where "It's not evened out; there are less whites than blacks" (10). A white sixth-grade girl liked the fact that HPES was "integrated and we get to have a lot of fun. It's different from other schools. It helps you get to know the people who, 'cause when you grow up you get to be with more people than just your same color" (101).

However, when I asked, "If you could change one thing, what would you change?" the same girl said, "It probably would be the fighting. Everybody's always fighting." Other children echoed her senti-ment: "Well, there's a lot of fighting around. A lot of people like to fight. I don't like violence at all—unless it's in the movies where nobody gets hurt—like if a car crashed and a person is stuck up in a tree, and he's not hurt, now that's OK" (31 wb 6th). A fourth-grade black girl said, "Change the rules, no fighting, hittin', and no popping girls in the head" (18). A newcomer in the sixth grade put it this way:

> I like it better at my other school because it was only one class going to PE [physical education] at one time. The teacher could handle it. Here half the people aren't playin' 'cause it's too rowdy. I mean I like basketball you play, uh, with friends, but when you play at school, it gets a little rowdy. Every-body's in there pushin' in, arguments, and . . . (69 wb).

A fourth-grader stated emphatically: "If I could, I'd make no fighting. Fighting would be *stopped!* In my class, you see, there's this boy named Anthony, and in my sister's class, she has got that girl named Robin. She always picks on Anthony" (66 wb). Some children even went to the nurse's office to avoid classroom fracases.

126

TROUBLE FOR FIGHTERS

Too much or too dramatic aggression got an individual into trouble with authorities. The student was sent to the principal's office. When a black parent was called in, he or she usually "whupped" the child. As previously mentioned, working parents became enraged when they had to take off time from work and lose income because of their offspring's misbehavior. "They beat the shit out of them," said a black parent. Sometimes repeated fighting led to a child being suspended or sent to a special school. Too much fighting can cause a child to lose friends or be unable to make them.

Meddlin' could crystallize into a pattern of more serious confrontation than what occurs at the elementary school level. In a longitudinal study of aggression beginning with six hundred third-graders in 1955, studied again in the thirteenth grade and then at age thirty, a major finding was that aggression at age eight is the best predictor we have of aggression at age nineteen irrespective of IQ, social class, or parents' aggressiveness.[10] Moreover, those rated as the most aggressive at that time were three times more likely than their less aggressive classmates to be convicted of serious crimes by age thirty.[11] Aggression led to jail, the psychiatric hospital, automobile mishaps, and alcohol and drug use. Consequently, aggression hurt not only victims of the aggressive acts but also the perpetrators.[12] Once a style of aggressive response develops, it tends to persist; besides, "aggressiveness is transmitted across generations within families."[13]

FRIEND OR FOE?

Ambivalence was a pervading source of anxiety and occasional discomfort for blacks and whites: "Hey man, com'on. All of a sudden, they play. It's just like magic. A kid might have sort of a frowny smile. I'll run. Sometimes it means I'm going to get you. Sometimes it means I want to play with you" (white fourth-grade boy).

Not only were there undesirable consequences of children's meddlin' each other, but meddlin' also created difficulties for adults in a setting that on the surface had appeared ideal. There was a high turnover of teachers for a variety of interrelated reasons, and at least one teacher left HPES during the school year for poor health. Middle-class Anglo and black teachers often experience culture shock when they are the target of children's physical or verbal abuse or are deprecated for efforts to be sympathetic. Baffled, hurt, and unable to understand or cope with the violence directed toward them, some teachers emotionally withdraw or find jobs elsewhere.[14] They suffer anxiety symptoms similar to the combat fatigue suffered by soldiers. The president of the National Educational Association refers to the problem as teacher burnout.[15] Critics of urban schools often fail to recognize that children have an effect on teachers who must adjust to them. Teachers' expectations of children's school performance frequently stem from the youngsters' failure to pay attention to lessons when teachers have tried their best to teach.[16]

Shared experiences, interests, reciprocity, communicative style, and empathy make up the mortar of friendship and lead to positive interactions. The greater the overlap in these areas, the easier it is for harmonious social relations to take place.[17]

The HPES children's experience of more black than white aggression led some blacks and whites to dislike blacks. Children who followed the rules found their self-concept and beliefs about being a student challenged when black children defied school authorities, since youngsters seek support for their behavior from classmates as well as authority figures. Some blacks, especially from middle-class backgrounds who share middle-class cultural values, feel embarrassed by being identified with the black group.

Certainly, there were incidents where a middle-class child perceived aggression when a low-income child had no harmful intention; for example, the latter wanted a particular place in line and had learned that pushing was an effective way of getting a place. In chapter 3, I had pointed out that some black children intruded into others' personal space out of curiosity rather than meddlin'.

All people use classification to guide their response to, and expectations of, individuals in the course of social interaction. The senses contribute to abstract thought: When we perceive an object, we grasp its essential qualities. Skin color is an obvious mark of identification, and sometimes also coinciding with culture, class, and aggressiveness, color becomes a clue to behavior. Children categorize aggressors as dumb, physical, mean, and unpredictable. Discovering aggression in one black child and then another and still a third and fourth, a youngster learns to abstract and generalize.

Color biases result from at least three conditions.[18] First, there is an individual developmental pattern common to all human beings. Second, each individual has personal experiences; meddlin' experiences fall into this category. And third, each individual learns from the attitudes, beliefs, and verbal and nonverbal behavior of parents, peers, and individuals presented in the mass media.

Children's responses to color have a biological base. Color differences are highly salient stimuli to the visually oriented Homo sapiens, and color terms white and black are generally the most frequently used color terms in all human languages. During the early days of human life, infants respond to differences in brightness of stimuli.[19] By six months, of age, they distinguish hue,[20] and children become aware of skin color differences at the age of four. French and Italian youngsters preferred white over black stimuli perhaps because of the diurnal nature of Homo sapiens.[22]

Youngsters pick up racial attitudes, beliefs, and behavior from verbal and nonverbal actions of adults in their environment. The courts are also responsible for creating color awareness by requiring the assignment of teachers and students on the basis of race in order to eliminate racial discrimination in public education.[23] The espousal of cultural pluralism, the emphasis on each group recognizing its racial identity in order to create strong group solidarity and gain equitable power; and the adversary climate of affirmative action and racial representation to achieve quality also emphasize color.

At HPES, the differential discipline teachers impose highlights color distinction:

> I think sometimes the teachers aren't fair, 'cause when, you know, like, a lot of black people say a lot of stuff and say some bad words and stuff, and she lets 'em get away with it, and then a white person says something, and she starts raising cain and all that. You know what I mean? And that's kinda unfair I think (76 wb 6th).

Another white child said:

> If they're not so good a student, and they in trouble all the time, then they should get in trouble more than I should. If there's a gang of them, the ones that are ganging up on the one should get in trouble, not just the one person. Like there's about twelve blacks against the whites (106 wg 6th).

A sixth-grader recognized the dilemma:

> They have to be treated more carefully; you never know what they are going to do. I remember a teacher was walking some wild ones extra careful. They're the toughest. John and Edward; they're both wild ones. And they started getting riled up. The teacher kept a good watch. And before you know it, as soon as they got in the bathroom, there was a big fight. Next thing you know, Edward was lying on the floor; his nose was bleeding (16 wb).

At HPES, teachers expected white children to have middle-class training and understand and correctly respond to white middle-class adult directions. For example, at an assembly with the U.S. Drum and Bugle Corps, teachers would stop white children from rhythmically moving or drumming in their seats while they ignored black children drumming, dancing, or shoulder shimmying. Class awareness often leads some white teachers who know that a black child's parents are professionals to treat the child like a white middle-class youngster.

The color coding of human groups suggests that because the color is different and the words designating the groups are different, human groups are therefore different. Color words acquire certain affective meanings in everyday use. Words with nonracial references become associated with a group in some people's mind (for example, the word "black" is associated with badness—a black mark is a censure, a blacklist is a catalog of undesirable people, a black sheep is deviant, the black market refers to illegal trade, a blackball is a negative vote, blackmail is extortion, and so on). The word white is associated with such characteristics as purity, angels, and cleanliness; a white lie is a harmless fib. Moby Dick, sickliness, and death are less common meanings of white.

In sum, children may develop a preference for light over dark because they are members of a species that is active primarily during the daylight and people that are socialized in American culture. Various cultural and individual experiences, including life in a desegregated school, shape the subsequent development of their concepts and behavior.

Another consequence of low-income black aggression may be that the kind of law-and-order cult that emerged in response to the 1960s' black revolt will develop among victims of meddlin'. The bitterness of an unpleasant experience may linger and subsequent interactions of the same confirm existing antipathies.

A consequence of black children's greater meddlin' is separatism between the races and social classes. That is, one finds segregation in a desegregated setting. Games and spatial areas become the province of special groups. *Children initiated situations of segregation* in contrast to adult efforts to eliminate segregation based on such factors as historical legacy, mutual interests, and neighborhood networks.

In free play (not directed by school staff), children expressed feelings and attitudes using particular communication patterns, which were generally understood or enjoyed by only the cultural group to which children belonged and by some children of other groups with whom they had interacted over a period of time. Because it is easier to understand people and get along when rules and assumptions are understood and accepted, individuals who share similar cultures are more likely to play and work together.[24] Thus children often align themselves on the bases of neighborhood groups or identification with a school previously attended. These friendships tend to persist and cliques are not particularly open to newcomers.

Voluntary seating patterns at HPES observed over the school year revealed blacks seated with blacks and whites with whites. Only occasionally in a group was there a person of another color. Another indicator of separatism was that black and white children usually mentioned youngsters of their own color when they named the brightest, toughest, or dumbest. Children thought in both terms of their immediate friendship group and the school setting. Concerning the latter, recall that both black and white children perceived and named low-income black children as engaging in more meddlin' at school. In reference to gender, however, they used she or he. Although blacks and whites rarely sought each other's company, they seemed willing and able to interact with each other harmoniously when they in a situation that required such behavior (bullies excepted).

A few whites interacted socially in an integrated fashion, but they expressed wariness when a black person became angry and rallied the black gang. In response to the question, "Are you afraid of anyone at school," a white girl said:

> At times. Sometimes if there's gangs. Tina's tall, and Gogo, she is bigger than I am, and they just, they're the biggest at school, so you're kind of afraid of 'em, and when there's a gang of black kids against whites and the whites against the blacks, I think the blacks can stand a lot more if they're in a fight—'cause I've been in that situation two or three times.

"What happened?" I asked.

> Well, we were outside, and the word got around that Tracy was mad at me, and so we walked in the gym, and she kicked me. So I kicked her back. And she kicked me, and it made me mad. So I kicked her real hard, and she fell down, and the other ones started up on me and started hittin' me in the head. And she hit me in the back, and I ran to the bathroom, and so after that we fought. My face was all red, and so the next day I didn't go to school 'cause . . . Sometimes friends take up for me, and sometimes they don't because they think you can do it yourself (106 wg 6th).

Since white children may not know what to do or say to black classmates, they sometimes block them out of their consciousness. In a majority-black school, whites "often ignore black classmates who would come between them and white friends. For white children in the school, blacks are often invisible. . . . Black children seemed very aware of their peers and rarely ignored them under any circumstance."[25] An older boy when pressed said, "Well, I just don't have anything in common with black kids. They have totally different interests than me. We get along by ignoring one another."[26]

Black pride, identity, boundaries, and neighborhood loyalty vis-à-vis the white establishment coalesces in dances HPES black girls perform[27] during recess on warm sunny days when they spontaneously organize ring plays, line plays, and cheers that combine dance and song. A leader sings a phrase that the group answers or merely leads the performers. Movements accompany and accent the song text or illustrate it. Hand clapping or other body percussion punctuate the performance to create a syncopated rhythm within the song and dance. In one instance, when a white girl wished to join the black girls in one of the dances, a black girl stepped back, put her hands on her hips, looked the white girl up and down about the hips and feet, and with a disbelieving scowl said loudly for all to hear: "Show me you can dance!" Everyone looked at the white girl who merely withdrew to the side lines.

Later, a different white girl joined the "Check Me" ring play in which the name of each participant standing in the circle was singled out in turn, going to the right. One girl's name was called by the girl to her immediate left; she identified herself, sang a refrain, and then called on the next girl to her right.

> Check [*clap*], check [*clap*], check [*clap*]
> My name is Tina,
> I am a Pisces.
> I want you to [*clap*]
> check, check, check
> to check out Bridgette.
> Check [*clap*], check [*clap*], check.
> My name is Bridgette . . .

When it was the white girl's turn to be called, the black girl just passed her by and called out the next black girl. Ignored and rejected, the white girl called out, "I can do it too!" No one paid attention. Not all white children appreciate the black dances or are unhappy about being excluded. One remarked, "They always do that crap!"

The dancers could have been "contesting," gaming, where the only rule is that there are no permanently fixed rules: The object is to discover the paradigm of rules in existence and hence gain the advantage by redefining the paradign and its rules.[28] By recognizing only blacks, participants in this case redefined the rule of taking turns according to one's place in the circle. Alternatively, it could have been that the fixed rules included blacks only. Besides passing time, asserting camaraderie, providing amusement, and working through problems in a world the performers do not control, the dances distinguish insider-neighborhood children from the outsider-volunteers, who belong to a variety of other neighborhood communities. Occasionally, black boys joined in these dances. The very few black newcomers who were not part of the neighborhood group were excluded as were the white girls who tried to participate in the dances.

Dance themes, events, and participation criteria reflect general attitudes that have been held among blacks for generations,[29] as well as newer attitudes. Although children learned some of the dances from their mothers and older people, they also made up songs and dances to express their own era of black power and desegregation. One fourth-grade girl said she made up the words to a song called "Walking over People, I Don't Care, Shampoo, Shampoo." Girls formed a line, arms around each others' waists, and moved briskly in the play area singing and dancing. "Sock It" and "Power" were other favorites called cheers. These were blends of ring and line dances with high school, college, and professional football cheerleader dance routines. These dances reflect confrontation, both as game and real life. Ambiguous meaning creates the excitement.

The black girls' performances appear to be defensive structuring, ingroup bonding in an arena in which they can excel as a response to their awareness of past white oppression and exclusion of black people. Their dancing suggests a future of racial separation possibly carried on as in the past—or even a reversal of power relations, blacks superior to whites.[30] The white audience is put on its mettle. White children had the outsider status in informal children-delineated performance arenas at HPES that blacks have had in the broader arenas in the United States. What the national context offered in prestige for whites, the local context offered in recognition and power for blacks. Perhaps the black girls' dances are similar to the trickster tales of the slave folk culture that afforded their creators psychic relief, an arena of mastery, and a vision of a possible future.[31]

The differential use of space is meaningful. People sometimes strategically used space to demonstrate power[32] or increase the potential for comfortable interactions with peers. Places become endowed with sentiment. "Students are extremely concerned with territoriality."[33] Blacks continue to accept some boundaries that whites originally imposed. The

HPES school was located in a black neighborhood with a separate and equal history; therefore, black children felt they could be bosses. Therefore, restrooms were for toughs at HPES and elsewhere.[34]

> Well, if they [blacks] see you use the restroom or the toilet, they start laughin' and stuff. And they say, "Ah, he's usin' the toilet" and all that stuff; and sometimes you got to run in there and use the restroom and get 'fore they come in, 'cause they start takin' all over the place (79 wb 6th).

The restroom was an unpleasant area of teasing and harassment for weaker children. Black and white youngsters reported verbal assaults, intimidating threats, and physical abuse by black bullies. Such action deterred restroom use. Consequently, after school many black and white children rushed directly home with physical discomfort and even soiled underwear. The absence of toilet doors in the boys' restroom made some children feel self-conscious and vulnerable. Sometimes a child was "imprisoned" in the stall by several youngsters who blocked the exit to keep him from leaving. A sixth-grade white boy said, "When they try to jump over [the side wall] and their fingers overhang it, I chop their knuckles." Teachers and aides rarely entered the restroom. Most were female, and the boys claimed they got embarrassed by their presence. One sixth-grade white girl said, "Oh, this really gets me mad: Some people grab on to the top of the doors and look over at you." In mainstream American culture, the toilet is regarded as a very private space where the individual has protective refuge from others. Thus an individual strongly feels a sense of having been aggrieved when not left alone.

Football was also for the tough kids. Some black boys did not play; few whites did. As one white boy put it, "The blacks don't throw the ball to the whites." It was not just that the black boys practiced a lot: They argued over rules and got into fights over them. Each black contestant had his group of friends. One youngster said, "If he meddles me, I get my friends, and he gets his friends." A circle delineated the fighting space; the whites stayed on the outskirts of the mayhem.

At HPES, teachers and aides described some white boys as immature because they played make-believe games or engaged in spontaneous play among themselves rather than joining the organized sports games. However, it may be their *maturity* and sensitivity to reality that accounted for their behavior. A number of factors figured into their choice:

> Black boys dominated the organized sports games.

> Black lower-class game and spontaneous play rules differed from those of white and black middle-class children.

134

Lower-class black youngsters responded to losing, not getting the ball, and other similar events during the course of a game, at times with violence.

Blacks' response to an accidental push or kick often led to an aggressive retaliation or full fight.

Blacks did not tolerate poor athletes on the field, and not all children could be successful in the games blacks dominated.

White middle-class children usually learn to discuss disagreements and use words to win their way; thus lower-class black children's greater reliance on aggressiveness in conflict resolution contradicted middle-class ethics.

Not participating in certain types of play with members of another culture may be a rational strategy for coping with children who use play forms as vehicles to aggress and dominate. Indeed, implicit in some spontaneous play was the use of play aggression as an excuse for fighting, which a player actually sought.

The spontaneous play of "playing with play" (disrupting a social order and expected behaviors and creating disorder for the experience of power and control) worked to the disadvantage of children who had not developed a strong peer support group. Spontaneous play at HPES involved patron–client relationships and gang organization.

It is of interest to contrast a study of the play of nine-to-twelve-year-old Vietnamese refugee children in four San Francisco area schools[35] with the analysis of social interactions between black and white children at HPES. The HPES youngsters' social life suggests other possible explanations than those posited for the Vietnamese children's choice of play forms and interactions with black and white American children. At HPES, white volunteer children behaved like the Vietnamese in San Francisco, who chose rule-governed games over spontaneous play; they found security in games with rules known to teachers.

The seemingly structureless play activities of spontaneous chasing, wrestling, and taunting require the cultural sophistication of knowing the children's implicit rules so well they can be ignored or distorted. Spontaneous play does not have clearly defined predictability, boundaries, structure, rules, or roles for participants.

The Vietnamese refugee children fit Piaget's model of children after seven years of age adapting to the natural and social world and indulging less in symbolic distortions and transpositions. They play rule-governed games that continue into adulthood.[36] However, older American children often play "nonrule-governed games." They have learned the game rules and now enjoy turning over the rules, playing with more complex social rules and structures. Vietnamese and American children

135

also differ in their decision-making and conflict-resolution behavior in the school setting. Vietnamese stand back while Americans make decisions and settle conflicts.

Vietnamese children avoid spontaneous play with American peers because they do not understand the rules well enough to break them. The Vietnamese children retreat from the confusion of learning a new culture into the safety of rules, or they are pulled into a structure they can work within. Game players try to eliminate confusion: "The confused and intricate laws of ordinary life are replaced in this fixed space and for this given time by precise, arbitrary, unexceptionable rules that must be accepted as such and that govern the correct play of the game."[37] It may be that Vietnamese, like many white volunteer children at HPES, are aware that the school's culture differs from their own, do not approve of it, or fear to participate in it because of the violence, which hurts physically, and the norms, which hurt psychologically in contradicting home and teacher instruction.

Pluses and Minuses in the Integration Process

After this lengthy discussion of problems, causes, and consequences, I want to underscore the fact that children at HPES generally had pleasant experiences. Unquestionably, the school was an exciting, warm, creative, and educationally sound institution. Fun was the prevailing sentiment. And some black and white children and adults were friends by any criteria. Youngsters played together, sat close to each other, shared, visited at home, and their parents visited socially. Such relationships would not have had the opportunity to develop in a segregated school or a desegregated school where individuals were not making efforts to promote harmonious relations. Racial isolation not only prevents each group from learning shared beliefs and behavior but leads to genuine differences. In mixed settings, children learn to adjust to diversity and change, which characterize the real world of tempestuous "future shock."[38] Some low-income blacks may become aware of and learn dominant middle-class styles and values, whereas higher-income blacks and whites may eventually pick up assertiveness, a relaxed, rhythmic kinetic style, down-to-earth emotional expressiveness, and openness about life's realities. There exists what Piaget called "deferred imitation."[39] Some individuals learn to deal with others who are less overtly expressive, whereas those in turn learn how to handle a range of emotional expression, including the occasional middle-class person's explo-

136

sion. Blacks learn not to fear whites after 350 years of anxious race relations.

Blacks may learn the feeling of majority status in a heavily black school, whereas whites may gain an understanding of minority outsider problems. One researcher argues that everyone should have the experience of being a minority and a majority in order to develop a democratic society.[40] Some children's simultaneous verbalization of civil rights rhetoric and experience of being meddled and excluded from soccer games or dance play that contradicts equal opportunity suggest their hopes for the success of integration.

Although there are pluses in a multicultural setting, children's perceptions and realities must be brought into the open so that they can be dealt with. Many unpleasant incidents take place because participants do not understand what is happening or care about what is appropriate school behavior. Consequently, children initiate segregation in the adult-initiated desegregated setting.

Children's actions depend on many factors: personality and values; physical capabilities; the prowess to stand up and fight, bluff, or deflect aggression; home, peer, and school learning; and situational pressures.

At HPES and everywhere people deliberately or inadvertently meddle each other because of perceptions they have of each other and themselves. Some of the perceptions are fantasies; others are not. Child's play aggression and actual aggression are the channelization of fantasies, anxieties, and frustrations. The impotent become potent; the physically or psychically brutalized transform into brutalizers. Some children resort to violence in response to seemingly minor trespasses upon their person, space, or property. With malice aforethought, other children use a trivial provocation or create one in order to hurt a child. Many youngsters and teachers are frightened; some children are allowed to disrupt their fellow students' education. Yet children learn best when there is a climate of security.

Chapter 6 focused on what children perceived to be the greatest dissonance in the school. The problems of meddlin' are magnified manifold in other schools across the nation, especially in schools located in large urban areas. Earlier chapters provided the historical context and some of the reasons for meddlin'. Most children engage occasionally in disruptive school behavior and encounter the universal problems of adjusting to new people, situations, grade levels, teachers, and classmates. However, from children's perspectives—validated by research observations—blacks engaged in a greater amount of aggression and did so more dramatically.

Guided by holistic, comparative, and communication theory perspectives described in chapter 1, I recognize that aggression is a fundamental message that requires a response to the causes as well as the manifestations. If responded to sensitively, aggression can be reduced because the factors precipitating it will be correspondingly decreased or ameliorated. At play in HPES were various forms of communication; cultural differences; bases and patterns of categorizing experiences and people; the self-fulfilling prophecy; self-preservation and the search for human dignity; race relations; human maturation; and the interweaving of black and white, low-income and middle-income, neighbors and strangers, children and adults. In such a context, when we are oblivious to or distort messages being sent and received, problems become exacerbated.

During my involvement in the school and subsequently thereafter, HPES was experiencing growth and development. Parents and staff members who became aware of the problems that were identified have been taking steps to ameliorate them. Many of these are included in chapter 8. Under the collaborative efforts of school, family, and neighborhood, HPES children have matured. Change *is* possible!

The following chapters focus on ways of increasing the number of children who have the opportunity to interact freely with those of different cultures and to share similar interests in an environment where they can successfully pursue academic goals without being diverted by the hidden survival curriculum of their social world. The problem is not merely desegregation but also the decline of excellence in education generally and the minority plight. Recall that 40 percent of seventeen-year-old minority youths are functionally illiterate; the related unemployment rate soars to 40 percent.

NOTES

1. Schofield and Sagar 1977:146.
2. Gregory 1964:41.
3. Killiam 1973:101–2.
4. Piaget 1951:131.
5. Aldis 1975:52. This trait is associated with black educational achievement and such middle class attitudes and behavior as knowing where to find jobs, wanting integration, and having checking accounts. It is also related to internal control, the degree to which individuals feel the power to control their environment (Crain and Weisman 1972:72). High internal control is associated with inhibiting aggression, planning for the future, and being generally "middle class" in attitude toward achievement.

6. See Sutton-Smith 1977.
7. Gordon 1977.
8. Schafft 1976:72.
9. Silverstein and Krate 1975:217.
10. Eron et al. 1971; Lefkowitz et al. 1977:192.
11. Lefkowitz et al. 1983; Eron 1983.
12. Walder et al. 1983.
13. Huesmann et al. 1984:1131.
14. Bloch 1978; Brodsky 1977.
15. Serrin 1979; Dworkin 1986.
16. Silverstein and Krate 1975:223–24; Metz 1978.
17. Cf. Scherer et al. 1975:156–57.
18. Williams and Morland 1976.
19. Hershenson 1964.
20. Fagan 1974.
21. Proshansky and Newton 1968.
22. Best, Naylor, and Williams 1975.
23. Williams and Moreland 1976:28.
24. See White 1977; Rosenbaum and Presser 1978; and Wax 1980:92–93, 103–5, 111 on children-initiated separatism in desegregated schools.
25. Schafft 1976:80.
26. Ibid., 81.
27. See chapter 2, Hanna 1986b, 1987, 1988b.
28. Farrer 1981.
29. Cf. Jones and Hawes 1972.
30. Corsaro (1979) points out that nursery school children have clear conceptions of honor, prestige, and status as power. See Giroux (1983) on children's resistance to the status quo.
31. Cf. Levine 1977.
32. "Space can be considered as a resource and thus control over space and a greater ability to use it for attaining one's goals can be a major benefit" (Baldassare 1978:44). Metz (1978:221–22) found that black students in a desegregated high school mobilized as a large group and then walked to school and clustered on the school steps. In this territory they had staked out, they left but a narrow passageway to the school entrance. Scherer and Slawski (1978) discovered that basketball and football were black and swimming and golf were white; female track was black, but male track was white. Clement et al. (1979); Polgar (1978); and Collins and Noblit (1978) also describe patterns of informal segregation that predominate in the schools they studied. See Crain et al. 1982:58.
33. Crain et al. 1982:58.
34. Cf. Schafft 1976:64.
35. Robinson 1978.
36. Piaget 1926:142.
37. Callois 1961:7.
38. Toffler 1970.
39. Gruber and Voneche 1978.
40. Willie 1978.

139

7

IDEALISM AND REALITY: PRESCRIPTIVE NEEDS IN THE NATIONAL CONTEXT

AN analysis in comparative perspective of HPES student comments and researcher observations of school life (set within theoretical perspectives of social communication and the history of the school setting) reveals what it is like to be a student in a low-income urban school. Discussion of the broader wellsprings of a student-experienced problem, meddlin'—more generally, the clash of socioeconomic styles that coincide with desegregation—and the implications of such disabling dissonance within the school followed. Disconcerting for me as a parent and then a researcher was the discovery that a process, desegregation, that I thought was working well in a favored magnet school urgently needed improvement, as did schooling elsewhere. The difficulties detailed are more than getting-started problems—they are widespread and of long duration. Moreover, they point to the broader issue of effective education for what has been called the underclass.[1]

At the National Forum on Excellence in Education, December 8, 1983, President Reagan, speaking of education in general, called for restoring "good, old-fashioned discipline." He equated student aggression against the teacher or self with chemical abuse and other such unlawful acts as physical assault of peers, robbery, theft, and property destruction. "In too many schools across the land, teachers can't teach because they lack the authority to make students take tests and hand in homework . . . quiet down their class. In some schools, teachers suffer verbal and physical abuse."[2] How one applied good old-fashioned discipline without additional money in a new era of changed lifestyles, economic dislocation, and socioeconomic expectations is a question not answered by merely restricting students' rights and reemphasizing their responsibilities. Because school officials have been subject to personal legal liability in instances where disciplinary actions have been taken (*Wood* v. *Strickland* 420 U.S. 308, 1975), the Department of Justice has filed "friend of the court" briefs in appropriate cases in order to increase the authority of teachers, principals, and school administrators in dealing with school discipline problems.

Yet the problem of disruptive school behavior goes beyond criminal acts and disobeying teachers to a counterschool culture and a behavioral style that are less apparent than a bloody knife fight or the smell of marijuana. The problem, as illustrated by the HPES case, has many manifestations and various causes. It requires a multipronged approach to solve it.

Low-income populations have specific needs. The Cabinet Council on the Human Resources Working Group on School Violence/Discipline stated that minorities bear the brunt of violent and disruptive schools and "urban school violence and indiscipline may be at the heart of the busing controversy which has so distorted public debate over American education and has so distracted the country from its real agenda—for black and white children alike—of academic exccllence."[3]

Desegregation is assumed to be working[4] if: There is a mix of black and white, there are no media reports of violence, schools allocate special resources to assist the process of desegregation and promote multiculturalism, and desegregation is begun with young children. The HPES children's story challenges this assumption. The school setting, *segregated or desegregated,* in which children meet has built-in pressures of comparison, embarrassment, shame, anxiety, and self-doubt that lead some youngsters to behave in ways that are not conducive to succeeding academically. In desegregated schools, this behavior tends to interfere with interracial and inter–social-class friendships. Moreover, and of critical importance, the society in which schools exist has inequities that limit youngsters' aspirations and shape social relations. Therefore education cannot adequately bring about effective change without reforms in the broader society that envelopes and meshes with the school.

Education is collective action and requires an integrated administrative, political, community, and parental effort to effect educational change.

> Learning is a dynamic process which, in public education operating at its best, creates a constructive synergism among teachers and students, extending to parents, administrators, community members, public officials and citizens. At worst, public education masks a game of manipulative control, where teachers, students, administrators, parents, community groups, and public officials vie with one another for power and resources to achieve particular ends in a destructive spiral of social interaction.[5]

141

Likewise, on the basis of a massive study involving 27,000 individuals who provided data and thirty-eight schools (thirteen high, thirteen elementary, and twelve middle schools), John Goodlad, the study's director, called the agenda of school improvement formidable. He, too, supports a holistic approach: "Significant improvement will come about not by tackling these problem areas one by one, but by addressing all of them as a system.[6]

The following diagram on educational change shows system elements that affect our children's education and indicates their points of impact, relationships, and chapters that discuss the various exchanges. Of course, in a discussion, it is necessary to separate the elements from the whole.

Even if schools alone cannot solve society's problems, steps can be taken to foster values and behavior that most people have a stake in perpetuating and to improve teaching and learning in schools generally and specifically with low-income students. Chapter 6 discussed some of the implications of children's disruptive school behavior within the school. There are serious implications beyond the school that this chapter addresses. It also discusses some needs for those who have contact directly with youngsters. Then we turn to strategies for the teacher on the "firing line" in the classroom (chapter 8) and finally, the other institutions that affect teaching and learning (chapter 9).

My practical involvement in communities and schools across the country in the late 1970s and 1980s alerted me to the problem that what should be common knowledge has not been broadly diffused. Shockingly enough, naïveté reigns among many parents, teachers, and policy makers.

The prescriptive strategies in the last three chapters, a synthesis not available elsewhere, are based on what HPES students, teachers, parents, and administrators and RISD personnel believed to be effective; my observations; assessments of policies in other schools; and literature on the theoretical bases of communication and social interaction presented in chapter 1. For the most part, the prescriptive strategies are of a clinical nature and attempt to take into account competing interests.[7] That is, they are not scientifically evaluated strategies so that we can know with certainty what actually works under specific conditions.

Victimizing Progress

By mandating desegregation without considering unintended consequences, policy makers have unwittingly instituted a plan that fails to

Figure 7.1

EDUCATIONAL CHANGE [a]

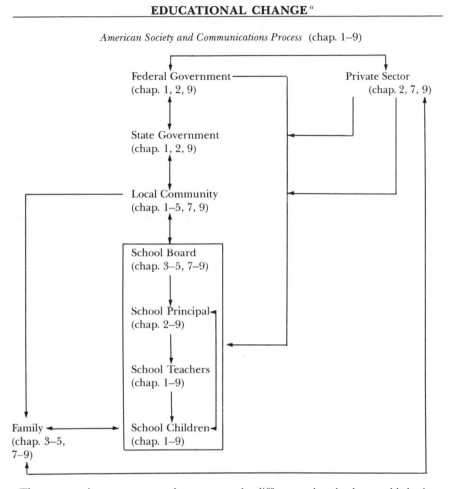

American Society and Communications Process (chap. 1–9)

[a]These categories encompass and are crosscut by different cultural values and behaviors, although middle-class culture dominates the government, private sector, and school structures.

provide equal educational opportunity. The emphasis on racial ratios and such material things as physical facilities, books, and science equipment have neglected nonmaterial resources—knowledge of dominant ways of thinking and the hidden dimension of mutually shared values, communication styles, and social networks, as well as the impact of the economy.[8]

The result of ignoring key problems in education appears to be a drift toward a more socioeconomically stratified society as those with the financial means send their children to private schools or move to other neighborhoods rather than have their youngsters attend desegregated public schools. Schools then lose many white students, are forced to change curricula, reducing the academic subjects offered, and experience budgetary difficulties as the middle-class exodus erodes the local tax base and state legislative allocations for public education. Parents with children in private schools often do not support taxes for public education. This compounds the problem of the public education budget squeeze, which eliminates "expendable frills" and makes private schools or affluent suburban systems even more attractive to parents who want the "three Rs" and more arts and sports for their children.

Coupled with the lack of support for public education is a decreasing interest in support for public services that support the poor outside the school. The *Los Angeles Times* and CBS published a poll that identified why Californians voted for Proposition 13, the Jarvis–Gann tax-cut amendment. Of the services inflation-weary voters felt could most easily be curtailed, most cited services to the poor. The majority believe that minorities have been excessive in demands for jobs, housing, education, transit, and so on.[9] Three years later, President Reagan's policies appeared to subscribe to this sentiment.

An elite private school population makes available a pool of resources for professional and managerial positions, whereas public schools provide for lower-level positions. The gap between the two groups could widen if the opportunity for the lower class to learn the hidden curricula of the middle class and for low-income talented individuals to gain training for higher socioeconomic positions decreased. Although some people think that a widening gap between rich and poor would lead to the poor white and black finding a common cause and changing the economic system, the history of black–white social relations lacks strong precedent for such a development.

Discussing low-income black students' disruptive school behavior sometimes leads to emotional charges of subverting civil rights. However, ignoring or denying children's perceptions and experiences, which prevents dealing with and perhaps resolving the difficulties, is surely more subversive and harmful; it merely leads to maintaining the status quo.

Some adults at HPES and other schools minimize the dissonance problem by saying that difficulties exist beyond the school, so children in schools with low-income students are learning about real life. Yet an alternative philosophy holds that the school should perpetuate society's positive traditions and learning, coping, and problem-solving skills.

Generational Credibility Gap

Adult–child differences exist and often need translation.[10] We assume that our children's school experiences are similar to our own. When I asked HPES parents and school personnel or other adults a question about education, their replies often began with: "I remember when I was in ——— grade. . . ."

As adults, however, we usually overspecialize in the vocal and auditory channels of communication. Teaching emphasizes the verbal mode that is the primary way of conducting social life. Although the nonverbal plays an important role, it lies largely outside our awareness and only recently have there been research and courses on nonverbal behavior.[11] Consequently, adults do not pay much attention to what occurs nonverbally among children whose senses of sight, touch, movement, smell, and space are especially active and whose language skills are unsophisticated. While adults tend to regard the body as a platform for the head, children, as illustrated at HPES, tend to regard the body as an instrument of action, including aggression. "Adult nonverbal behavior differs from that of children most clearly in the negative realm."[12]

Not only do children rely heavily on multichanneled communication that adults forget, but children's experiences today are enmeshed in a different milieu—one of an increased lack of discipline and faith in school and society. Moreover, children's peer interactions in a new and unique era of black assertiveness create generational differences.

Parents who do not hear stories assume all is well with their children. Some adults believe so strongly in integration, the irrelevance of color, and equality that a child cannot report everyday happenings without getting disapproving responses. Thus, the child learns to keep quiet and harbors stresses that erupt in different ways.

The taboo on discussing race or color and the differences that coincide with these, as well as the denial of differences, creates an even greater generational credibility gap. When forced to live out their parents' idealistic dreams, children cannot help but lose trust in naïve parental pronouncements. Parents and teachers tell children not to consider racial distinctions in making friends. Experience, however, teaches youngsters that color is an important ingredient in parents' friendship groups and acquaintances, as well as their own.

145

As was sometimes true at HPES, children may keep traumas secret from parents whom they perceive as insensitive to their experiences. Some parents maintain that fear of blacks is a fantasy generated by a lack of contact. One mother, a civil rights activist, told me, "I did not know any black person other than the maid in our home in day-to-day living." The maid was docile, kind, and subservient. Other adults interacted with middle-class blacks or repressed unpleasant experiences. Consequently, stories of aggression by "those darling black children," particularly in the first and second grades, fall on deaf adult ears.

A longitudinal study of U.S. high school seniors' and sophomores' perceptions of misbehavior suggests that school administrators understated the level of fighting among students and students' feeling of security in school. Fewer than 6 percent of the high school administrators reported student fighting as a moderate problem, but more than 35 percent of the sophomores said that students often fight in more than 15 percent of the high schools.[13]

Breaking Taboos: White Liberals

Many whites find it difficult to discuss cultural differences, for they were brought up to believe in the United States as a great melting pot where diverse backgrounds and life styles blend. Some white parents maintain a public integrationist stance by sending their children to magnet schools like HPES. Breaking the taboo about discussing race-relations problems shakes their confidence in their choice to voluntarily bus their children to desegregated schools as well as in their ability to guide and protect their children.

Indicative of white children's awareness of taboos is the fact that most whom I interviewed did not mention the word black. However, it was evident that they were speaking about blacks from the names of the children mentioned as bullies or tough or by comparisons with their former neighborhood school.

White parents interested in promoting integration should try to interact with black parents, most of whom share the same goals for their children. Whites may have to take the initiative to visit with blacks at school activities and continue their efforts despite occasional rebuffs. Some bridge-building activities include parents supporting school teams and the school holding curricular and extracurricular events at times when working parents are able to attend.

White parents who know black English dialect, sensitivities, and problems can better guide and protect their children, who may experience uncomfortable provoked or unprovoked encounters. Parents may need to teach their children assertiveness and alliance behavior—to use strong-suit tactics and develop in areas where they have shortcomings, as I had to help my youngsters. Children can develop creative and adaptive skills relevant to all areas of life. For example, from their early development, children learn reconnaissance behavior in which they scan a scene (first a street they have to cross and later a classroom in which they must work) and then act appropriately.

In addition, whites need to become aware of how they inadvertently offend blacks. For example, a volunteer parent at HPES knew several white parents who needed child care in order to assist teachers at the school. She asked some of the Hamilton Park neighborhood mothers whom she knew to be at home caring for their own children if they would babysit for the white children at the same time because baby-sitters are difficult to find during school hours and the neighborhood was convenient for the volunteers. Blacks took offense because they did not want the status of maid: "We are tired of raising white folks' babies!"

What are some of the other faux pas that cause discomfort and prevent good will attempts between the races? Here is a black perspective on verbal communications that should be considered in social interaction:[14]

At social occasions talk about race relations and jobs must be an exchange of give and take.

"Some of my best friends are . . ." Such a statement has too much display in the claim.

"But the Irish (Jews, Italians . . .) did it, why can't you?" Blacks resent these comparisons; the implication is that if blacks had worked harder, their fate would have been more favorable. But the slave stigma remained with blacks who could not get lost in a white crowd as other ethnic groups could.

"A credit to his race . . ." The assumption of this praise is that blacks need crediting. Talent and technique are insulted if an individual is praised as a black ——— (fill in whatever). If one is crediting blacks, one should credit whites.

"What do you people want?" The assumption is that blacks want something different from what white people want.

"The first black to . . ." The hoopla confirms tokenism in many cases.

147

"It's for your own good" is a patronizing statement. It implies that blacks do not know their own best interests.

"Violence will get you nowhere." Whites imply that black violence is special, yet blacks think of white slavemaster brutality, the underworld, Vietnam, and so forth.

"How come the others didn't make it?" Whites use a few success examples to deny that things are gloomy for the majority of blacks.

"We only want to help." The problem is that the liberal's help turns into domination.

"If he's qualified . . ." The liberal might substitute white for black and see how things work out.

"It's not because you're black." Yet blacks receive an overdose of insensitive, rude, or offensive behavior.

Breaking Taboos: Concerned Blacks

Harvard political scientist Martin Kilson said that many blacks had drawn "an ethnic *cordon sanitaire* around entire areas of the black experience. Now, some blacks are breaking the code of silence that meant such things as black violence and inferior academic performance were either peremptorily blamed on white racism or ignored. Candid discussion is a step toward constructive problem-solving action.[15]

Building positive social relations is not a one-way process in any multicultural setting. Many whites assume that the minority group member is supposed to pursue integration into the majority while the majority member has the prerogative of rejecting the advances.[16] However, many blacks at HPES and elsewhere resent the lack of reverse cultural deference. Blacks, sensitive to the sincerity of whites, do not want to subject themselves to racism or being patronized; therefore they sometimes rebuff and call insincere or patronizing white overtures. Blacks need to help whites become aware of their inadvertent offensiveness.

For children to succeed in school, support from home is important. Therefore, it behooves black parents to work cooperatively with the school and white parents for the child's benefit.[17]

It is in the interest of black children for their parents to bear in mind that black attack or ostracism can reinforce negative perceptions among whites and create them where they never existed. Black parents who hear what their children say about who aggresses and misbehaves and listen to black psychiatrists without accusing them of selling out to prejudiced whites may gain helpful perspectives. Calling everything that goes amiss for children racism makes them feel they are "drowning in a sea of ill feeling with no allies or potential."[18]

Adults do not always realize that strict teachers and rigorous discipline of the past no longer characterize schools. Black parents could recognize that however well behaved their children are in their presence, black and white children in a number of schools, including HPES, perceive (and observations confirm) black children most often to be the fighters, bullies, and classroom disruptors.[19] When aggressors brag about their victimization and children discuss it, this communication reinforces the victim's and others' notion of black toughness. Couple the experience and aftermath of talking about aggressive behavior with the stereotypic lore about blacks, and the need for countervailing experiences to moderate these becomes essential.

Some black families are able to translate high educational aspirations for their children into school success, whereas others are unable to achieve desired outcomes. On the basis of ten case studies of low-income black families in urban ghettoes, including single-parent families dependent on public welfare, the home's hidden curriculum appears to be an important influence on children's school success.[20] Parents of high achievers were assertive in their efforts to attain information about their children's progress in school. In contrast, parents of low achievers tended to avoid contact with school personnel unless summoned to the school by authority figures. Parents of high achievers were more optimistic and copers, had frequent parent–child dialogues, encouraged academic pursuits, including homework and other educational activities in the home, and had contacts with other achievement-oriented people, set clear and consistent behavioral limits, consistently monitored how children use time, and required tasks and leadership roles for the child in the home. In the evaluation of compensatory education for disadvantaged children, the amount of reading done at home bore significant and consistent relations to achievement.[21]

Parents who follow these guidelines are well advised to seek alliances with other parents using a similar approach to child rearing: It is difficult to be the only parent in the neighborhood requiring one's child to behave in a certain way.

Breaking Taboos: Teachers

Some HPES teachers, typical of the profession nationwide, are reluctant to report black children's misbehavior, for they would be admitting that they are unable to control their students. Fear of losing a job, of hurting the cause of integration, and of black parents to whom children threaten to complain are other constraints.

When children discover and discuss black–white differences, some teachers may become embarrassed instead of actively treating the subject. It is often assumed that children know the implications of the words they use, even racial epithets, when in fact they may not. The meanings of words also change over time.

Teachers have to be aware that blacks distrust white people until proved trustworthy. As we were chatting, a sixth-grade black girl made the point:

> I'm not trying to make fun of your color or nothing, but my mother said, if you can find a good white person that'd be your good friend, she said, you're one lucky person and I think Ms. Mann [sixth-grade teacher] is the kind of person my mother is talking about.

I asked, "So you don't think there are too many of them?" "Well," she answered, "I haven't met them yet!"

"If you were training teachers who might have black children in their classes, what would you want them to know?" I asked a sixth-grader who had been at HPES since its inception. "I want them to know it may not be easy havin' both colors together, because they might not be used to each other. Or I want them to know that they can be nice to different kids, and the kids will be nice to them" (93 bg).

Of course, teachers will be more likely to break the taboos on reporting misbehavior and discussing sensitive matters when they have the support of parents, administrators, and the community. This support can benefit both the youngsters who misbehave, and those who are the victims of the misbehavior.

NOTES

1. Auletta 1982.
2. Quoted in Weisman 1983.
3. 1984:11–12.
4. The criteria for successful desegregation vary. Maintaining a numerical racial balance may satisfy the courts; a boost in academic achievement may satisfy the educational agencies. Quality or orderly education may be the criterion of success for local communities. Willie (1978) said the goal of desegregation is the control, understanding and patience children acquire in integrated settings and the understanding of the functions of the court in a democratic society in promoting justice and equity.

5. Comfort 1982:150.

6. Goodlad 1984:271.

7. Blalock (1979:13–18) points out that there are many alternative and sometimes conflicting values in the American creed at stake in any power struggle between opposing groups. For example, economic values include equality of opportunity, rewarding achievements, maximizing efficiency of production, free enterprise, maximizing opportunities for one's children, and protecting the unsuccessful and incapable. Political–legal values include freedom of speech, religion, press, and physical movement; legal equality; personal security and protection of private property; the minimization of internal conflict; federalism and decentralization of power; and change through the system. Social values encompass the integrity of family, other primary groups, and voluntary associations. Each side in a contest is likely to stress the set of values that it perceives to be most threatened. Prescriptive strategies attempt to take into account competing interests.

8. See Mungham and Person 1976; Willis 1977. The troubles attributed to working-class adolescents in England have economic origins and represent working-class frustration. Similarly, Everhart (1983) sees school work assigned to students as a labor process from which students lack assurance of benefiting and therefore become alienated. Larkin (1979) describes the economic patterns that impinge on the affluent suburban youth in the United States.

9. Kraft 1978.

10. MacKay 1973; Wood et al. 1971; Cicourel et al. 1974.

11. Davis 1982.

12. La France and Mayo 1978b:221.

13. DiPrete et al. 1982.

14. Rush and Clark 1971.

15. McGrath and Weathers 1985.

16. Kochman 1971:53.

17. Rich 1985 provides parents with suggestions to help their children at home.

18. Comer and Poussaint 1975:227.

19. In a personal communication, Jack Daniel (May 20, 1983), said blacks with whom he associated often engaged in brutal self-criticism as well as criticism of large segments of blacks—so much so that the label super black was developed for those who thought they were blacker than others. He noted the popularity among some blacks of the Last Poets' critical recording of "Niggers Are Afraid of the Revolution," Sonia Sanchez's poem criticizing sex in the name of revolution, Malcom X's discussion of "House versus the Field Negro," Don L. Lee's criticism of the notion that being black is "cool," E. Franklin Frazier's *Black Bourgeoisie*, Harold Cruse's *Crisis of the Negro Intellectual*, Carter G. Woodson's *Mis-Education of the Negro*, and Carl Rowan's critical comments in his daily radio reports.

20. Clark 1983.

21. Wang et al. 1981.

8

Keeping Iron-Clad Conviction from Rusting Out: Some Strategies for the Classroom

In chapters 2 and 3, cultural differences between modal blacks and whites and low-income and middle-income youngsters at HPES were revealed in comments on what they like and do not like about the school, and what they think is appropriate behavior from the school authorities' point of view and from their own. Cultural (socioeconomic-class) differences in classroom performance, work patterns, bases for accepting authority, and the use of aggression to express friendship, anger, frustration, and insubordination become clear from children's remarks and research observations of what they were doing.

What are the possibilities of bridging gaps in understanding, differences in values and behavior, and misuse of rules as adaptive responses? Differences are often adaptations to the kinds of relations that occur between people. What can be done to fulfill the public's expectations of the school as a vehicle for positive change? In this chapter, I draw on approaches that seemed to work at HPES as well as on solutions used elsewhere in the United States.[1] I observed the short-term success of some of these means of handling problems, and teachers, children, and parents believed they worked. When observations and reports agree about a strategy, it offers promise.

Classroom research conducted in the last ten to fifteen years has developed clear and detailed information about how successful teachers organize and manage their classrooms. However, there is less information about methods of handling students and chronic disruption. In general, classroom management implies good instruction, organized, planned, and varied activities, and cost-effectiveness.

A word of caution is in order: There are diverse philosophic attitudes and procedures for coping with disruptive student behavior.[3] Few are tested in ways that enable us to predict results confidently.

Researchers may find one result in an experimental setting and a contrary one in an observational study.[4] While many strategies apply to any classroom, some are specific to coping with cultural dissonances; understanding children's perceptions is crucial to the success of any strategy.

Meshing Academic and Social Learning

Although the teacher's mission is to teach the academic subjects of reading, writing, math, music, and art, and counselors specialize in social relations and adjustment, we know that children's academic progress intertwines with feelings about themselves and their peers. Thus consideration of children's thinking and feeling helps in classroom management, individual and group performance, and teacher–student encounters. Students' perceptions about the world affect how the teacher will reach the child to successfully communicate substantive material.

Some parents, teachers, and administrators underestimate the complexity and subtlety of the social knowledge a child needs to interact successfully among multicultural peers, asserting that "kids pick up" the common sense principles of social performance. Some children do so in the same way others learn to read without formal instruction, but judging by the number who do not have the requisite skills, the acquisition cannot be taken for granted. Furthermore, self-starters in reading and social engineering may need work on the subtleties of language arts and social relations, and there are reasons for dictionaries, style manuals, and etiquette books written for adults. Many of the rules middle-class whites and blacks take for granted are tacit; therefore, learning may be imprecise, inconsistent, and indeterminate when rules are not made explicit. Similarly, low-income cultural rules may be implicit. Middle-class children who are picked on may, for example, need instruction in such *survival skills* as patron–client relationships in order to get along. (Observe the current popularity of adult self-defense courses.) Since some children handle problems physically, it is important to establish rules and handle quarrels in a calm setting and *interweave lessons of compromise, tolerance, and self-control with relevant material on human relations in past and current history.*

Almost every lesson has the potential for introducing value concepts and exploring how people get along with each other. Because learning occurs when it is related to a *child's own experience*, it is sound teaching to link children's everyday experience to the issues of the American Revolution, the use of complete sentences, or simple arithmetic. The children at HPES and elsewhere whose role models are pimps and drug peddlars can benefit from knowing about the death rate among criminals and the horrors of prison life.

Discovering Multicultural Styles

It helps children adjust at the *beginning of school* if the teacher introduces them to each other as individuals, focuses on multicultural similarities and differences—including those personally sensitive and politically volatile. If a school has introduced busing for desegregation, the subject should be discussed. *Orientation* to the school's culture is, of course, appropriate. As a white HPES boy pointed out, "No one tells you the rules of the school" (79).

"If you could change one thing at Pacesetter, what would it be?" I asked. A boy's response indicated that some blacks acted as if volunteer white busing to the formerly all-black school was an unwanted invasion.

> They think that since we came over from our school, some of the black people there, they think that they should be rude to everybody. What I like is some of the black people and a lot of them are nice friends, and some of them like me, but there's just a few who don't like me (79 wb 6th).

Children entering the school in the *middle of the year* need orientation and so do their parents. Teachers or counselors can privately orient newcomers, or school personnel can take advantage of a new arrival and use the occasion for an introduction as well as a review with all the students who may forget the appropriate values and behavior, problems that exist, and ways of handling conflict. Adjustment to the social dynamics at HPES takes up to a year, as some children astutely commented. A white boy whose best friend is black said, "He acts pretty good. He doesn't say anything, but last year he did. Like he sits down and doesn't say, "Hey boy!" and stuff like that" (105 wb 2d). Another student, a black girl, observed:

> Some are just actin' like it [tough] 'cause they're scared. When they had the integration, I was the meanest black kid that ever went to school. I don't know why. I just got a first bad impression, and I did it, and that's why nobody liked me until the beginning of last year. Everybody thinks that a black person is . . . fighter.

I asked, "So, from what you know now, what would you have done when they began desegregation?"

154

I'd have showed them around the school, and I'd been nice to 'em and everything. Well, first of all, I think that you should team 'em up. Well, if you know somebody who loves soccer and likes baseball but hates math, then you should, you know, sort of latch him up with another person of a different race (67 6th).

It is not only children in a desegregated school who need introductions to, and explanations of, multicultural similarities and differences, children throughout the *school district* also need appropriate orientations. One white boy proposed the following:

Yeah. Like sometimes gettin' the kids together and talking to them. You know, our teacher does that, and I think that's pretty good. And also one day, I don't know if this could be done, about three schools, you know, one school all whites, not all white but mostly white people, if they could come, we could talk to 'em about these things. And maybe it would put some sense into their head about, you know, that all black people aren't bad, and then they would think that they are good or something. But you know, they say they're no good, and all this stuff. Then they watch all these shows like with Bill Cosby and stuff like that, and they think they're really real funny and real good, and somebody told 'em, "How come you watch this show?" And all that they just go—"Oh, I just watch it, it's a good show" (79 6th).

About his neighborhood he said:

If I went back to my old school, they'd make fun of me. They'd say things like, "you're half nigger" and all that. And some of my friends, one of my friends does, you know. I try and keep him from callin' 'em that. And you know, I tell 'em that some of 'em are real good people, and they don't believe me (79 wb 6th).

Children need *reviews of social relations* just as they need reviews of language and math facts, so that as an incident arises, the teacher can lead the students back to the issues first discussed in the getting-to-know-you session.

The *nature of prejudice and racism* should also be taught.[5] By glossing over racial problems, the school, parents, teachers, and children are unprepared to cope with troubles that eventually break out. Letting boys and girls comment on what difference variations make can be painful, but comparison occurs even if it is not verbalized. Conclusions drawn are often unlike those the teacher might help children reach. Like sexual information, lore about outsiders picked up on the street is often distorted, and misconceptions often create unnecessary anxieties and fears. Children need to learn that some cultural dissonances result from dif-

155

ferent historical backgrounds and social, political, and economic factors shape values and behavior. Perceptual differences often cause misunderstandings that lead to flair-ups or counterproductive adult behavior. Intervention to remedy the crisis may be costly in time and emotion; however, such outbursts may have long-lasting repercussions.

Educators can catch those "teachable moments" or create them; for instance, if a child touches a hot stove and is burned, the supervising adult should take the time to explain that some things are not to be touched. *Role-playing* can create teachable moments and help youngsters understand that behavior is caused and consequential, develop sensitivity to the feelings and attitudes of others, and clarify their own values by contrasting them with those held by others. In dramatic play, role-players try out a situation or stage a confrontation that the teacher outlines. A scene may be replayed several times, each time with new actors. Discussing among students the reality of the situation and responses will provide insights into what people do, why, and with what consequences. Youngsters can thus help each other and the teacher "see." Because youngsters find their peers' unfamiliar behavior exciting, they pay attention.[6]

Much of what is perceived as aggression, invasion of personal space, especially in restrooms, is merely curiosity about someone who looks different. I have described several incidents at HPES involving same-sex encounters. A *science lesson* should address the issue of skin pigmentation, of *observed and covered body parts,* and what all humans have in common anatomically and physiologically.

Children need to learn to *interpret body language* and distinguish between play and nonplay. Although happiness is judged by facial expression, anger by content-free vocalization, chest and abdominal musculature, and hand gestures, there may be cultural variation. Children, even more than adults, manifest a variety of bodily ways of initiating friendship, showing anger, and reflecting dislike.[7]

The fact that college students consistently decode nonverbal messages with greater than chance accuracy suggests the salience of body language. However, expressions are also frequently misinterpreted.[8] Therefore, if nonverbal modes cause difficulty within cultures, a possibility for even more misunderstanding between cultures exists. Even smiles differ by region.[9] As with verbal language, nonverbal translation is a recognized remedy for potential intercultural misunderstanding.

When children *share likes and dislikes* in classroom discussions, those who are different in some aspects can identify youngsters with whom they share interests. Having children state, "What bugs me about ———

(boys, girls, blacks, whites, and so forth)" can help students identify cultural dissonances that everyone can then work toward ameliorating.

One of the HPES counselors focused on *action and reaction* in a weekly classroom session. In this exercise, a child acts in any manner toward another child who then reacts. The children's explanations of what happened introduce them to different ways of interpreting behavior and therefore possibilities for misunderstanding, as well as to synonyms, homonyms, antonyms, and guides to effective social relations. Other getting-to-know-you techniques include playlets, having children draw pictures and then explain them, and writing poems and essays.

Individualizing Activities

Although engaged in a firing-line operation with little spare time, a teacher should, nevertheless, *review a child's previous year's record* with great caution for two reasons. First, children grow and change. Second, overreactive teachers' rigidly held expectations affect children's performances in a self-fulfilling prophecy. Yet past achievement scores, performance records, and reports of difficulties sensitized allegedly effective HPES teachers to the nature of potential skirmishes and how to deal with them early in the semester in order to guide the child in the most constructive way.

If a child did well in the past, it is important to expect similar kinds of performance. Children with high IQs and achievement test scores who are nonperformers will produce with a minimum of effort if that is what satisfies a teacher.[10] If children did not do well in the past, teachers should explore alternative reasons for continued poor performance. Teachers must always be *alert to signs of major breakthroughs* in order to keep a child challenged and motivated. Some HPES teachers found that slow learners are more successful with structured written work than classroom discussion: The student's mistakes are then not publicly visible.[11]

At HPES, there were some children with *medical and mental health problems* that required special techniques and approaches. If emotionally disturbed or hyperkinetic youngsters on medication miss taking the appropriate dosage at the correct time, their misbehavior requires the administration of medicine, not lessons in individual responsibility nor punishment. As a sixth-grade black boy said, "The wild ones have to be treated more carefully; you never know what they are going to do" (16).

It is important that such labels as emotionally disturbed, minimal brain damage, and hyperkinetic do not screen out what is actually occurring and become a substitute for effort on the parts of both teacher and student.

Soliciting *parental guidance* for insights may help a teacher. Explaining to other children that certain individuals have problems related to illness and need their assistance can make classroom activities flow more smoothly. Children can knowingly avoid behavior that easily triggers some bullies.

The HPES program of individualized instruction, with its emphasis on each child's own growth in an ability group, helped cope with low academic self-esteem and aspirations as well as school's high expectations. Children's hostility and aggression toward each other are often related to failure and frustration in learning.[12]

In trying to ascertain why a child is not succeeding academically, the school has to take into account the *search for dignity and the teacher's role in awarding it* for successful academic pursuits. This award may irritate children who have a counterschool reward system that devalues work and personnel by disrupting classroom tasks and pressures peers to do likewise. The HPES had its share of such disruptions. Schools, like other American work institutions, tend to single out a few individuals as the best, while treating the others as an undifferentiated mass.[13] For example, some teachers are inclined to give greater attention to students who appear more intelligent because they seem more valuable and worth the time.[14] The hierarchy of social legitimacy in American society originates in calculations of a person's socially productive work. Youngsters whom teachers actively approve rather than merely tolerate confirm to the teachers their power to affect others and the legitimacy and dignity of the teaching profession. At HPES, hostility toward academically-motivated youngsters surfaced among low-income children in the second grade, perhaps earlier. They referred to the "goody goodies" with hostile images of weakness—punk, motha-fucker, fag, dick-kisser.

Many low-income youngsters lose any expectation that school will help them. This was certainly true for whites in one Boston school:

> By the time the children are ten or eleven, the split between the many and the few who are expected to "make something of themselves" is out in the open; the aloofness developing in the second grade has become open hostility by the sixth. Among the boys, this hostility is expressed by images which fuse sex and status. Boys like Fred and Vincent are described by the "ordinary" students as effeminate and weak, as "suck-ups." The kids mean by this both that the Freds and Vincents are getting somewhere in school because they are so docile, and that only a homosexual would be so weak; the

image of a "suck-up" crystallizes this self-demeaning, effeminate behavior that to them marks off a student whom the institution can respect.[15]

Similarly among working-class whites in Sheffield[16] and Birmingham, England, the school serves as a stimulus for an anticulture of "boys" as opposed to "ear 'oles" or what are called creeps, arse creepers, teachers' pets. These latter are considered despicable for conforming to school norms, lacking assertiveness and autonomy, and "most of all for their inability to create 'fun' for themselves, to 'have a laff.' "[17]

Earlier, I noted that children who are not academically competitive, whether because of native intelligence, individual choice, inadequate training, or peer pressure often communicate through their behavior that academic performance is not meaningful to them and therefore their self-worth cannot be measured by it. The saving-face activities of these youngsters is "an attempt to create amongst themselves badges of dignity that those in authority can't destroy."[18] In unity there is strength; consequently, a child pursuing academic success and gaining the teacher's approval is viewed by friends as betraying the group, seeking self-development, and leaving the group behind. Low-income children in a white ethnic school felt betrayed because those who were getting approval directed their power and that approval "not towards aiding them, but towards escaping the situation and progressing by them-selves."[19] The situation at HPES is similar to that found in white work-ing-class school settings: A child demonstrating ability, thereby putting others in the background, is penalized by losing peer affection.

Some children who know they have ability and want to pursue the lure of personal academic advancement are caught in the crossfire of conflicting demands—peer conformity, collective coping skills, and the need to belong versus school goals of individual academic achievement. When the teacher tells a child to work on an assignment quietly and alone, but at the same time a peer asks the child to collaborate, the child faces conflict.[20] Consequently, for the sake of those who would like to partake of the formal school culture, the administration might transfer the few children who initiate disruptions to a different classroom away from a provocative setting.

The teacher's task of communicating to each child that he or she is *respected as an individual while at the same time reinforcing academic achieve-ment* is a difficult one. The importance of that task has been substantiated in the finding[21] that impersonality is associated with school violence and vandalism: Anonymity spells trouble. In assessing an individual's poten-tial, the teacher may want to provide *some private study activities for a student apart from the purview of the child's peers*. It is not sufficient for a teacher to believe a child can succeed and expect the child to do so. The child must have evidence of success that is recognized by universal criteria or self-doubt reigns. Black students elsewhere continued to believe in the popular culture's Tarzanlike images of their heritage in spite of an African study unit designed to dispell stereotypic nonsense; the need for continual positive recognition from the school culture is apparent.[22]

Modifying Teacher Style

Interrelated features of teacher style contributed to successful classroom management—preventing misbehavior.[23] *"Withitness and overlapping"* refer to a teacher communicating knowledge of children's actions to them and attending to two issues at the same time when both are present; this is similar to having eyes behind one's head and obviously requires a high level of energy and a juggling-act ability. The black HPES principal jokingly told teachers, "Don't smile until Christmas!" Teachers must be especially alert while students test them to see what they can get away with.

Preventing misbehavior involves never leaving a class unsupervised; to do otherwise would invite aggression. Adjustment to school during the first fifteen minutes of class may be critical in setting the atmosphere for the entire day. A child may have left a conflict at home or had fights on the way to school. Children often become carried away when they gather together during a class break or recess or before an anticipated assembly. A teacher's quiet touch on an excited child's shoulder accompanied by a friendly "take it easy" is usually more effective than shouting in helping students control themselves.[24]

Some teacher responses to disruptions by slow learners enable the instructor to avoid teaching children who are difficult to reach and permit students to play peer group politics.[25] Teachers must be aware of mutually gratifying diversionary tactics to avoid some learning–teaching tasks.

"Smoothness and momentum," how teachers manage movement during class activity and between transitions, are useful in controlling pupil deviance.[26] Smoothness refers to the absence of "dangles," which occur when a teacher begins an activity, leaves it in midair by turning to another activity, and then finally returns to the original activity. For example, if a teacher tells students to put away their spelling papers, take out their math books, and then asks youngsters about work in spelling. What appears logical to a teacher may not be so to the child, especially

one who works with many teachers and must learn a variety of expectations and cues.

In addition to having a smooth flow in the classroom and moving toward or touching a child who begins to misbehave, reducing the number of rules may limit deviance. It helps both student and teacher if the school has a consistent written policy, and if *children and parents contribute to making the rules,* for they will then have a stake in their enforcement.[27] At HPES, each class or grade had its own penalties for misbehavior. Generally accepting the class rules, children mentioned them in response to the question, "If a child misbehaves, what do *you* think the teacher should do?" Second-graders, knowing the penalities their teachers imposed, for example, said that a child who had misbehaved should sit in the corner or put his or her head down.

A third teaching style that contributes to successful classroom management is *"group alerting and accountability."*[28] Group alerting involves teachers' attempts to include nonreciting children in a recitation and then keep their attention. A person who conveyed warmth through posture, smiling, and eye contact, and responding to responses with "mm-hmm" was found to increase the amount of talking another person did.[29] Teachers pause and look around, pick children randomly, or intersperse group responses with individual ones to create suspense so that a child does not know who will be called on next. When a youngster does not answer fully, another may then be called on.

Accountability refers to the degree to which the teacher expects children to be responsible for their performances during recitation sessions. The HPES teachers used such accountability techniques as asking children to show their answers, recite in unison, or raise their hands if prepared to perform.

"Variety and challenge" within the subject matter is the fourth feature that contributes to effective classroom functioning. As children grow, they master one thing, then feeling comfortable, seek the next thrill— which may mean breaking rules. Incorporating thrill-seeking in learning academic subjects fulfills several needs simultaneously. Children draw on a variety of resources in play, such as exceeding limits, violating conventions, upsetting expectations, taking apart things that go together, or using an object incongruously. Furthermore, "risking the consequences of transgressing the boundaries of the permissible or the possible appears to be the source of pleasure."[30] A stimulating environment that arouses children is more likely to be conducive to successful school performance.

Games and contests in academic work when—as in play—there are no penalties for losing, may satisfy children's exploratory needs. Moreover,

HPES students often mentioned "She lets us play games" in describing what they like best about their favorite teacher. Providing situations in which grades are not averaged in the total report card score encourages constructive risk taking, creative work, and moving beyond what a child finds to be secure. As in play, particularly in chase games and play aggression, there should be safe, time-out havens where children can recoup by resting or physically releasing tension that builds up.

"For the healthy, a monotonous environment eventually produces discomfort, irritation, and attempts to vary it."[31] Since children easily become restless, teachers can vary activities by using sensory or motor skills, such as writing, reading aloud, working individually, alternating tasks by skill requirements (comprehension, selective recognition, memory, and creativity), and providing interludes of gross motor activities or quiet away from the classroom. Although teachers need prepared lessons, improvised strategies must sometimes supplant the best made plans.

Since boys are more disruptive than girls and enjoy manipulating objects, teachers should attempt to masculinize some classroom activity. This would engage the boys' attention and provide girls with opportunities they might not otherwise have.[32]

Making *academic material relevant to children's immediate concerns as well as future career opportunities* is important. When low-income blacks have high interest, they do as well as whites.[33] The HPES fourth grade had an economics unit in which children engaged in occupational role-playing with the respective incomes and budgets for adult life expenditures. In the process, the students discovered what it cost for a range of housing options and what an individual could afford on the basis of particular employment opportunities. By comparing occupational benefits and past and present opportunities for minorities, children can evaluate the possible payoff of current academic efforts. Low-income blacks' confidence in such a payoff, however, depends on seeing successful adults who came from backgrounds similar to their own.

Balancing Assimilation with Cultural Pluralism and Ability Grouping

In the United States, assimilation refers to the gradual absorption of minorities into the dominant group culture. Assimilationist practices include separating immigrant, nonstandard English speakers from their native tongues and customs. Assimilation alters basic values and eventually transforms personal identities, which not all ethnic group members from central and southern Europe in the past have desired. Yet many of the Jews, Germans, Poles, Italians, and Irish who escaped foreign and domestic oppression and abject conditions of poverty viewed the assimilationist public schools as the gate to opportunity, which they were.[34] Such immigrants held the public schools in awe, demanded respect for the teachers, and were willing to pay the price of having their children lose cultural and religious traditions.

Cultural pluralism, on the other hand, is relativistic and celebrates bilingualism and ethnic identity. However, proponents of this orientation often do not consider that the unmodified public existence of an autonomous minority culture may be a barrier to opportunities controlled by the majority. This is especially so if such manifestations as meddlin' violate notions of appropriateness in dominant American culture.[35] Thus, in what is called structural pluralism, some of the assumed equally valid ways of living can be responsible for isolating various groups from the mainstream economic and political structures of society.

The issue of assimilation versus cultural pluralism within the schools centers on communication styles, human relations, incentive motivation, and teaching and curriculum. Cultural pluralists sometimes see the school as a place where minority culture clashes with Anglo culture, confounding some of the traits required for living in a Western industrial technological, capitalist system with what is adequate for rural, preindustrial, or low-level technological development. Certain economic systems require specific values and skills wherever they operate and whatever the color of the participants.[36]

Consequently, it may be wisest *to provide all individuals with the opportunity for choice* by teaching the skills that allow a person access to socioeconomic mobility with the possibility of code switching (being able to operate in one or another culture at will). Therefore, desegregation should include, in addition to attempts to equalize the quality of the physical plant and teaching and foster respect for achievements by different groups, *access to mainstream communicative modes, codes, and processes*—explicit knowledge of what the middle class knows implicitly.

Children who cannot exhibit the socially competent behavior expected of dominant American culture may be labeled behavior problems, hyperactive, or slow. Individuals as a group create and sustain the context of interaction by communicating in various ways. There is a need for junctions between contexts to be marked so that participants in a given situation know when the context has changed, and further, that criteria for appropriate behavior have changed.[37]

Civil rights advocates in multicultural education often claim that tracking, streaming, or *ability grouping* within a school is a deliberate subterfuge for segregation in desegregation, a maneuver to maintain the status quo. The sorting processes are blamed for negative influences on intergroup relations and dooming low achievers to failure. However, research findings on ability grouping are equivocal because instructional and organizational methods have been confounded. For example, quality of instruction may lead to academic achievement irrespective of the ethnic composition of student groups.[38] In those studies that found lower academic self-evaluation among individuals in low- and average-ability groups than in heterogeneous groups, it is not clear whether students were questioned before or after they had taken examinations based on classroom work.

Certainly, any system has room for improvement. It is not tracking per se but being locked into a track or providing inadequate instruction, problem-solving skills, and curriculum in the low track that are detrimental. At HPES, teachers continually regrouped children in response to their growth and achievement. Children readily know who is academically superior whether they are in the same or different classroom space.[39] A stigma can be attached to poor achievement in a homogeneous or heterogeneous group. In fact, heterogeneity within an academic class has led to low-achieving blacks becoming discouraged with their comparative lack of success and misbehaving, while middle-class blacks and whites resent them and are bored with the classroom's slower pace and drawn-out explanations.[40]

Black youngsters with high academic ability who are in high-ability groups have the opportunity to work free from counterschool pressures and to have contacts based on shared interest. In such environments, black and white students report more interracial contact. When peers of opposite races perform at comparable achievement levels, a potential source of strain is absent.

Those people who espouse heterogeneous grouping overlook the *rights of individuals to human dignity*. Illustrative is the case of the HPES sixth-grade black male nonreader whose three more advanced nonreader peers ridiculed him. Only when the perceptive special education teacher worked privately with the boy, did he learn to read. He even asked to have more individualized reading instruction as his reward. Some argue that isolating black students in special education courses stigmatizes them but so, too, does the spoken or unspoken charge of dummy. Students enrolled in a special ABC program started in 1963 by a group of independent school head masters seeking bright, ambitious minority group youth cited "the fears of 'looking bad' in front of classmates" as an impediment to learning.[41] Therefore, separation from peer pressure may be essential for a child's equal opportunity. This must be coupled with continual evaluation of a child's progress and procedures to move a child to appropriate groups.

Of course, schools can emphasize the *contribution of all groups to American culture;* however, focusing on exotic characteristics of ethnic groups alone is likely to reenforce stereotypes and misconceptions.[42] Some black middle-class people have come to view certain aspects of black culture—such as chitlins, gospel music, and feeling the spirit—as inferior. In a Philadelphia school, officials banned children's spontaneous playground dancing that was similar to what I saw at HPES. "The dances were labeled as lewd, fresh, inappropriate for school, disrespectful, and too sexual." The principal announced over the school loudspeaker: "Nice girls don't do that."[43] There was little recognition of dance as cognitive communication drawing on the same mental processes required in academic achievement.[44]

While ethnic solidarity was a valuable asset for groups entering American society at the poverty level, as most immigrants did, after attaining social mobility perceived ethnic cohesiveness can be a handicap to entering the mainstream, an acknowledgment of lower-class antecedents, a denial of the American experience, and a divisive mechanism. What is necessary is "respecting cultural and language differences, . . . sensitivity to practices which are demeaning and denigrating, and concentrating attention . . . on the ways in which acculturation can occur without major personal dislocation."[45]

American culture can also become more open and encompass other cultures so that acculturation, the continuous contact of members of different cultures, with mutual borrowing, occurs. Middle-class youngsters can learn to become more physically and emotionally expressive, become rhythmic, accept the body without shame, and be assertive and capable of surviving adversity. Whites have already borrowed many things from black culture—music, dance, humor, and vernacular expressions. Many of America's unique jazz, folk, and social dance and music forms draw on black influences. White fiddlers in the eighteenth and nineteenth centuries took the 3-3-2 syncopation from black rhythm.

Encouraging blacks and whites to know the history and achievement of black people can occur without creating the impression that blacks can achieve in only certain areas that have been open to them in the past. Such black publications as *Ebony, Crisis, Jet, Black World Digest,* and *The Black Panther* illustrate the range of activities in which blacks participate.

Teaching the dominant culture's language and communicative styles can be done without denigrating a child's own cultural and communicative styles and thereby damaging the child's self-concept. New cultural patterns should be acquired with respect for existing ones that are not contradictory. Just as we recognize the need for Sunday dress or work clothes at times, there is also a need for specific behavior in certain settings and at certain times. White teachers are sometimes "afraid to apply the same standards to black students" and therefore do not teach them so well.[46] For teaching and learning to occur, discipline is essential, and some subcultural differences must be rejected.

The school's competence goals may differ from the competence goals for which children have been socialized. Teachers can *build on what children already know in order to help them acquire what they need to know.* This often requires modifying curriculum, text selection, and teaching strategy to meet the needs of different children who may be in the same classroom.

Since the call and response pattern is integral to black verbal and nonverbal communications, it may be that low-income black students who listen passively are not learning. Teachers should desire some "noisy" behavior from black youngsters; it means "they diggin' on what you saying."[47] In English instruction, teachers could build on the feature of tonal semantics in black English by using rhymes and rhyming patterns. Teachers' understanding of the dialect may help them distinguish between learning problems and simply rendering a sentence in black English, for example, deleting the *r*, deleting *s* in the third person, and substituting *d* for the initial *th*.

Structuring Cooperation: Jigsaw Puzzle and Tournament Learning

Integration, psychologists have found, is achieved by mixing black and white students under conditions that lead to positive social relations. The conditions necessary for a major program of school integration include equal access to sources of social status as well as physical facilities and materials, equal status contact, cooperation on shared goals, and support for positive relations.[48] Children's values and behavior, including communicative styles, also must be taken into account. As the story of HPES suggests, children learn what they live.

The equal status contact theory overlooks children's awareness that their peers may have different abilities, evaluations of these, and criteria for social status. Even youngsters who begin their childhood in low-income settings and then move into middle-class neighborhoods may carry with them the values and behavior patterns of their former community. Desegregation is a necessary but not sufficient condition for integration. Interracial contact can lead to either greater prejudice and rejection or increased respect and acceptance, depending on the circumstances in which it occurs.

Studies of military and housing desegration have shown that interracial attitudes toward blacks and whites living and working together become more positive after people have actually engaged in small-group activities. In response to the question of how he made friends, a HPES black student in the sixth grade expressed a sentiment held by many of the children: "Well, we have in our class, when we have groups to work together, and then when the teacher puts you in groups, that's how then you make friends; that's how" (115).

At HPES and elsewhere, some black and white children with neutral or positive attitudes toward blacks developed negative attitudes after experiencing low-income-style interactions in which they were hurt or frightened. Therefore, structuring cooperative work and play is important for overcoming negative views. Cooperative patterns also build on a black mode of learning in cooperative contexts where the leadership role falls to the person who is best suited for it. (See chapter 3.)

Conscious or unconscious expectation of white superiority held by whites and blacks helps account for white domination in biracial cooperative academic activity.[49] Although contact theory in psychology posits that positive relations will evolve if a cooperative equal environment is created, expectation theory suggests that even in such an environment biased expectations on the part of both whites and blacks may lead to continued white dominance unless active steps are taken to reverse the perhaps unconscious expectations. In this regard, tracking makes it easier to produce equal status relationships.[50] The smaller the ability and social class differences, the less race serves as a basis for dominance and more equal is the actual performance.

Interdependence, not just being part of a small group, increases interracial friendship.[51] A productive technique that involves a small group of students who depend on each other's strength for learning required material uses the principle of the jigsaw puzzle: Each child has a piece of information, and it takes all group members to put the puzzle together. No one can do well without the aid of everyone else in the group. Through this technique, children learn to teach and listen to one other and how to draw out a child and to ask the questions that make it easier for a child to explain his or her ideas.

Competition is prevalent in dominant and minority group cultures, therefore suppressing competitive performance in the classroom would be tantamount to keeping the lid on a pressure cooker. But the *competi-*

tive spirit can be organized to downplay cultural and social class differences. At HPES, mixed groups worked on social studies projects, assembly presentations, and economic production and distribution (organizing a popcorn sale, advertising, shopping for ingredients, making the popcorn, packaging it, and selling it) in cooperative teams.

There are several other approaches that foster small-group cooperation and also frequently have positive effects on academic achievement.[52] In the teams–games–tournaments approach, students, divided into groups, compete academically for prizes awarded according to a system in which performance standards are based on each individual's previous level of academic success. Thus each youngster is stimulated to work at his or her own pace.

Seating patterns can foster cooperative work and create the potential for friendship. Teachers may inadvertently promote separatism in an attempt to comply with children's desire to choose their own seats next to friends. Black HPES children, for the most part, had friendships based on long-term neighborhood interactions. Children who belonged to a neighborhood group were judged conceited or deviant if they chose to sit with others. Therefore, the opportunity for making interracial friendships depends on teachers structuring situations that foster them. More than one child said, "We became friends because we were partners." Of course, a child who disrupts another's work must be seated away from other youngsters.

Interracial friendship involves more than social contact at any age. Previously established friendships on the bases of similar interests and neighborhood networks often preclude the willingness to make new friends voluntarily. Just as I observed at HPES, so also in five desegregated schools studied by Murray L. Wax, "the stigma attached to those few who venture out and seek friendships among members of other groups is often so strong that many are discouraged at the outset."[53] Without social intervention that occasionally brings children with similar interests together and uses small structured cooperative team tasks where each person has equal status, segregation in desegregation is likely to persist.

Refereeing Potential Conflict Activities

In unsupervised play, children respond to social dynamics and learn to express themselves, govern each other, escape from adult social restraints, experiment with feelings, pursue self-interest, and act independently. As children argue about rules, add new ones, agree to exceptions, and censure those who violate rules, they explore the need for regulations, publicize them, and suggest how they can be made effective. While children play with rules, they discover what they can get away with, and the consequences of lawlessness become apparent when disagreements and fights dissolve a game.

Yet in a multicultural setting in which members of both cultures want to play a game that usually has set rules, fights may occur because of disagreements or interpretations of them to the extent that the game becomes one of "black versus white." It is useful, therefore, to *structure cooperation on the playground and have an adult referee,* who can help form teams on the basis of alphabetical order rather than black and white and call the plays in games children voluntarily choose. The adult can, to some extent, control the outcome of a game so that extreme imbalances do not occur. In addition, the authority figure can ameliorate a player's frustration by controlling the game at crucial times and including children who would otherwise be overlooked by their peers. Games that involve eliminating players may be harsh and hazardous for disturbed youngsters. Because negative peer interaction feeds on itself, with one hostile communication leading to another, the best method is to divert aggression in its incipient stages. Proper social behavior can be reinforced and praised—even videotaped. Children love to see themselves, as I was reminded each time I videotaped HPES classrooms and playgrounds. After viewing interactions, rules can be discussed, reviewed, and clarified.

Recognizing Ripple Effects of Discipline

How should a teacher handle a child who misbehaves? Since a teacher works with a group, taking account of the effect on other children of a teacher's action to stop misbehavior is important. When a teacher follows a regimen of *praising appropriate behavior and ignoring inappropriate behavior* that does not prevent teaching and learning, problems tend to diminish. A distinction should be made between manners and serious disruption.

By allowing some forbidden activities in class in return for concentration, the developmental teachers got their students to work seriously for a larger proportion of their time in class than did teachers who officially required them to work all the time but were pushed by constant disruptions into using up their resources for control on matters other than directly academic effort.[54]

169

The basis on which children receive rewards has effects on their cooperation with one another. Recognition for good social relations usually encourages more of the same. On the other hand, teachers should spot potentially disruptive behavior early and not allow youngsters to get away with misbehavior that impedes the academic process.[55]

As at HPES, some teachers in Boston white working-class schools believed that many of their charges, due to family background and past school performance, would resist following rules that educated adults view as logical and beneficial. These teachers "unwittingly set in motion in the classroom a vicious circle that produces exactly the kind of behavior they expect"[56] by insisting on rigid order and discipline—an example of self-fulfilling prophecy at work.[56]

When youngsters misbehave, teachers should *focus on the act rather than the person*. If a child is labeled deviant and so treated, the child may respond repetitively in accord with the expectation—another example of self-fulfilling prophecy.

Punishing an entire class for the misbehavior of a few obvious deviants was considered *unfair* by HPES black and white children as well as their parents (PIP survey). A sixth-grader remarked: "Well, a lot of times, when a child misbehaves, a lot of teachers, they take it out on the whole class. And I think the teacher should just punish him by sending him to the office or out of the room or something like that" (112 bg).

Twice at fourth-grade recess, I observed a teacher's assistant keep four classes standing in inclement weather (once in a brutally hot Texas sun and the other time in a drizzle) until all members of the classes were properly lined up. On one occasion, six black boys sat on a sheltered stoop enjoying the rain's frizzing effect on the adult woman's blond hair as well as their power over peers. Such events lead to antiblack sentiment. "I get blamed for what they do and I don't like it!" I heard from black and white children. Punishing an entire class for the misbehavior of a few is based on the assumption that peer pressure will bring the recalcitrants back to the fold. It usually works in homogeneous middle-class settings. However, in mixed classrooms where the low-income children's rule is that a child must be prepared to fight whomever he or she tells what to do, it is difficult for peer pressure to alter recalcitrant behavior.

Because children seek peer approval, a child needs an *opportunity to save face* when losing a challenge to the teacher. Therefore, it is best to speak with the child privately about misbehavior and any subsequent praiseworthy improvement. A teacher's well-intentioned overinvolvement with a child singles out that individual and can alienate the youngster from others. Effective teacher–student interaction requires establishing trust and keeping confidences. Of course, in cases of extremely disruptive behavior, placing a child who is performing for peers in an area devoid of social or other reinforcement and stimulation is necessary.

Involving students in the teacher's behavior interventions helps preclude counteractions by students.[57] Since peer groups have leaders, coopting these individuals in positive classroom actions is advantageous. This is discussed further in the section on providing channels for aggression.

A school that expects blacks to be more physical and condones their behavior at the same time that it restricts the same actions performed by whites is promoting black-white distinctions and behavior counter to successful school and later work performance. Such a school tends to convey the attitude that it is afraid of blacks. A teacher who allows a child to harm another with impunity may reinforce aggression. Other youngsters learn how to be aggressive and what the possible outcomes can be. Thus the school action may generalize and legitimize aggressive street behavior.

Authorities—firm, impartial, and compassionate—who consistently and *evenhandedly mete out punishment in accord with policies that are clearly communicated* to staff, pupils, parents, and community are likely to preclude contention.[58] Some white students in an urban high school attributed an interracial fight to the school's unfair way of enforcing its rules. Blacks were "let off easy," and white resentment toward blacks smoldered and then flared up. A white student put it this way: "This school lets them blacks do whatever they feel like. The teachers and administrators let the blacks cut up in classes and run this place. If we don't behave, they throw us out or call our parents. The blacks get away with murder."[59]

Another factor in providing a peaceful environment is the visibility and availability to students and staff of the principals as a resource in disciplinary matters. Teachers have disciplined classrooms when they regiment their classes and swiftly punish offenses from the outset to create a myth of coercive control. Establishing a routine and using structured written work were techniques used to quiet a class of students. At HPES, guardians of disruptive children were sometimes contacted.

Providing Counseling

Because a teacher works with a relatively large group of youngsters, there is limited time to counsel a student who has difficulties in social and academic performances stemming from low-income conditions and values or other causes. With the required parental permission, black and white counselors at HPES tested and worked with children individually and in small groups. They had parent conferences, intervened in crises, and recommended outside assistance as necessary. The discipline room teacher also counseled students. In addition, counselors met with each regular class once a week for lessons on affective learning.

Counselors, in collaborative arrangements with other classroom teachers, worked out contracts (written agreements) with students to help them develop self-monitoring and self-control techniques. Because certain behavior cannot be controlled by the school authorities, the school seeks to kindle students' motivation so that they find working on and completing school tasks to be inherently satisfying or regard these tasks as part of acquiring valued skills.

Counselors can *build on teachers' social relations lessons, focus on unique problems* that come to their attention, and expand children's affective and social relations learning. Bullies often meet the criteria for emotionally disturbed children and need counseling. The Joint Commission on the Mental Health of Children and Youth's criteria are "(a) impairment of age-relevant capacity to realistically perceive the external environment, (b) inadequate impulse control, (c) a lack of rewarding interpersonal relationships, and (d) failure to achieve appropriate learning levels."[61]

Coping with Aggression

Children and teachers have to learn to behave in such a way that their environment is not dominated by the fear, chaos, destruction, and violence that have been documented in many schools.

Senator Birch Bayh introduced the Juvenile Delinquency in the Schools Act of April 9, 1975:

> Our preliminary study [this did not include HPES, but it does indicate that problems at HPES are actually greater elsewhere] . . . has produced compelling evidence that . . . [the] level of violence and vandalism is reaching crisis proportions which seriously threaten the ability of our educational system to carry out its primary function. Although the level of violence directed against teachers . . . is indeed alarming, the principal victims of the rising tide of crime in our schools are . . . the students.[62]

All youngsters are entitled to access to school facilities, including restrooms, stairs, and halls.[63]

Coping with aggression at the elementary level is critical to ameliorating violence in higher grades, which has become overwhelming nationwide. The Texas Federation of Teachers requested that the 1979 legislature provide funds for security personnel to combat violence in public schools: Teachers have been mugged, raped, and attacked by students. Although these things were happening all over the state, they were being covered up.[64] Similarly in schools elsewhere in the United States, adults often try to maintain students' ignorance of others' violent misdeeds so that they will not use them as examples.[65] When children are anxious and afraid, the stress affects their performance. Moreover, school violence uses up tax dollars.

The NIE Violence and Vandalism in the Schools report stated that about 10 percent of the student body was responsible for classroom disruption. Consequently, there is a strong argument for the need to recognize "that the limits to the right of students to remain in school for educational purposes are reached when their presence jeopardizes the education of classmates."[66]

Some basic long-term organizing principles of social life resist immediate adult influence. Two HPES children's comments suggest the problem:

> There used to be a whole bunch of fights around here, and everybody would fight. Even I would fight so the teacher would stop it. And Mr. Griffin [black principal] is saying to the teachers to let them [the youngsters] fight 'cause if they want to fight, they'll fight. They won't stop; teacher's can't teach them to stop fighting (64 wg 4th).

A sixth-grader explained:

> Nobody wants to stop it—you can't stop it. Some people like to watch fights, to go and tell other people, I guess. If it's a small kid, we'll stop it. If it's like a bully on a little kid, then they can stop it (85 wb).

Younger children have usually not developed a repertoire of defensive strategies and need adult protection.[67] If a child is taught to fight at home and in the neighborhood, then the school must insist that although fighting is one way of handling a problem, it is not the acceptable way at school or on a job. Of course, *reducing the causes of anger* is critical. There must be opportunities for children to succeed at tasks without ridicule, as well as much talk and dramatic mime about frustrations and how to deal with them.

Researchers/clinicians offer the following advice to white parents, which also applies to teachers.[68] When a black child bullies a white child, the adult should first determine if the child is provoking the attack in some way, such as exhibiting a rejecting or condescending attitude or demonstrating verbal or physical hostility. Parents should work out arrangements so that children are able to know one another as individuals rather than groups. Psychologists suggest parents instruct their children to tell blacks, "Look, if you'll be fair with me, I'll be fair with you."

How should name calling which triggers fights be handled? Psychiatrists suggest telling the child that the name-caller must have some problems. A black child attacked by a black can say, "Blacks who feel good about themselves do not call each other names."[69] Children should be told that if they fight every time they experience injustices, they may not have time for anything else.

Parents teach their children to fight in neighborhoods where not fighting would make the child a constant victim. Black parents can try to help children learn ways of working out their problems through talk and compromise rather than by physically abusing each other. "You can explain that an offer not to fight but a willingness to fight if you must can 'save face' and cut down on the number of black children who victimize each other."[70]

Omnipresent supervising adults interrupting misbehavior and *singling out ringleaders of rough play and leading them away* discourage aggression. Yet incidents occur in spite of the genuine efforts of the most sensitive and intelligent master teachers. If a fight breaks out, the antidote is for adults to *stop the fracas* and separate the children by shrieking at the combatants and moving other youngsters away from harm or keeping them from joining the melee.[71] At the same time, two dependable children should be sent for help, one to a strong adult (for example, a physical education instructor) and the other to a nearby teacher. Younger combatants can be physically separated by grasping their arms and speaking calmly. But this demands care, in the interests of both students and teachers. Some HPES teachers have masterfully separated fighters; others have been bloodied.

A school staff member should *determine the cause of a fight.* Ignoring the reasons may fuel further violence. Anecdotal records help identify underlying causes not at first apparent. At HPES, the principal would ask each participant to provide an account of who, what, where, why, and how. Then she discussed with each participant the other's perspective and how such situations could be handled in the future in light of their new understanding.

My discovery of my own naïveté about the children's world through open-ended questions leads me to the suggestion that teachers should

174

periodically *ask children what they like best* about the classroom or school and *what they would change* if they could change one thing. In this way, a teacher can identify both problems and solutions. Furthermore, a difficult child can be the subject of a *case study* wherein teachers who observe the youngster meet to discuss what patterns occur and their possible causes and cures.

Aggression is rewarding in itself if it (1) reduces tension produced by such emotional arousal factors as anger; (2) helps an individual obtain material resources; or (3) helps the individual obtain such immaterial needs as status in the group, control of adults, and self-esteem. If aggressors obtain rewards from their victims (such as crying, fleeing, toys, or candy) or gain status among peers, the likelihood of further aggression will increase. Negative consequences, such as the victim's counterattack or a teacher's censure, result in temporary suppression of aggressive acts.

> [For] punishment to be an effective inhibitor . . . aggression has to be constantly, consistently, and immediately punished . . . punishment may be somewhat effective because it can lead to anxiety (i.e., fear of future punishment), which will inhibit the undesirable response regardless of the controlling agent's presence.[72]

A tough kid put it this way:

> I'm not callin' myself Superman, you know, but I'm, well, the people know that I don't mess around. Well, they come to me 'cause I'm the strongest, you know, in this whole school. Really. All right. Okay, so I just lifted a hundred and five pounds, so's they come to me and say, "I lift more than you." And then they hit me, and they think they can whup me. And you know, so I just ignore it and just go on to my class, 'cause if I fight 'em, if I stay there like a dummy and fight 'em, then that lessens my chance of keepin' going to school. 'Cause I know the next time I go to the office, I'm going home (91 bb 6th).

Children need restraints. As Harrison-Ross and Wyden put it in their study of the black child:

> They need a structure in their lives. When everyone bows before them and acts scared of them, these kids become terrified. Because they know even if their parents don't just know how unsure and inexperienced they are. They're bluffing. And they're dying to have their bluff called.[73]

Children living with aggression outside school need nonaggressive models, counseling, and vigilance.

175

Should the school provide substitute *channels for aggression?* There is little evidence that substitute activities (for example, sports) or displaced aggression against harmless objects (for example, chopping wood) have cathartic effects (that is, consequences that decrease aggressive motivation).[74] Vicarious experience may well increase aggressive behavior. On the other hand, permitting stylized, disciplined, ethical, and rule-governed fighting and establishing rank, as in the Oriental martial arts, might not reinforce aggression so much as control and dampen its negative aspects and provide new values. One child (69 wb 6th) thought youngsters fought to determine who was tougher; therefore, he thought weight lifting or rope climbing could be another way of deciding who was the strongest.

Some HPES teachers constructively channeled the energy, need for recognition, and potential leadership of aggressive youngsters by making them guards or "teachers" (teaching assistants) and allowing them to contribute to disciplinary policy making and gain a stake in the school system. The children enjoyed responsibility for helping their younger peers learn and act according to school norms. Teachers need to make sure that the youngster's charges are protected: *Teaching tough children responsibility* could be like asking the fox to guard the chicken coop. In a twenty-year study, aggressive children were viewed as unpopular and lacking leadership qualities; thus promoting prosocial behavior is essential.[75] While the school can work with aggressive and passive children to change the behavior of the one group and protect the other, bullies whose behavior cannot be modified may need special institutions designed for incorrigibles.

Due to the heightened public perception of increased crime nationwide, many people are seeking survival skills. However, if assertiveness training is insufficient for frightened children, they, too, may need to attend a different school. Indeed, this is a reason the middle class withdraws children from public schools.

Altering Passivity

Due to a lack of assertiveness and an expectation of bullying, a child may behave in a way that encourages aggression. At the same time that a teacher provides a climate for student success, activity, tension release, and negotiation to prevent bullying, a teacher can provide *assertiveness training for meek children* to prevent them from giving clues that stimulate bullying. "What do you do to stop a bully from meddlin' you?" I asked. A sixth-grade black girl said, "You talk to 'um mean, and they stop be mean" (108). An assertive tone and stance deter much abuse according to several white children: "You will not touch me or hurt me!" A child who is friendly to a bully and identifies with something the youngster likes can help the bully lower the barrier to friendliness.

Helping children become more assertive involves encouragement and praise without embarrassing the child. If a withdrawn child suddenly rises to self-defense against a bully or some kind of attack, a teacher should not intervene unless there is the possibility of injury or embarrassment that would deter the child from future self-assertion. Two problems that might develop involve the withdrawn child overshooting the mark and becoming aggressive beyond what is desirable, or becoming overly dependent on an adult.[75]

A black middle-class mother was concerned that her son was the target of aggression. The boy asserted, "I'm not going to hit him; he can beat me up." His mother replied, "I want him to be able to defend himself." By taking the victim's role, the boy was providing reinforcement for the aggressor.

Whites may be afraid to stand up to blacks for fear blacks will call them racist. *Assertiveness training for teachers* counsels them to make eye contact, use a child's first name in a command, and place a hand on a youngster's shoulder.[77]

Having an "Out-to-Lunch Bunch"

Ms. Mann was one of many teachers at HPES who had a reputation among children and parents as a successful teacher. Several black children praised her for helping them reform. I asked her what she did to transform bullies and disobedient children. She said that consistency and firmness were critical. At the beginning of each semester, she called each parent and indicated that she was glad that adult's child was in her room.

> Since every child has both strengths and weaknesses, I mention one or two positive things about the child and suggest halfway a problem I anticipate. I tell the parent, "I'm going to do my part; I'd like you to back me up." About the second month, before the end of October, I have a conference with the parent, and the child is present. I lead in with the positive and have facts to back the negative. We go over the child's work habits.

She said a teacher has to know when to be soft and when to apply the pressure. The knowledge depends on sensitivity, experience, and intuition. "I give the kids *lots of love*. The first time a child misbehaves, I talk to the child *in private* and say, 'I'm here to see you succeed; I'm not here to see you fail. You are a neat person. I like you a lot. Let's see what we can do about the problem.'" She works out a *plan with the child* according to the needs they both identify. The second time the child misbehaves, Ms. Mann speaks privately with the child and reviews the plan they developed; the third time, a punishment is in order.

One of Ms. Mann's students explained:

> Ms. Mann has a plan book—a calendar. If you're bad and you should know better, you get your name in the book. People who have not gotten their names in the book get to go out to lunch, be part of the *"out-to-lunch bunch"* on Friday at the end of the month [reward]. There are three ways to get your name out of the book [redemption]. One way is to stay in from recess for three days. A second way is to stay in and clean up the classroom. A third way is to have to copy a dictionary page [and Ms. Mann just happened to choose the page with "cooperation" on it!].

Ms. Mann is a good story teller and motivates children to finish work so there is time for her to tell a story. She judiciously uses humor and peer pressure. She said to a child, "I know you did your work; you don't want to get a zero." Then she emptied his desk drawer looking for work she knew was not done; she did this to four children with a straight face. Their peers were hilarious. Everyone did the work thereafter.

Summary

COPING WITH BEHAVIOR THAT DISRUPTS THE CLASSROOM

Mesh Academic and Social Learning
> Teach survival skills, for example, patron–client relationships.
> Interweave lessons of compromise, tolerance, and self-control with historical material and children's experience.

Individualize Activities
> Provide beginning- and middle-of-the-year orientation and reviews as needed.
> Explain the nature of prejudice and racism.
> Use role-playing techniques.
> Give science lesson on observed and covered body parts.
> Interpret body language.
> Discuss angry words and their meanings.

Let children share likes and dislikes to discover mutual interests.
Use action and reaction exercises to reveal different ways of interpreting the same behavior.

Discover Multicultural Styles

Review a child's previous record.
Be alert to major changes.
Solicit parents' guidance.
Recognize a child's search for dignity and the teacher's role in that process.
Respect the child as an individual while reinforcing academic achievement.
Work privately with troubled youngsters.

Modify Instructional Style

Practice "withitness" and attend to issues that present themselves.
Supervise classroom at all times.
Give clear, noncontradictory directions.
Involve children and parents in making procedural rules.
Use group-alerting and accountability techniques.
Provide variety and challenges, for example, games and contests.
Make academic material relevant to children's immediate concerns and future career opportunities.

Balance Assimilation with Cultural Pluralism and Ability Grouping

Explain the need and provide an opportunity for code switching.
Use ability grouping to recognize the need for human dignity.
Emphasize the contribution of all groups and their common needs.
Build on what children know, then advance them to what they need to know.

Structure Cooperation: Jigsaw Puzzle and Tournament Learning

Build on the individual's strength.
Make each person necessary to complete a task.
Provide seating patterns.

Referee Potential Conflict Activities

Structure cooperation on the playground.
Provide an adult referee.
Praise cooperation.

Recognize Ripple Effects of Discipline

Praise appropriate and ignore some inappropriate behavior.
Spot disruptive behavior early.
Focus on the misdeed, not on the person who misbehaved.

179

Punish misbehaving children rather than the entire class.
Provide opportunities to save face.
Involve students in behavior interventions.
Mete out punishment consistently and evenhandedly.

Provide Counseling
Build on teachers' social relations lessons.
Handle unique problems.

Cope with Aggression
Supervise children.
Reduce causes of anger.
Isolate ringleaders of aggression.
Diffuse explosive situations.
Investigate the cause of a fight.
Involve students in preventing problems.
Use a case study approach for a disruptive child.
Teach bullies responsibility.

Alter Passivity
Provide assertiveness training for meek children and teachers.
Explain children's behavior that stimulates bullying.

Have an "Out-to-Lunch Bunch"
Contact parent or guardian at the beginning of the year to indicate
the teacher's interest in the child and the desire for parental
cooperation.
Give love.
Speak privately to a misbehaving child; work out a behavior plan with
the child; if the child misbehaves again, review the plan; punish
the child for the third misbehavior.
Have opportunities for canceling the penalty for a misdeed.
Provide rewards for good behavior.

NOTES

1. Ronald Emonds, assistant to the New York City school chancellor for
instruction, Michael Rutter, Richard Murmane, and George Weber argue that
there should be a strong principal; clear teaching objectives in school; a school
climate that is safe, orderly, attractive, serious, and one that avoids the intrusion
of security measures; high expectations for all students; and the use of standardized tests to measure progress and make plans (Fiske 1979). The features of a
school that Rutter (1979:194) believes make it more likely students will share the
school's education perspective include "(1) general conditions for, and staff
attitudes to, the pupils; (2) shared activities between staff and pupils; (3) pupil

positions of responsibility within the school system; and (4) success and achievement." See also National Institute of Education 1978 and Olweus 1978:169–92 on handling aggression in Sweden.

2. Brophy 1982.

3. Cf. Davis's 1974 summary.

4. Kounin 1970.

5. See Grambs 1968; Banks 1981.

6. See Shaftel and Shaftel 1982 for guidance in using role-playing.

7. See Hanna 1983a. Perhaps nonverbal communication can be viewed as a second language with the same potential for successful teaching and learning as a verbal second language (see literature on bilingual education: Cazden et al. 1972; Simoes 1976; McLaughlin 1982).

8. Speer 1972:42.

9. Seaford 1975.

10. Karlin and Berger 1972:132ff.

11. Metz 1978:102–5; see also Fiske 1980.

12. Comer and Poussaint 1975:200.

13. Clark's study (1977) confirms the need to treat the concerns of all students, those who perform academically and those who do not. Poor black and white vocational students felt neglected and stigmatized. They resented resources given to college-bound students. Poor whites, in addition, felt excluded from the bounty given to blacks. The poor, feeling alienated, disenfranchised, and powerless, rebelled and rioted.

14. Sennett and Cobb 1973:265.

15. Ibid.: 82.

16. Hakken 1978.

17. Willis 1975:19, 1977.

18. Sennett and Cobb 1973:84.

19. Ibid.:270.

20. See Bateson 1972 on the double bind.

21. National Institute of Education 1978:9.

22. Giles 1972.

23. Kounin 1970 refers to withitness, overlapping, smoothness, momentary variety, and challenge); cf. Rutter 1979.

24. DeBruyn 1978.

25. McDermott and Gospodinoff 1979.

26. Kounin 1970.

27. See O'Neil 1985.

28. Kounin 1970.

29. Reece and Whitman 1962.

30. Garvey 1977:106.

31. Banks et al. 1978.

32. Millar 1968:114.

33. Raspberry 1979a; Restak 1979.

34. Ravitch 1978a.

35. In preparation for a litigious society, the school requires verbal negotiation of conflict. Training programs often overlook the children's worlds; Thus survival for some children requires physically striking out first.

36. See Rist (1978) and Gumperz (1978:15) who summarize some of the issues.

37. Shultz and Florio 1979.

38. Cf. Rosenbaum 1980.

39. See Scarr and Weinberg (1978) on genetic contribution.

40. In their twenty-year longitudinal study of aggression of school children (mostly white), Lefkowitz et al. (1977:79) found that low IQs consistently correlated with high aggression. A low IQ makes school work frustrating and is a condition that limits a child's ability to learn a variety of socially acceptable behaviors. Cf. Wolf 1981:119–25.

41. Williams, L. 1979.

42. Banks 1977:19–20.

43. Gilmore 1983:239.

44. Hanna 1983b, 1986b, 1987, 1988a.

45. Grambs 1979:6.

46. Coleman in Feinberg 1978.

47. Smitherman 1977:200; pp. 106–7 suggests the kinds of acknowledgment expressed.

48. Following Allport (1954), Pettigrew (1971:64, 275 ff; 1974) and Pettigrew and Back (1967) specify conditions for integration. Weigel et al. (1975), and Aronson (1975), Aronson et al. (1978), and Cohen and Roper (1972) found that students who work together in small groups like each other more.

49. Cohen and Roper 1972.

50. Cohen 1980:273.

51. Aronson et al. 1978.

52. Slavin 1980.

53. Wax 1980:114–15, 120.

54. Metz 1978:115–16.

55. Rutter 1979.

56. Sennett and Cobb 1973:83.

57. Rubel 1977.

58. National Institute of Education 1978:148.

59. Quoted in Clark 1977:100.

60. Metz 1978.

61. Long et al. 1976:86.

62. Quoted in National Committee for Citizens in Education, nd:5.

63. Scherer and Slawski 1979:141ff.

64. *Dallas Times Herald* 1978; Stumbo 1978.

65. Metz 1978.

66. National Institute of Education 1978:38.

67. See Henry (1957) on the ways teachers can organize emotions to encourage or deflect intragroup aggression.

68. Comer and Poussaint 1975:119.

69. Ibid., 200.

70. Ibid., 189.

71. Karlin and Berger 1972:106–10, 115.

72. Scherer et al. 1975:92–3.

73. Harrison-Ross and Wyden 1973:182.

74. Scherer et al. 1975:106.

75. Lefkowitz et al. 1977:192. Woodson 1981 discusses successful alternative community-based programs for youngsters inadequately served by the public schools.

76. Comer and Poussaint 1975:210.

77. Lubow and Copeland 1978.

9

LEADERSHIP AND POLICY: PRINCIPALS, GOVERNMENT, AND THE PRIVATE SECTOR

I have mentioned the taboos against talking about disruptive school behavior in desegregated and low-income settings throughout the United States. Some apparently effective strategies that are used by teachers and staff at HPES and elsewhere have been sketched. But a school does not exist as an isolated entity and cannot solve society's problems alone. The school has only a minimum of control over many of the problems it encounters; especially significant is the historical, socioeconomic context that shapes the cultures from which children come to school.

The American public school is a product of the nineteenth century, during which time providing minority people with such civic services as education was regarded as a nonpriority issue because of scarce resources; today budget deficits, a nongrowth economy, and the Gramm-Rudman-Hollings Congressional spending ceiling limit resources for minority education.[1] I do not fully accept Patterson's critique of the doctrine of equal educational opportunity, namely, that

> the educational institution is not and cannot be an agent of social change, that it invariably reflects the society in which it exists, its main role being to pass on traditional values and skills and to certify those who, for reasons having little to do with their education, are destined to be successful.[2]

Notwithstanding this context, schools need the efforts of other social institutions and key individuals. The constraints and pressures from inside and outside the educational system under which schools and administrators operate usually make it exceedingly difficult to depart from existing patterns of behavior and implement innovations.[3]

For teaching and learning to occur most effectively in public educa-

183

tion, local, state, and federal policy makers have roles to play in developing programs and allocating resources. These include considering community-developed innovative school alternatives if there is evidence that they work. Dominant people in the private sector can also make a difference to disruptive school behavior in America.

Principals

Among the school factors that seem to affect children's achievement one of the most important is a principal who seriously solicits and considers staff views and emphasizes acquiring reading and math skills, continually evaluates pupils' progress, maintains high expectations for students and supports teachers.[4] Since principals hire and reward teachers, teachers respond to what they perceive as their boss's wishes. Principals thus establish the climate of a school. Students and parents find these leaders both a threat and a protection, since principals have the power to destroy a student's or teacher's career, serve as moral and behavioral guardians responsible for inculcating appropriate values and skills, and provide for orderly instruction and school behavior.

A principal is constrained by an organizational system that has been described as "loosely coupled." As researchers have pointed out,[5] a principal must work within the macrostructure of the school's system-wide edicts, the school board's and administration's control of budget and staffing lines, and union contracts and negotiations. Working within such a macrostructure, and without tenure or a union, principals are more vulnerable than teachers if they choose to disobey policy made by their superiors. Principals also experience constraints within the microstructure, the organization of the school that the principal supervises and the immediate community of parents. Because direct commands are not always enforceable, a principal needs to communicate expectations clearly and use rewards and punishment to gain the support of staff and students to meet the goals. Initiating and carrying out change requires a principal also to be a good expediter and mediator.

A principal is the key liaison with the community. By providing resources for counselors who work with students and parents, and support services such as typing and mailing announcements, meeting rooms and custodial maintenance after an assembly for community-related events, the principals at HPES facilitated the participation of parents and concerned community members in school problem-solving activities. Public-relations activity by the principal can also encourage parent–teacher associations and private-sector organizations to contribute to the development of school programs and to supply services and materials that would not otherwise be available.

Liaison takes time and resources. When a child justifies behavior contrary to school policy by saying, "My momma told me . . ." the school has little possibility of changing that behavior without the parent's intervention.[6] The bureaucratization and professionalization of public education turned many of its spokespeople against interference by parents. Possibly because they are defensive about their insecure professional status and self-image, teachers tend to be receptive to parents who are obsequious, appreciative, and uncritical or accept their need for autonomy. But now, the public education system is beginning to recognize that it cannot succeed without parental support.[7] Schools can survey parents about their attitudes and ideas for solving problems. Principals can find sponsors, such as the initiator of the Parents in Pacesetter organization described in chapter 3, to facilitate cross-racial and cross-socioeconomic-class contacts. Potential mediators, often living voluntarily in integrated areas and socializing with white and black, can help bridge the gulf between otherwise separate groups.

Because adults are often not at home when a child returns from school, principals can take the lead in helping organize a form of school or community group, or some combination of these, to provide supervised study hall facilities and tutors to assist youngsters with such matters as homework, learning problems, and citizenship accountability. *The Home-School Connection* describes select partnership programs in large cities.[8] In some programs, community people go into the home and work with the school as a parent substitute and a role model for a youngster. The Maryland Montgomery County National Association for the Advancement of Colored People initiated an after-school and Saturday program to provide community volunteer one-on-one aid for youngsters.

Effective leadership is required in preventing problems. For school construction, often under principals' guidance, the following recommendations,[9] designed to stimulate people's better instincts and reduce opportunities for "wreck-reation," are apt: An exposed rock–cement mixture, slanted cedar siding, and a deeply groved surface would make walls unsuitable for graffiti. Such construction would interfere with the user's perception of a wall as an empty inviting "picture plain" waiting to be filled as well as a person's learned writing behavior of keeping letters the same size and moving horizontally from left to right on a relatively smooth and constant contrast background. Using bracing across toilet flanges along the top would discourage students climbing on doors in order to infringe on their peers' privacy, as occurred at HPES.

Special Programs

Leadership at various governmental and private-sector levels is essential to long-range planning for needed programs that encompass a continual evaluation of academic achievement, social relations, and occupational needs while at the same time remaining flexible to meet the unanticipated.

If it is true that socioeconomic class is a critical determining variable in academic success, then there are several possibilities. One is to homogenize culture and change our economic system—an unlikely national/local policy choice. Another approach is for leaders to promote such programs as federal Headstart for preschool children, Title 1 compensatory school programs, competency-based curriculum, children working at their own level in individualized programs, and instruction in test-taking skills. These programs have helped youngsters go through school without needing special education and with the preparation that propelled them on to college or steady, skilled jobs.[10] Some critics of enrichment strategies thought these programs would provide incentives for the continued concentration of blacks in the cities and the flight of white residents and businesses. However, at least for a time, the energy crisis and the poor state of the economy actually attracted middle-class white consumers, tax payers, and services to the cities.[11]

There is a need for alternative organizational structures to educate youngsters with such a strong counterschool culture that they do not fit into the typical school's routine of set periods. "Schools without walls" that draw on community resources and on-the-job training are possible schooling substitutes.

Student leadership training programs are essential. Youngsters acquire a stake in the system when they actively participate in decision-making, rule enforcement, curriculum, and instructional style. For example, student peer conflict mediation and counseling through Project Smart (School Mediators Alternative and Resolution Team) has cut student suspension, homicide, and suicide rates. Approximately 20,000 peer counseling programs exist in elementary and upper schools nationwide, and there is a journal called *Peer Facilitation Quarterly*.[12]

Retired athletes and military veterans should receive special training to teach math and science (subjects in which there is a teacher shortage), tutor during and after school, and help create an orderly and safe school climate for learning. They not only have acquired relevant skills but also can be very influential in the lives of young people, many of whom admire the physical strength and accomplishments of these role models.

Another area for attention centers on students' physical and emo-

186

calls attention to the need to build into court-mandated plans an *evalua-tion-adaptation component* rooted in the human experience in order to cope with unintended consequences in the development of a unique social experiment. Without identification, problems cannot be addressed by policies to achieve the goals for which they were designed.

Disaggregating the diverse groupings called white and black is appropriate where possible.[18] At HPES, middle-class blacks were excluded because they lived outside the HPES area. Contact with a range of social classes among the black minority helps dispell stereotypes and provide models for black achievement.[19]

Socioeconomic class considerations cast doubt on the value of deseg-regating school faculty. It is questionable whether members of a given ethnic group, ipso facto, communicate most effectively with those of the same ethnic group.[20] In fact, a probable reason for the failure of teach-ers to be effective with low-income black pupils is that teachers, both black and white, are middle class and view the world differently from their low-income students. Consequently, teacher assignments on the basis of early background or experience in low-income settings may be more useful than merely ethnic similarity.

Given the attitudes about territorial possession and turf that exist, the choice of facility for desegregation might best be a *neutral setting,* that is, a new school, even if an old building, in which there is no existing community and set of attitudes that lead to the perception of another group disrupting or displacing the status quo when desegregation is introduced. Recall that HPES was located in a black community and formerly black-controlled school and the black girl's remark to the white girl, "You in soul country now!"

As research findings reveal, effective desegregation involves a com-posite of factors. Illustrative is the long-term Project Concern study that followed a group of low-income black students from four inner-city elementary schools, who were bused into sixty predominantly white schools in thirteen suburbs of Hartford, to high school graduation. Males were more likely to graduate from high school, and if they at-tended college, they completed more years there. They perceived less discrimination in college and other areas of adult life, experienced less difficulty with police, and fought less as adults. Females were less likely to have children before age eighteen. Black participants in desegregation had closer interracial social contacts and higher-level jobs than blacks who attended segregated schools.[21] Note that benefits of desegregation to blacks occurred under specific conditions: A few blacks were bused voluntarily into a school with a virtually all-white student body and staff.

189

Desegregation occurred with the support of the black youngsters' home and community. The program had a high dropout rate, which suggests that more kinds of support efforts were needed.

A good education is more important than integration for many blacks. Busing in Wilcox County, Alabama, has led to an antibusing lawsuit that charges the federal and state governments with irreparable harm and child abuse on behalf of four black women whose children ride a bus to Pine Hill High School, which experienced an exodus of white students to private academies.[22] The assumption that all black schooling is harmful overlooks those schools destroyed by desegregation. For example, Dunbar High School in Washington, D.C., from 1870 to 1955 sent three-fourths of its graduates to college at a time when college attendance for most white Americans was the exception rather than the rule. "To the extent that racial balance policy obviates efforts toward quality education for students of color, such a policy is pernicious and therefore a violation of equal protection."[23]

Choice in education has been suggested as an alternative to forced busing for desegregation.[24] Currently, in order to send your child to the public school of your choice, you have to live in that particular district. Poor people have limited choice of place of residence and consequently, of school as well. Furthermore, if the well-to-do dislike the assigned public school, they can send their children to private schools; poor people do not usually have this option. As the quintessential self-serving monopoly, public schools have no incentive to win families they already have. The solution to this predicament is to give the have-nots the liberty and responsibility that works for the wealthy to educate their children. Thus the state could issue vouchers (on a sliding-scale value comparable to that used for taxation) to parents to be cashed by the school they select. By permitting voluntary transfers across district lines, the choice plan would provide opportunities for racial desegregation; indeed, incentives for desegregation could be included in the voucher system. Such a proposal inevitably evokes fears of the destruction of public education. Yet given its general decline, which is creating a serious situation for low-income blacks, it would appear to be worthwhile trying several small-scale experiments of different designs.[25]

Thus Congress could mandate that nothing be done to prevent voluntary integration, and that a child have the choice of free transportation to attend a school in another neighborhood inhabited predominantly by those of another race, when a court has determined that intentional racial discrimination in educational opportunities has occurred.[26] The middle class is more receptive to receiving low-income children in middle-class schools than to sending its youngsters to schools in low-income neighborhoods where the aggression level is likely to be higher.

Magnet schools such as HPES that address the problems described should be supported. These schools could be included in voucher or incentive plans.[27] Financial incentives could be given to both sending and receiving districts for students who choose to transfer across district lines. Support is needed to cover the transportation cost, the extra burden of educating a child outside of its tax district, and the loss of state aid that a sending district would normally receive.

Education and Economy

Chapter 5 noted some trends in American society that offer a context for understanding disruptive school behavior: the increasing separation between the student's family and community accompanying the consolidated school system, decrease in respect for authority, and emphasis on children's rights. Another trend is the middle-class response to changing American economic organization; For example, changes since the 1950s in a suburban, affluent, middle-class, mostly white high school are ramifications of a postscarcity, leisure-oriented society that has overtaken the bourgeois, Protestant culture of productivity, capital accumulation, thrift, individual enterprise, emotional restraint, sexual repressiveness, a patriarchal nuclear family, and punctuality.[28] Large corporations eclipse entrepreneurial life and the bourgeois culture that had served to fetter consumption. Advertising, commodity consumption, and hedonistic pleasure, coupled with installment buying, assault older values and behavior. Child-socialization patterns have also changed. Paternalism became divested from the middle-class family and recognized in the corporation or in bureaucracy, which had much greater potency than father.[29]

Much of middle-class youth, who had the most to gain from the system, rebelled against it. Why?[30] Some students tend to feel guilty because they do not envision being able to fulfill their lives through meaningful work as opportunities dwindle. Like blue-collar labor, white-collar work is becoming subdivided and routinized. "Motivation for school attendance is primarily negative. It is not couched so much in terms of what rewards can be gained for continued effort, but what happens if one drops out."[31] Furthermore, youth must also compete with peers for increasingly scarce resources.

The attitude neither of low-income nor of middle-class youth toward education is enthusiastic, to say the least; obviously, some environmental change is called for. In the history of educational reform, business leadership has contributed to various developments out of self-interest. The private sector relies on schools to recreate conditions of existence, have a strong national defense, mold the labor and managerial supply, control students until they are ready for the labor market, credential levels of competence, and sort individuals into subsequent occupations and social positions.[32]

The private sector has a dramatic stake in the quality of education and consequently gains when youngsters of all social classes are committed to the system and benefiting from it. Unless action is taken quickly to increase educational and social opportunities for poor children, the economy will be in jeopardy when millions of young Americans reach working age without skills or any hope of employment.[33] The Business Advisory Committee of the Education Commission of the States speaks of at least 15 percent of Americans between the ages of sixteen and nineteen as unlikely to become productive adults because they are "disconnected" from society.[34]

Social malaise has costs—skyrocketing dependence on welfare, epidemic crime in the street and home, security of the office, law enforcement, prisons, increasingly violent political conflict, and a non-tax-paying population. Moreover, in the future, if the current number of jobs remains stable and the fertility rate continues as it is (down to 1.9 in 1980 from 3.8 per married couple in the late 1950s), literate and well-educated people will be in high demand.[35] The deterioration of the labor force results in a further decline in American competitiveness in the world market and a loss in sales and profits.

Education is essential in this era of social dislocation due to computerized automation in manufacturing and commerce. The history of the fate of millions of people whose lives have been either destroyed or blighted because they were unable to find a viable role in the economy and society into which they were born is shocking.[36] *Age of Triage* explores the cultural forces at work that made for *both* unemployment and genocide.

Because the positive motivation of low-income students toward academic achievement is affected by their perceived potential employment opportunities and the school does not usually provide jobs, the private sector can provide such immediate rewards for academic success.[37]

Moreover, business can give attention to the development of human capital just as it does to other forms of capital.[38] To that end, there are such programs as Adopt-a-School and Partnerships in Education. In 1984 there were more than 46,000 corporate and community sponsors in 2,058 school districts according to a U.S. Department of Education survey of 16,746 school districts. Atlantic Richfield Corporation has a full-time coordinator of volunteer services in Los Angeles. Business can provide such services as individual tutoring, providing state-of-the-art equipment that schools cannot afford, instruction in using this equipment, public relations to explain business activities and employment needs. A New York foundation, the Commonwealth Fund, has developed the Career Beginnings program to deal with dropouts and other troubled students to help them succeed as workers and students. The program attempts to fill the gap in the life styles of minority students who lack a family member or network of adults to help them plan for life after high school. Students in the program obtain salaried summer jobs and work with an adult mentor.[39] Graduates of six elementary schools, about 425 students in some of New York City's poorest and toughest neighborhoods where dropout rates are among the highest, will have their college education paid for if they graduate from high school. Donors provide tutoring programs and support, college scholarships, and guidance.[40] It is important to counter the isolation of the school from the economic sector and bridge the gap between educational outcomes and business requirements for employee skills.

The Challenge

This book reports adult-validated children's perceptions of what it is like to be a student in a desegregated magnet school that is located in a black neighborhood and has bused volunteer white children. The school is a proving ground for what many people think education should be. There are more positive than negative academic and social learning experiences at HPES. My study has focused on the negative in order to identify problems in education that demand attention. In evaluating social policy for the "natives," the "native"'s view is important. Children construct reality from stimuli in their environment; their perceptions often contradict adult ideals and policies meant to realize those ideals. How children feel about themselves and each other in the world they know affects their schoolwork. Since their early life experiences have an impact on later life values, beliefs, and behavior, difficulties they face need to be tackled.

Problems found in a model school occur in greater number and intensity and with greater impact elsewhere, as indicated in the discussion and references throughout this book. What we dislike will not disappear by pretending that it does not exist, or complaining that it is present and blaming others. We must strive to take an unflinching look at the distasteful and work toward altering it.

193

At the level of the individual learner, accidents of birth into a particular race and social class bear on different patterns of socialization, childhood peer group influence, academic achievement, and adult employment. At the level of the school, the facility's physical and substantive attributes and participants' attitudes and behavior contribute to a climate that affects the nature of social relations and schooling. At the level of the external environment, opportunities in the economy affect teaching and learning. Prescriptive strategies for educational equal opportunity must consider the concept of culturally disadvantaged or deprived youth in tandem with the structure of limited opportunity.

The costs of prescriptive strategies for parents and the school can, in large measure, be met within existing expenditures for PTA activities and teacher in-service meetings and training as well as teacher training. Other strategies do involve additional expeditures or reallocation of resources. Time and energy are essential to ameliorate dissonance arising from historical and economic patterns and to realize the American dream. An ignored underclass will ultimately sap the resources and strength of the entire society; angry have-nots will prey on those who have. Just as it took a complex of social forces to produce antischool culture conditions, it will take a range of remedies to dissolve them.

Summary

A SCHOOL SYSTEM'S GUIDE TO IMPROVING THE ACADEMIC ACHIEVEMENTS OF MINORITY STUDENTS

I. *Problem*

    A. Counterschool culture with deep roots and web of causes.
      1. Peer pressure against doing what is required for academic achievement.
      2. Low individual academic motivation with attitudes and behavior established since early childhood.
    B. Home environment unsupportive of academic achievement (for example, broken home, low education of guardian, working guardian not available to assist child).
    C. Past approaches generally unidimensional or too narrowly focused and unsuccessful (magnet schools, special education, tutoring, counseling services, low student to teacher ratios, higher teacher salaries, longer school day, tracking, eliminating tracking, reduced class size, minimum standards,

upgrading instructional materials, raising teacher qualifications, short in-service training on minority culture, hiring black teachers and administrators, sensitivity sessions on prejudice and teacher expectations, busing for desegregation, improved physical facilities, and so forth).

D. School personnel handicapped.
    1. Inadequate training to deal with the problem.
    2. Time is overcommitted.

II. *Need: Multipronged Effort* (see Figure 7.1, "Educational Changes").

Applied ethnographer/coordinator employed to work with schools in implementing process described below.

Informal use by coordinator of advisory group comprised of representatives from local and state governments, the community, school, and academe.

A. Offer head start program and continued reinforcement/enrichment for new school cohort.

B. Elicit perspectives, participation, and accountability of groups involved (Harvard University Project on Technology, Work, and Character; family-therapy and community-based reform-home models of *working with* individuals rather than *doing to* or *for* them).
    1. Elicit participation of school personnel.
    2. Coopt peer leaders of current student classes.
        a. Elicit their suggestions for changing climate.
        b. Elicit their aid to tutor younger students, maintain school rules, and promote academic interest.
    3. Involve community, family members, and local heroes (such as athletes, entertainers, and so forth) in providing suggestions and aid.
    4. Involve government and business leaders in providing suggestions and aid (for example, equipment, tutors, afterschool and summer jobs).

C. Establish reward system (based on student, school, community, business, and government recommendations).

D. Mesh academic learning with fun—based on student views (for example, competition between gangs, classes, schools).

III. *Progress toward Meeting Need*
    A. Needs Assessment
        1. Meet with school system administration to ascertain specific problems, actions taken, difficulties encountered or

anticipated, possibilities, and constraints (budget, person-nel, community sensitivities; note minority diversity based on social class).

2. Meet with principals to explain and modify process described herein if necessary.

3. In each school, meet with principal, principal and teach-ers, teachers in groups and individually.

   a. Elicit perceptions of problems and possible solutions to change school climate.

   b. Elicit identification of minority student diversity, leaders, toughs.

4. Meet with minority low academic achievers, especially leaders, to elicit perceptions of problems and possible solutions.

5. Meet with community members to elicit perceptions and identify sponsors.

6. Meet with business community leaders to elicit percep-tions.

7. Observe school (classroom and outside classroom) and minority student communities to identify unnoticed problems.

B. Program Development

1. Synthesize information and develop a plan based on reported research findings in book and school-specific findings.

2. Meet with school administration to review and modify plan.

3. Meet with each principal concerning implementation.

4. Meet with principal and teachers to explain "their" plan.

5. Offer workshop.

   a. Detail problems based on what is known (see Table 3.1, Cultural Duality in School).

   b. Describe approaches to problem-solving (see Sum-mary, Chap. 8, "Coping with Behavior That Disrupts the Classroom").

   c. Set up communication network and regular meetings to share new knowledge.

6. Meet with student groups to explain "their" plan.

7. Meet with community group members to explain "their" plan.

   a. Establish majority–minority relations group to pro-mote cooperation.

196

      b.   Involve minority members as tutors and disciplinarians in in-school and after-school programs.
    8.   Modify plan to improve academic achievements of minority students in accord with input from various meetings and disseminate information on modification.
C.   Evaluation
    1.   Keep detailed records on procedure for
        a.   Continual evaluation and modification of approach
        b.   Preparation of published handbook that can be used for other coordinators to follow in an effort to improve the academic achievements of minority students and for teacher/administrator training.
    2.   Use standardized tests and develop instruments for short-term evaluation.

NOTES

1.   Weinberg 1977:349.
2.   Patterson 1978:23.
3.   Polk and Shafter 1972:264.
4.   See Weber 1971; Wellisch et al. 1978:190–94; and Rutter et al. 1979.
5.   See Noblitt and Johnston 1982.
6.   Lightfoot (1978:20–42) describes tensions between schools and black families.
7.   See Krug 1976; Hechinger 1979b.
8.   Collins et al. 1982.
9.   Wise 1982.
10.   Maeroff 1980; Rubin 1980.
11.   Frey 1979.
12.   Dullea 1987.
13.   Dr. Leroy Taylor quoted in Fisher 1987.
14.   Cf. Hill-Burnett 1978.
15.   Sedlacek and Brooks 1976:49.
16.   Spindler 1982.
17.   Barbash 1980:A2.
18.   Cf. Williams, R. 1977:109.
19.   Cf. Dunaway 1979; Pettigrew 1974:381–84. The advisability of the courts considering a mix of students from families of different income, educational, and occupational backgrounds, as well as the racial composition of school faculties, at the high school level is suggested by Lieske's (1978) study of a sample of 119 American cities during the late 1960s. He found that school violence seems more likely to occur where the social conditions for blacks are better absolutely and relative to whites, where blacks, "having surmounted basic survival and security needs, no longer feel threatened by white socioeconomic and political reprisals (59 percent of the reported school disorders analyzed in his study originated in organized protests and demonstrations, not the more recent

individual and criminal outbreaks of school violence). "School disorders are much more likely to occur in cities where black and white students come into frequent and daily contact" (ibid., 91). When blacks are represented on school faculties in proportion to the black student population, violence is less likely. Lieske (ibid., 96) concluded that

> blacks who cross the poverty threshold and approach whites in social status are more likely to develop a heightened sense of racial identity and consciousness, a militant "riot ideology," and a greater propensity to translate their social and political emancipation into aggressive riot behavior.

The implication is that racial school desegregation along class-stratified lines may not necessarily be more conducive to greater racial harmony as assumed by the equal-status assumption of contact theory. However, as Lieske (ibid., 97) points out, his study analyzed disorders in the context of the 1960s civil rights struggle when such disturbances and their justification were much more widespread than they are now.

20. Landis et al. 1975:141.

21. Crain et al. 1985 MS.

22. Prugh 1979.

23. Newby 1979:22.

24. Coons and Sugarman 1978; Abrams et al. 1978; Coons 1980.

25. See Cohen and Farrar (1977) on a trial of the voucher system in Alum Rock, California. Because of the dynamics of the school superintendent's goal of decentralizing and financing schools and the Office of Economic Opportunity's desire for a test of consumer sovereignty, the case was not a clear test. It did, however, reveal the need to help parents make choices. "Most parents failed to become more autonomous, powerful, or involved" (p. 89).

26. Cuddy 1982.

27. Coleman 1981.

28. Larkin 1979.

29. Ibid., 43–45.

30. Ibid., 57–58.

31. Ibid., 60.

32. According to some perspectives, the guiding force in the history of education has been less educating children than maintaining social peace, prosperity, and the status quo of the leadership within the context of private property and governmental structures that support it. See, for example, Bowles and Gintis 1976; Nasaw 1979:241–42.

33. Levin 1985.

34. Business Advisory Committee, Education Commission of the States 1985.

35. Butz et al. 1982.

36. Rubenstein 1983.

37. Shabecoff 1980. The failure of students in a Jewish afternoon school, according to Schoem (1982), is due to the parents' and their own perception that there was no compelling material reward to be expected from this education.

More than eight million factory jobs have been lost since 1979 according to the Bureau of Labor Statistics in 1985. Joblessness among teenagers has expanded steadily over the last thirty years despite numerous efforts to combat it. In 1954, the overall youth unemployment rate was 12.6 percent; in 1984, in the midst of a national economic resurgence, it reached 18.9 percent. For young blacks, it was 43 percent. In 1986, the figures were 19 percent for all youth, 39 percent for nonwhites.

38. Levine 1985.
39. Maeroff 1986.
40. Rohter 1986.

APPENDICES

Letter to Faculty and Staff

September 19, 1977

To: Faculty and Staff of Pacesetter

From: Judith Lynne Hanna, Ph.D., Research Scientist, the University of Texas at Dallas

Subject: Project Understanding: A Study of Communication

A number of teachers, staff, and students have asked who I am and what I am doing. To the students, I say, "I'm doing a story about Hamilton Park—what it's like to be a student. Would you like to help me?" "How?" they ask. I answer, "You can write a little story about (or tell me) what it's like to be a student at Hamilton Park."

I would like all the members of the faculty and the staff to know the goals of the study I am working on and the ways we can, working together, help teachers at Pacesetter and elsewhere improve teaching effectiveness and harmonious social relations between student and student, as well as between student and teacher. In the study, I am trying to:

1. Describe the ways children communicate (verbally and with "body language"),
2. Compare their words and actions, and
3. Identify communications that students of a particular culture do not perceive or understand.

200

To do this, I will be observing children, asking questions, taking notes, and occasionally recording behavior with audiovisual equipment.

Children's comments, along with my training in education (as a teacher in the Los Angeles, Lansing, and Gill School systems and a consultant for the New York, Philadelphia, and Englewood systems) and anthropology (I studied with Margaret Mead at Columbia), alerted me to the need for this study. Discussions with parents and children at Pacesetter, elsewhere in RISD, and across the United States, and with Pacesetter and RISD administrators have confirmed the need.

By having information about the way people in different cultures (cultures based on common ethnicity, class, sex, and/or age, and so forth) express themselves and communicate, teachers may choose to modify some teaching and discipline techniques in order to reach some students more effectively, eliminate some stressful situations, and additionally promote intercultural understanding.

Sharing your experiences and insights with me will help us achieve the goal of improved communication—the basis of education and social relations. Individual names and practices, and so forth, will of course remain strictly confidential. I will try to talk with many of you as soon as research time permits. If you wish to arrange a time to talk with me, please leave a message with your alternative free times in my box in the teachers' lounge.

I wish to take this opportunity to thank all of you who have made me feel welcome at Pacesetter and have helped to get this study off to a promising start.

Judy

Letter to Parents

HAMILTON PARK ELEMENTARY
"The Pacesetter School"
8301 Towns Street
Dallas, TX 75243

RICHARDSON INDEPENDENT SCHOOL DISTRICT

October 14, 1977

Dear Parent,

Project Understanding is underway at Hamilton Park Elementary School to better prepare educators to teach students and promote harmony among students. We are studying ways of communication. Communication includes verbal (written and spoken) and nonverbal (body) languages. As part of the project, students may be asked questions, videotaped, photographed, and/or asked to comment on pictures. At no time will any student or teacher be identified by name.

Any parent who has questions about the study may contact Judith Lynne Hanna, Ph.D. (690-2981), one of our Hamilton Park parents who is helping us. We welcome your help, too!

We hope you will permit your child to participate in what promises to be a most enjoyable activity. It's fun to see yourself on television!

Sincerely,

Mrs. Phyllis Owen
Principal

James Griffin
Principal

I give permission for my child,_____, to
(please print child's name)
participate in Project Understanding.

Parent's signature _____

Observation Report Form

Communication in a Multicultural School   Date of write-up: _____

Date of Event _____   Commentary

Time _____

Place _____

General Event _____

Children present _____

Adults present _____

Visual record _____

Audio record _____

Themes: _____

Time   Who   What

Project Understanding: Interview Schedule

Begin with, "I am writing a story about HPES. I am interested in students' views, and I have some questions to ask you."

O. *How long have you been at HPES?*

A. *What do you like best about HPES?*

B. *If you could change one thing, what would you change? (What don't you like about HPES?)*

1. How can you tell if a child (kid) wants to be your friend?

    (What does the child do?
    How does the child look?
    What do you do?

    a. Do all kids act the same way if they want to be friends?
    b. How do they act differently?
    c. How do you make friends?

2. How can you tell if a child is mad?

   (What does the child do?
   How does the child look?)

   a. Do all kids act the same way when they are mad?
   b. How do they act differently?
   c. How do you act when a child gets mad?
   d. How do you act when you get mad?

3. If a child is bothering you (bugging, messing with, meddlin' you), how do you let the child know you want her or him to stop?

   a. Do you act the same at home? (If not, how?)
   b. Do you act the same at school? In class, the hall, toilet, on the playground?

4. a. When a child picks on (bugs, messes with, meddles) your friend, what do you do?
   b. How do you know a child is picking on (bugging, messing with, meddlin') your friend?

5. What do you do to put a child down (tease, get the best of someone)?

6. a. What is your idea of a nice (favorite) teacher? (How does the teacher act, look?)
   b. What is your idea of a mean teacher? (How does the teacher act, look?)

7. If a child misbehaves, what do you think a teacher should do?

   a. If they do the same wrong thing, should boys be treated differently from girls? (If so, how?)
   b. If they do the same wrong thing, should neighborhood (black) children be treated differently from volunteer (white) children? (If so, how?)

8. a. The school has rules, but what do you think is bad behavior in the classroom?
   b. What do you think is bad behavior on the playground? in the hall? toilet?
   c. What do you think is bad behavior at home?

9. Think of the toughest (strongest) child in your grade:

   a. What does the child do?
   b. Is the child a bully?
   c. What is a bully?

10. Think of the neatest, smartest, most admirable child in your grade: How does the child act?

204

11. Think of the dumbest child in your grade: How does the child act?

12. Think of the child who does the best school work: How does the child act?

13. Are you afraid of anyone at school? (If so, why?)

14. What do you think causes fights? (when, where, what, why, how?)

C. *What did you think of these questions?*
D. *Do they give me an idea of what it's like to be a student at HPES?*
E. *What other questions would you ask to find out what it's like to be a student at HPES? Ask the child the question(s) suggested.*

Discipline Referral Report Form
(Project Understanding)

Child identification (name or code): _____
Grade: 1   2   3   4   5   6
Homeroom teacher: _____
Sex: M   F
Volunteer/Neighborhood
Years of attendance at HPES: 1   2   3   4   5   6

Referral history: 1st time, 2d, 3d, 4th

Date of misconduct: _____
Place of misconduct: _____
Complainant: _____

Date of conference with child: _____

Type of misconduct:

_____ verbal abuse toward a child
_____   "   "   "   an adult
         type (name calling, profanity, mimicking, sassing)
         content _____
_____ vocal abuse toward a child
              "   "   "   an adult

205

    type (laugh, screech) _____
_____ physical abuse toward a child
_____   "   "   "   an adult
    action _____
    body part used in abuse _____
    body part abused _____
_____ noisy (talking, beating on door)
_____ physically restless (wanders about)
_____ destroys property
_____ takes other's property
    kind of property_____
_____ uncooperative general attitude
_____ does not do work

Interaction role:
_____ initiates actions that cause problems
_____ reacts to situations in ways that cause problems

Affect involved in problem:
_____ happy
_____ anger
_____ withdrawn (hides)
_____ other

Special problem:
_____ on medication
_____ sees psychologist
_____ sees school counselor
_____ sees resource teacher

Additional comments:

Parents for Improving Pacesetter (PIP) Letters and Forms

February 21, 1978

Dear Parent,

    We are a group of parents who believe in the Hamilton Park Pacesetter Program. We feel, however, that there are a number of things about the school that could be improved. After meeting and discussing these problems, we decided to turn to you, *all* the parents at Hamilton Park. WE NEED YOUR OPINIONS, YOUR COMPLAINTS AND YOUR SUGGESTIONS. We want to work *with* teachers and administrators in making this school one of the best in the nation, but first we must identify the areas that need improvement. We need a list that represents the feelings of the majority of the students and their parents, not just this committee. If you believe in this school and if you or your child has a specific concern or suggestion, then please, list it on the next two pages under the appropriate heading and send this form back to us. YOU DO NOT HAVE TO SIGN THIS FORM. NO ONE HAS TO KNOW WHO SENT IT. Please, just mail it back to: The PIP Committee, Hamilton Park School, 8301 Towns St., Dallas, Texas 75243. If you do not wish to mail it, you can drop it off in the box inside Mr. Griffin's office or send it back to school with your child. Feel free to use as much paper as you need in writing your comments. We want you to be as detailed as possible.

We plan to schedule some meetings with the faculty and administration to work on these various problems. If you wish to be included in one or more of these meetings, then please check the box marked YES at the end of this letter and state which areas are of interest to you. We will need your name and phone number or you may call Judy Nassif at 348-3173.

Complaining among ourselves is not going to change anything or give us a better understanding of the situation. We must work together with each other and the faculty if we ever hope to make Hamilton Park the great school it was designed to be. We need you, we are counting on you. Thank you for your cooperation.

Sincerely,

The PIP Committee*

*PIP Committee: Linda Bradbury, Minnie Champ, Marsha Friedman, Judy Hanna, George Nassif, Judy Nassif, Rita Robinson, George Smith, Lurlene Terrell.

February 21, 1978

Dear STUDENTS OF HAMILTON PARK,

WE NEED YOU! We are a group of parents who want to make Hamilton Park the best school in the entire country. We know that some of you and your folks are unhappy about a few of the things at the school. We are interested in your problems and we want to know your feelings, so please take this letter home to your parents or guardians and talk to them about it. They will fill out the form and send it back to us, but it is up to you to let them know how you feel. We know we can count on each and every one of you to get this letter home and see that your folks fill it out.

Thanks, PACESETTERS, you're going to help make Hamilton Park the very best school ever!

Your friends,

Parents for Improving
Pacesetter Committee

P.S. We need to have these forms returned by February 28.

PLEASE RETURN BY FEBRUARY 28, 1978

SUGGESTED AREAS FOR IMPROVEMENT

1. Busing:

2. Curriculum (subject matter being taught):

3. Communication (parent-teacher, student-teacher, student-student, etc.):

4. Discipline:

5. Division of students in math and reading groups:

208

6. Extended Day:

7. Field trips and assemblies:

8. Homework:

9. Neighborhood and volunteer student relations:

10. School policies (examples: lunch money, restrooms, medical attention, recess, and so forth):

11. Special education, counseling programs, diagnostic testing:

12. Student safety:

13. Teachers and principals:

14. Other:

☐ YES, I want to participate in one or more of the meetings. I am interested in the following areas:_____

☐ YES, I am interested in being a member of this committee.

Name: _____ Grade _____ Date: _____
     You do not have to sign   Child or children's
                                       grade level

PLEASE RETURN BY FEBRUARY 28, 1978

Social Interaction Observation Guide

Observer:
Date of Coding:

AV Identification
  Type:
  Date:
  Place:
  Basis of Choice of Subject:

Key Subject
  Name:
  Grade: Homeroom teacher:
  Sex: Male/Female
  Volunteer/Neighborhood

Number of Interactants: __bb __wb   __b&b __w&b
                           __bg __wg   __b&g __w&g

Situational Context (constraint on behavior): __teacher's presence or directive
                                                     __weather
                                                     __termination of recess
                                                     __other

Action Description:
Time:_____   Activity Sequences:
Type of Play (these may alternate)
__organized game: __soccer __baseball __football __jump rope __other
_____informal play
_____play equipment (swing, seesaw)
_____body exploration, part (for example, hair, skin)_____
_____play aggression, _____fight _____chase _____capture
_____vertigo (twirling, spinning)
_____sudden spurt of energy, hop_____ skip_____ other_____
_____stunts, balancing on rail_____, other_____
_____dance _____phrase of two movements _____cheer _____ring play
    _____line play

Interactive Modes:
_____leader gives direction
_____greeting in nonagonistic manner
_____greeting in agonistic manner (slapping)
_____aggressive attack

bite
choke
embrace
gesture threateningly
hit
hold
kick
pinch
pull
push
spit
throw
touch
trip
twist
wrestle

_____number of contacts
_____length of time

Body part:_____
hair
head
face
hand
arm
shoulder
chest
back
waist
buttocks
groin
thigh
leg
ankle
feet

_____number of parts touched

Active Reaction:
_____follows leader
_____greeting in nonagonistic manner
_____greeting in agonistic manner

Passive Interaction:
_____taking it, submission
_____contact avoidance (moving away, withdrawing)

211

Affect (play signal):_____
  happy (smile, laughter)
  serious (concentrates on someone or thing, gaze focus)
  anxious (tense movement, tense laughter or smile)
  angry (agonistic gestures, bites lip, clenches fist)
  aversive (withdraws, moves away, turns up nose, grimaces)

Verbalizations:_____
  affirmation (ok, um-hmm)
  possession (it's mine)
  negative comment
  imperative (command)
  insult (curse word, your mama)
  criticism (that's not nice)
  praise
  threat to tell teacher (I'm gonna tell)
  threat (I'll beat you up)
  suggestion (let's)
  protest (stop)
  encouragement (go on get it)

212

WORKS CITED

Selected references on desegregation are asterisked for newcomers to the subject.

Abrahams, Roger D., and John F. Szwed. 1975. Black English: An Essay Review. *American Anthropologist* 77, no. 2:329–35.

Abrams, Carol; John E. Coons; and Stephen D. Sugarman. 1978. School Integration through Carrots Not Sticks. *Theory into Practice* 17, no. 1:23–31.

Aldis, Owen. 1975. *Play Fighting.* New York: Academic Press.

Alihan, M. 1970. *Corporate Etiquette.* New York: Mentor.

Allport, Gordon, W. 1954. *The Nature of Prejudice.* Cambridge, Mass.: Addison-Wesley.

*Armor, David. 1972. The Evidence on Busing. *Public Interest* 28:90–96.

Arnez, Nancy L. 1978. Implementation as a Discriminatory Process. *Journal of Negro Education* 47, no. 1:28–45.

Aronson, Elliot. 1975. Busing and Racial Tension: The Jigsaw Route to Learning and Liking. *Psychology Today* 8, no. 9:43–50.

Aronson, Elliot; Nancy Blaney; Cookie Stephen; Jev Sikes; and Matthew Snapp. 1978. *The Jigsaw Classroom.* Beverly Hills: Sage.

Auletta, Ken. 1982. *The Underclass.* New York: Vintage.

Averch, Harry A.; Stephen J. Carroll; Theodore S. Donaldson; Herbert J. Kiesling; and John Pincus. 1972. *How Effective Is Schooling? A Critical Review and Synthesis of Research Findings.* Santa Monica, Calif.: Rand Corp.

Baldassare, Mark. 1978. Human Spatial Behavior. *Annual Review of Sociology* 4:29–56.

Banks, James A. 1977. *Multiethnic Education: Practices and Promises.* Bloomington, Ind.: Phi Delta Kappa Educational Foundation.

———. 1981. *Multiethnic Education: Theory and Practice.* Boston: Allyn and Bacon.

Banks, W. Curtis; Gregory V. McQuater; and Janet L. Hubbard. 1978. Toward a Reconceptualization of the Social–Cognitive Bases of Achievement Orientations in Blacks." *Review of Educational Research* 48, no. 3:381–97.

Barbash, Fred. 1980. Three Justices Flay School Busing Plans. *Washington Post,* January 22, p. A2.

Barringer, Felicity. 1980. Students at California School Find They Can Profit from Education. *Washington Post,* November 3, p. A2.

Bateson, Gregory. 1972. *Steps to an Ecology of Mind.* New York: Balantine.

Baxter, J.D. 1970. Interpersonal Spacing in Natural Settings. *Sociometry* 33:444–56.

213

*Bell, Derrick, ed. 1980. *Shades of Brown: New Perspectivs on School Desegregation.* New York: Teachers College Press.

Berger, Peter L. 1978. *Ethics and the New Class.* Washington, D.C.: Ethics and Public Policy Center, Georgetown University. Reprint 9.

Bernstein, Basil. 1970. A Sociolinguistic Approach to Socialization: With Some Reference to Educability. In *Language and Poverty: Perspectives on a Theme,* Frederick Williams, ed. Chicago: Markham, 25–61.

———. 1972. *Class, Codes, and Social Control. Theoretical Papers.* London: Routledge and Kegan Paul.

———. 1975. *Class, Codes and Control:* vol. 3, *Towards a Therapy of Educational Transmissions.* London: Routledge and Kegan Paul.

Best, D. L.; C. E. Naylor; and J. E. Williams. 1975. Extension of Color Bias Research to Young French and Italian Children. *Journal of Cross-Cultural Psychology* 6:390–405.

Biddle, Wayne, and Margot Slade. 1982. SAT Scores in Black and White. *New York Times,* October 10, section 4, p. 8.

Birdwhistell, Ray L. 1970. *Kinesics and Context: Essays on Body Motion Communication.* Philadelphia: University of Pennsylvania Press.

Blakely, Mary M. 1983. Southeast Asian Refugee Parents: An Inquiry into Home–School Communication and Understanding. *Anthropology and Education Quarterly* 14, no. 1:43–68.

Blalock, Herbert M., Jr. 1979. *Black–White Relations in the 1980s.* New York: Praeger.

Blank, Rolf K.; Robert A. Dentler; D. Catherine Baltzell; and Kent Chabotar. 1983. *Survey of Magnet Schools: Analyzing a Model for Quality Integrated Education.* Report no. 300-81-0420 for the U.S. Washington, D.C.: Dept. of Education, Office of Planning, Budget, and Evaluation.

Bloch, Alfred M. 1978. Combat Neurosis in Inner-City Schools. *American Journal of Psychiatry* 135, no. 10:1189–92.

Bloom, Lois. 1976. Child Language and the Origins of Language. In *Origins and Evolution of Language and Speech,* Stevan R. Harnad, Horst D. Steklis, Jane Lancaster, eds. New York: Annals of the New York Academy of Sciences no. 280:170–172.

Blumer, Herbert. 1969. *Symbolic Interactionism: Perspective and Method.* Englewood Cliffs, N.J.: Prentice-Hall.

Bowles, Samuel, and Herbert Gintis. 1976. *Schooling in Capitalist America.* New York: Basic Books.

Bradley, Laurence A., and Gifford W. Bradley. 1977. The Academic Achievement of Black Students in Desegregated Schools: A Critical Review. *Review of Educational Research* 47:399–449.

Brannigan, Christopher R., and David A. Humphries. 1972. Human Nonverbal Behaviour: A Means of Communication. In *Ethological Studies of Child Behaviour,* N. Blurton-Jones, ed. Cambridge, Eng.: University Press, 27–63.

Brodsky, Carroll M. 1977. Long-Term Work Stress in Teachers and Prison Guards. *Journal of Occupational Medicine* 19, no. 2:133–38.

Brophy, Jere. 1982. Classroom Mangagement and Learning. *American Education* (March): 20–3.

Brophy, Jere E., and Thomas L. Good. 1974. *Teacher–Student Relationships: Causes and Consequences.* New York: Holt, Rinehart, and Winston.

Burgess, John. 1981. "Rainbow" Generates Rosemary Hills Controversy. *Washington Post,* June 10, p. C1, 10.

Business Advisory Committee, Education Commission of the States. 1985. *Reconnecting Youth*. Washington, D.C.: Education Commission of the States.

Butz, William P., et al. 1982. *Demographic Challenges in America's Future*. Santa Monica, Calif.: Rand Corp.

Cabinet Council on Human Resources Working Group on School Violence/ Discipline. 1984. *Disorder in Our Public Schools*. U.S. Dept. of Education, office of the Deputy Secretary for Planning, Budget, and Evaluation memorandum.

Caditz, Judith. 1976. *White Liberals in Transition*. New York: Spectrum.

Caillois, Roger. 1961. *Man, Play, and Games*. New York: Free Press.

Cassell, Joan. 1977. The Relationship of Observer to Observed in Peer Group Research. *Human Organization* 36, no. 4:412–16.

———. 1978. *A Fieldwork Manual for Studying Desegregated Schools*. Washington, D.C.: National Institute of Education.

———. 1980. Ethical Principles for Conducting Fieldwork. *American Anthropologist* 82, no. 1:28–41.

Cassell, Joan, and Murray L. Wax, eds. 1980. Ethical Problems of Field Work. *Social Problems* 27, no. 3.

*Cataldo, Everett F.; Michael W. Giles; and Douglas S. Gatlin. 1978. *School Desegregation Policy: Compliance, Avoidance, and the Metropolitan Remedy*. Lexington, Mass.: Lexington Books.

Cazden, Courtney; Vera P. John; and Dell Hymes, eds. 1972. *Functions of Language in the Classroom*. New York: Teachers College Press.

Chance, Michael R. A., and Ray R. Larsen, eds. 1976. *The Social Structure of Attention*. New York: Wiley.

Cheek, Donald K. 1976. *Assertive Black . . . Puzzled White*. San Luis Obispo Calif.: Impact.

Children's Defense Fund. 1985. *Black and White Children in America: Key Facts*. Washington, D.C.

Chronicle of Higher Education. 1986. Black Anti-Semitism Is Said to Stem from White Fundamentalist Culture, April 23, p. 7.

Cicourel, Aaron V.; Kenneth H. Jennings; Sybillyn H. M. Jennings; Kenneth C. W. Leiter; Robert W. MacKay; Hugh Mehan; and David R. Roth. 1974. *Language Use and School Performance*. New York: Academic Press.

Clark, Kenneth B. 1965. *Dark Ghetto*. New York: Harper and Row.

Clark, Reginald. 1983. *Family Life and School Achievement: Why Poor Black Children Succeed or Fail*. Chicago: University of Chicago Press.

Clark, Wood Wilson, Jr. 1977. *"Violence in the Public Schools."* Ph.D. diss., University of California, Berkeley.

Clement, Dorothy; Margaret Eisenhart; and Joe R. Harding. 1979. Veneer of Harmony: Social–Race Relations in a Southern Desegregated School. In *Desegregated Schools: Appraisals of an American Experiment*, Ray C. Rist, ed. New York: Academic Press, 15–64.

Clymer, Adam. 1981. Polls Find Black–White Gaps on Variety of Issues. *New York Times*, August 28, p. B7.

Cohen, David K., and Eleanor Farrar. 1977. Power to the Parents: The Story of Education Vouchers. *Public Interest* 48:72–97.

Cohen, Elizabeth G. 1980. Design and Redesign of the Desegregated School: Problems of Status, Power, and Conflict. In *School Desegregation: Past, Present, and Future*, Walter G. Stephan and Joe R. Feagin, eds. New York: Plenum, 251–80.

Cohen, Elizabeth G., and Susan S. Roper. 1972. Modification of Interracial Interaction Disability: An Application of Status Characteristics Theory. *American Sociological Review* 36:643–57.

Coleman, James S., Ernest Q. Campbell, et al. 1966. *Equality of Educational Opportunity.* Washington, D.C.: Government Printing Office.

———. 1981. The Role of Incentives in School Desegregation. In *Race and Schooling in the City,* Adam Yarmolinsky, Lance Liebman, and Corinne S. Schelling, eds. Cambridge: Harvard University Press, 182–93.

Coles, Robert. 1967. *The South Goes North.* Vol. 8 of *Children in Crisis.* Boston: Little, Brown, and Co.

Collins, Carter H.; Oliver Moles; and Mary Cross. 1982. *The Home–School Connection: Selected Partnership Programs in Large Cities.* Boston: Institute for Responsive Education.

Collins, Thomas W., and George W. Noblit. 1978. *Stratification and Resegregation: The Case of Crossover High School.* Report to the National Institute of Education.

Comer, James P., and Alvin F. Poussaint. 1975. *Black Child Care.* New York: Simon and Schuster.

Comfort, Louise K. 1982. *Education Policy and Evaluation: A Context for Change.* New York: Pergamon.

Congressional Research Service and Congressional Budget Office. 1985. *A Study of Trends and Policy, 1968–1984.* Washington, D.C.: Government Printing Office.

Connolly, Patrick Raymond. 1973. "An Investigation of Personal Space and Its Meaning among Black and White Americans." Ph.D. diss., University of Iowa.

Cook, Thomas; David Armor; Robert Crain; Norman Miller; Walter Stephan; Herbert Walberg; and Paul Wortman. 1984. *School Desegregation and Black Achievement.* Washington, D.C.: National Institute of Education.

Coons, John E., and Stephen D. Sugarman. 1978. *Education by Choice: The Case for Family Control.* Berkeley: University of California Press.

Coons, John E. 1980. My Turn: The Public-School Monopoly. *Newsweek,* June 9, p. 21.

Corsaro, William A. 1979. Young Children's Conception of Status and Role. *Sociology of Education* 52, no. 1:46–58.

Cosnow, Jeffrey E. 1979. Cultural Adaptation among Lower-Class Children. Paper presented at the annual meeting of the Society for Applied Anthropology, March.

Crain, R. L., and C. S. Weisman. 1972. *Discrimination, Personality, and Achievement: A Survey of Northern Blacks.* New York: Seminar Press.

Crain, Robert L., and Rita E. Mahard. 1978. *National Longitudinal Study: The Influence of High School Racial Composition on Black College Attendance and Test Performance.* Washington, D.C.: National Center for Educational Statistics, Government Printing Office.

*Crain, Robert L.; Rita E. Mahard; and Ruth E. Narot. 1982. *Making Desegregation Work: How Schools Create Social Climates.* Cambridge, Mass.: Ballinger.

Crain, Robert L., et al., 1985. Finding Niches: Desegregated Students Sixteen Years Later. Forthcoming unpublished report cited in *New York Times.* Study Finds Desegregation Is an Effective Social Tool. September 17, pp. C1, 13.

Cuddy, D. L. 1982. A Solution to Forced Busing. *Human Events,* (October 30): 12–13.

216

Curtis, Lynn A. 1975. *Violence, Race, and Culture.* Lexington, Mass.: D. C. Heath.

Dallas Times Herald. 1978. Teacher Seeks Funds to Hire Bodyguards. June 17, p. 26-C.

Damon, William. 1977. *The Social World of the Child.* San Francisco: Jossey-Bass.

Davis, Jean E. 1974. *Coping with Disruptive Behavior.* Washington, D.C.: National Education Association.

Davis, Martha, and Janet Skupien. 1982. *Body Movement and Nonverbal Communication: An Annotated Bibliography, 1971–1980.* Bloomington: Indiana University Press.

DeBruyn, Robert. 1978. Handling Stress . . . Ours and Students. *The Master Teacher* 8, no. 29 (March 27).

*Dentler, Robert A., and Marvin B. Scott. 1981. *Schools on Trial: An Inside Account of the Boston Desegregation Case.* Cambridge, Mass.: ABT Books.

Dillman, Caroline M. 1977. Ethical Problems in Social Science Research Peculiar to Participant Observation. *Human Organization* 36, no. 4: 405–7.

DiPrete, Thomas; with Chandra Muller; and Nora Schaeffer. 1982. *Discipline and Order in American High Schools.* Washington, D.C.: National Center for Educational Statistics.

Dollard, John; Leonard Doob; Neal E. Miller; O. H. Mowers; and Robert F. Sears. 1939. *Frustration and Aggression.* New Haven: Oxford University Press.

Dullea, Georgia. 1987. For the Conflicts of Youth, Help From a Peer. *New York Times,* February 9, pp. 1, B5.

Dunaway, David King. 1979. Halting White Flight. *New York Times,* January 4, p. A19.

Duncan, Starkey, Jr., and Donald W. Fiske. 1977. *Face-to-Face Interaction.* Hillsdale, N.J.: L. Erlbaum.

Dworkin, Anthony Gary. 1986. *Teacher Burnout in the Public Schools.* Albany: State University of New York Press.

Eckland, Bruce K., and Louise B. Henderson. 1981. *College Attainment Four Years after High School.* Washington, D.C.: National Center for Educational Statistics.

Eddy, Elizabeth M. 1965. *Walk the White Line: A Profile of Urban Education.* New York: Anchor.

———. 1975. Educational Innovation and Desegregation: A Case Study of Symbolic Realignment. *Human Organization* 34, no. 2: 163–72.

Epps, Edgar G. 1975. Impact of School Desegregation in Aspirations, Self-Concepts and Other Aspects of Personality. *Law and Contemporary Problems,* Spring 300-13.

Erickson, Frederick. 1975. Gatekeeping and the Melting Pot. *Harvard Educational Review* 45, no. 1: 44–70.

———. 1979. Talking down: Some Cultural Sources of Miscommunication in Interracial Interviews. In *Nonverbal Behavior: Applications and Cultural Implications,* Aaron Wolfgang, ed. New York: Academic Press, 100–26.

Erikson, Erik H. 1963. *Childhood and Society.* 2d ed. New York: W. W. Norton.

———. 1977. *Toys and Reason.* New York: W. W. Norton.

Eron, Leonard D. 1983. The Consistency of Aggressive Behavior Across Time and Situations. Paper presented at the annual meeting of the American Psychological Association.

Eron, Leonard D.; Leopold O. Walder; and Monroe M. Lefkowitz. 1971. *Learning of Aggression in Children.* Boston: Little, Brown, and Co.

217

Estes, Robert, and Kent Skipper. 1976. *Comprehensive Evaluation of the Pacesetter Program.* Richardson Independent School District contracted report, December.

Evans, Eli. 1978. The City, South and Carribean. *New York Times,* June 27, p. 27.

Everhart, Robert B. 1983. *Reading, Writing, and Resistance: Adolescence and Labor in a Junior High School.* Boston: Routledge and Kegan Paul.

Fagan, J. E., III. 1974. Infant Color Perception. *Science* 183:973–75.

Farb, Peter. 1974. *Word Play: What Happens When People Talk.* New York: Knopf.

Farrer, Claire R. 1981. Play and Interethnic Communication. In *The Anthropological Study of Play: Problems and Prospects.* Proceedings of the first annual meeting of the Association for the Anthropological Study of Play, David F. Lancy and B. Allan Tindall, eds. Cornwall, N.Y.: Leisure Press, 86–92.

Feinberg, Lawrence. 1978. Colemen Now Discounts Advantages of School Desegregation. *Washington Post,* September 18, pp. A1, 5.

———. 1979. College Board Tests Show a Black–White Disparity. *Washington Post,* December 9, p. A6.

———. 1980. D.C. Losing Middle-Income Black Families to Suburbs. *Washington Post,* April 6, pp. B1, B5.

Fine, Gary Alan, and Barry Glassner. 1979. Participant Observation with Children: Promise and Problems. *Urban Life* 8, no. 2:153–74.

Finkelstein, Neal, and Ron Haskins. 1983. Kindergarten Children Prefer Same-Color Peers. *Child Development* 54, no. 2:502–8.

Fisher, Marc. 1987. Confronting Teen-Age Sexuality: Dallas School Clinic Offers Birth Control Devices. *Washington Post,* April 14, pp. A1, 8.

Fiske, Edward B. 1979. Studies Challenge Assumed Limits on Improving Schools in Inner City. *New York Times,* December 26, pp. B1, 10.

———. 1980. New Teaching Method Produces Impressive Gains. *New York Times,* March 30, pp. 1, 37.

Flint, Jerry. 1979. Jobless Rate of Blacks Still Rising despite a Twenty-Five-Year Federal Effort. *New York Times,* March 13, pp. A1, B6.

Foster, Herbert L. 1974. *Ribbin', Jivin', and Playin' the Dozens: The Unrecognized Dilemma of Inner-City Schools.* Cambridge, Mass.: Ballinger.

Franklin, John Hope. 1978. *From Slavery to Freedom: A History of American Negroes.* 5th Ed. New York: Alfred Knopf.

Frey, William H. 1979. Central City White Flight: Racial and Nonracial Causes. *American Sociological Review* 44, no. 3:425–88.

Gallup Poll. 1978. Decline Continues in U.S. Religious, Racial Prejudice. *Washington Post,* November 23, p. A19.

Gallup, George. 1982. The Fourteenth Annual Gallup Poll of the Public's Attitudes toward the Public Schools. *Phi Delta Kappan* 64, no. 1:37–50.

Galloway, Charles M. 1976. *Silent Language in the Classroom.* Bloomington, Ind.: Phi Delta Kappa.

Gans, Herbert J. 1962. *The Urban Villagers: Group and Class in the Life of Italian-Americans.* New York: Free Press of Glencoe.

Garvey, Catherine. 1977. *Play.* Cambridge: Harvard University Press.

Gay, Geneva, and Roger D. Abrahams. 1973. Does the Pot Melt, Boil, or Brew? Black Children and White Assessment Procedures. *Journal of School Psychology* 2, no. 4:330–40.

Genovese, Eugene. 1974. *Roll Jordan Roll: The World the Slaves Made.* New York: Pantheon.

Gerard, Harold B., and Norman Miller, eds. 1975. *School Desegregation.* New York: Plenum.

Giles, Michael W. 1978. White Enrollment Stability of School Desegregation: A Two-Level Analysis. *American Sociological Review* 43, no. 6:848–64.

Giles, Raymond H., Jr. 1972. "Black and Ethnic Studies Programs at Public Schools: Elementary and Secondary." Ed.D. diss., University of Massachusetts.

Gilliam, Dorothy. 1978. Black Programming on TV "At Death's Door." *Dallas Times Herald,* May 17, pp. 1, 7.

Gilmore, Perry. 1983. Spelling "Mississippi": Recontextualizing a Literacy-Related Speech Event. *Anthropology and Education* 14, no. 4:235–55.

Giroux, Henry A. 1983. Theories of Reproduction and Resistance in the New Sociology of Education: A Critical Analysis. *Harvard Educational Review* 53, no. 30: 257–93.

Glick, Joseph; K. Alison; and Clarke Stewart, eds. 1978. *The Development of Social Understanding.* New York: Gardner.

Goffman, Erving. 1959. *The Presentation of Self in Everyday Life.* New York: Doubleday.

———. 1963. *Stigma: Notes on the Management of Spoiled Identity.* Englewood Cliffs, N.J.: Prentice-Hall.

———. 1974. *Frame Analysis: An Essay on the Organization of Experience.* Cambridge: Harvard University Press.

Gold, Martin, and David Mann. 1977. Can Alternative School Programs Lead to Greater Safety in American Schools? *Institute for Social Research Newsletter.* (October–November.)

Goodlad, John I. 1984. *A Place Called School.* New York: McGraw-Hill.

Goodman, John, Jr. 1979. Reasons for Moves out of and into Large Cities. *Journal of the American Planning Association* 45 (October):407–16.

Goodman, M. E. 1970. *The Culture of Childhood.* New York: Teachers College Press.

Goodwin, Marjorie Harnees. 1982. Processes of Dispute Management among Urban Black Children. *American Ethnologist* 9, no. 1:76–96.

Gordon, Milton M. 1978. *Human Nature, Class, and Ethnicity.* New York: Oxford University Press.

Gordon, Suzanne. 1977. Pain Is Good for You. *New York Times,* December 13, p. 43.

Goss, Emanuel V.; James O: Griffin; and Vivian T. Starks. 1966. *Hamilton Park High School Community Study Report: A Summary.* Hamilton Park, Tex.: Hamilton Park High School Community.

Grambs, Jean Dresden. 1968. *Intergroup Education: Methods and Materials.* Englewood Cliffs, N.J.: Prentice-Hall.

———. 1979. *Multicultural Education; Issues without Answers.* The IACTE monograph, no. 1. January.

Gregory, Dick. 1964. *Nigger.* New York: Pocket Cardinal.

Grier, William H., and Price M. Cobbs. 1968. *Black Rage.* New York: Basic Books.

Gruber, Howard E., and J. Jacques Voneche, eds. 1978. *The Essential Piaget: An Interpretive Reference and Guide.* New York: Basic Books.

Gumperz, John J. 1978. The Conversational Analysis of Interethnic Communication. In *Interethnic Communication* (Southern Anthropological Society Proceedings, No. 12) E. Lamar Ross, ed. Athens: The University of Georgia Press, 13–21.

219

Gustaitis, Rosa. 1979. Riding L.A.'s Troubled School Buses. *Washington Post,* June 10, p. D2.

Hakken, David. 1978. Workers' Education and the Reproduction of Working-Class Culture in Sheffield, England. Paper presented to the annual meeting of the American Anthropological Association.

Halberstadt, Amy G., 1985. Race, Socioeconomic Status, and Nonverbal Behavior. In *Multichannel Integrations of Nonverbal Behavior,* A. W. Siegman and S. Feldstein, ed. Hillsdale, N.J.: L. Erlbaum, 227–66.

Hall, Edward T. 1974. *Handbook for Proxemic Research.* Washington, D.C.: Society for the Anthropology of Visual Communication.

Hall, Stuart, and Tony Jefferson. 1976. *Resistance Through Rituals: Youth Subcultures in Postwar Britain.* London: Hutchinson.

Hall, William S., and Roy O. Freedle. 1975. *Culture and Language: The Black American Experience.* Washington, D.C.: Hemisphere.

Halle, David. 1978. Joking Relations and the Values of the Industrial Working Class. Paper presented at the American Anthropological Association.

Hanna, Judith Lynne. 1976. "The Anthropology of Dance Ritual: Nigeria's Ubakala Nkwa di Iche Iche." Ph.D. diss., Columbia University.

———. 1979. American Folk Dance. In *American Folklore Cassette Lecture Series,* Henning Cohen, ed. Deland, Fl.: Everitt Edwards.

———. 1980. African Dance Research: Past, Present, and Future. *Africana Journal* 11, no. 1:33–51.

———. 1982. Public Social Policy and the Children's World: Implications of Ethnographic Research for Desegregated Schooling. In *Doing the Ethnography of Schooling,* George D. Spindler, ed. New York: Holt, Rinehart, and Winston, 316–55.

———. 1983a. *The Performer–Audience Connection: Emotion to Metaphor in Dance and Society.* Austin: University of Texas Press.

———. 1983b. The Mentality and Matter of Dance. *Art Education* (special issue: Art and the Mind) 36, no. 2:42–46.

———. 1984. Black/White Nonverbal Differences, Dance, and Dissonance. In *Nonverbal Behavior: Perspectives, Applications, Intercultural Insights,* Aaron Wolfgang, ed. Toronto: C. J. Hogrefe, 349–85.

———. 1986a. Movement in African Performance. In *Theatrical Movement: A Bibliographic Anthology,* Bob Fleshman, ed. Metuchen, N.J.: Scarecrow. 561–85.

———. 1986b. Interethnic Communication in Children's Own Dance, Play, and Protest. In *Interethnic Communication* (vol. 10, International and Intercultural Communication Annual), Young K. Kim, ed. Newbury, Calif.: Sage, 176–98.

———. 1987. *To Dance Is Human: A Theory of Nonverbal Communication.* Chicago: University of Chicago Press. Original, University of Texas, 1979.

———. 1988a. *Dance, Sex, and Gender: Signs of Identity, Dominance, Defiance, and Desire.* Chicago: University of Chicago Press.

———. 1988b. *Dance and Stress: Resistance, Reduction, and Euphoria.* New York: AMS Press.

Hanna, Judith Lynne, and William John Hanna. 1981. *Urban Dynamics in Black Africa.* 2d ed. Hawthorne, N.Y.: Aldine.

Hare, Bruce R. 1977. Racial and Socioeconomic Variations in Preadolescent Area-Specific and General Esteem. *International Journal of Intercultural Relations* 1, no. 3.

220

————. 1978. Self-Perception and Academic Achievement: Variations in a Desegregated Setting. Paper presented at the annual meeting of the American Association of Psychiatry.

Harrington, Charles. 1973. Pupils, Peers, and Politics. In *Learning and Culture: Proceedings of the American Ethnological Society 1972*, Solon T. Kimball and Jacquetta H. Burnett, eds. Seattle: University of Washington Press, 131–62.

————. 1975. A Psychological Anthropologist's View of Ethnicity and Schooling. *IRCD Bulletin* 10, no. 4:2–12.

Harrison-Ross, Phyllis, and Barbara Wyden. 1973. *The Black Child*. Berkeley, Calif.: Medallion.

Havard, Bronson. 1978. Who Kills Whom in Dallas? *Dallas Times Herald*, June 30, p. B2.

Hawley, Willie D. 1980. *Increasing the Effectiveness of School Desegregation: Lessons from the Research*. Durham, N.C.: Center for Educational Policy, Institute of Policy Sciences and Public Affairs, Duke University.

Hazzard-Gordon, Katrina. 1983a. Afro-American Core Culture Social Dance: An Examination of Four Aspects of Meaning. *Dance Research Journal* 15, no. 2:21–26.

————. 1983b. "Atibas a Coming': The Rise of Social Dance Formation in Afro-American Culture." Ph.D. diss., Cornell University.

Hechinger, Fred M. 1979a. About Education: "Frills" in Schools Are Often Basic. *New York Times*, Janaury 23, p. C5.

———— 1979b. Teachers Now Seek Parental Participation. *New York Times*, November 20, p. C4.

————. 1980. Is One-Parent Household a Handicap for Pupils? *New York Times*, September 30, p. C1.

Heider, Eleanor Rosch. 1971. Style and Accuracy of Verbal Communications within and between Social Classes. *Journal of Personality and Social Psychology* 18:33–47.

Heinig, Ruth Miriam Beall. 1975. "A Descriptive Study of Teacher–Pupil Tactile Communication in Grades Four through Six." Ph.D. diss., University of Pittsburgh.

Henley, Nancy. 1977. *Body Politics: Power, Sex, and Nonverbal Communication*. Englewood Cliffs, N.J.: Prentice-Hall.

Henry, Jules. 1957. Attitude Organization in Elementary School Classrooms. *American Journal of Orthopsychiatry* 27, no. 1:117–33.

Hentoff, Nat. 1979. The Principal Principle. *Village Voice*, January 15, pp. 64–65.

Herbers, John. 1978. Black–White Split Persists a Decade after Warning. *New York Times*, February 26, p. 28.

————. 1979. Changes in Society Holding Black Youth in Jobless Web. *New York Times*, March 11, pp. 1, 44.

Herndon, James. 1968. *The Way It Spozed to Be*. New York: Simon and Shuster.

Hershenson, Maurice. 1964. Visual Discrimination in the Human Newborn. *Journal of Comparative and Physiological Psychology* 58:270–76.

Hill-Burnett, Jacquetta. 1978. Developing Anthropological Knowledge through Application. In *Applied Anthropology in America*, Elizabeth M. Eddy and William L. Partridge, eds. New York: Columbia University Press, 112–18.

Hochschild. Arlie Russell. 1979. Emotion, Work, Feeling, Rules, and Social Structure. *American Journal of Sociology* 85, no. 3:551–75.

Hollingshead, A. B. 1949. *Elmtown's Youth*. New York: Wiley.

Horowitz, Donald. 1977. *The Courts and Social Policy.* Washington, D.C.: Brookings Institution.

Huesmann, L. Rowell; Leonard D. Eron; and Monroe M. Lefkowitz. 1984. Stability of Aggression over Time and Generations. *Developmental Psychology* 20, no. 6: 1120–34.

Huizinga, Johan. 1955. *Homo Ludens: a Study of the Play Element in Culture.* Boston: Beacon.

Hurn, Christopher J. 1978. *The Limits and Possibilities of Schooling: An Introduction to the Sociology of Education.* Boston: Allyn and Bacon.

Ianni, Francis A. J.; Mercer Sullivan; Margaret Orr; Samuel Henry; and John Mavros. 1978. *A Field Study of Culture Contact and Desegregation in an Urban High School.* Report to National Institute of Education.

Jacob, Herbert, and Robert Lineberry. 1982. *Urban Crime.* Washington, D.C.: National Institute of Justice.

Johnson, Kenneth R. 1976. Black Kinesics: Some Nonverbal Communication Patterns in the Black Culture. In *Intercultural Communication: A Reader.* 2d ed. Larry A. Samovar and Richard E. Porter, eds. Belmont, Calif.: Wadsworth, 259–68.

Jones, Bessie, and Bess Lomax Hawes. 1972. *Step It down: Games, Plays, Songs, and Stories from the Afro-American Heritage.* New York: Harper and Row.

Jones, Lyle V. 1984. White–Black Achievement Differences: The Narrowing Gap. *American Psychologist* 39, no. 11:1207–13.

Kando, Thomas W. 1983. Report Shows Excessive Concern for Underdogs. *American Sociological Association Footnotes* (April 6).

Kardiner, Abram, and Lionel Ovesey. 1951. *The Mark of Oppression.* New York: Norton.

Karlin, Muriel Schoenbrun, and Regina Berger. 1972. *Discipline and the Disruptive Child: A Practical Guide for Elementary Teachers.* West Nyack, N.Y.: Parker.

Killian Lewis M. 1973. White Southerners. In *Through Different Eyes: Black and White Perspectives on American Race Relations,* Peter I. Rose, Stanley Rothman, and William J. Wilson, eds. New York: Oxford University Press, 89–113.

King, Martin Luther, Jr. 1967. *Where Do We Go from Here, Chaos or Community?* New York: Harper and Row.

Kluger, Richard. 1976. *Simple Justice: The History of Brown v. Board of Education and Black America's Struggle for Equality.* New York: Knopf.

Kochman, Thomas. 1971. Cross-culture Communication: Contrasting Perspectives, Conflicting Sensibilities. *Florida FL Reporter* 9:3–17.

———. 1977. Review of William W. Gage, ed. *Language in Its Social Setting.* Washington, D.C.: Anthropological Society of Washington, 1974, *Language in Society* 6, no. 1:49–64.

———. 1981. *Black and White: Styles in Conflict.* Chicago: University of Chicago Press.

Kounin, Jacob S. 1970. *Discipline and Group Management in Classrooms.* New York: Holt, Rinehart, and Winston.

Kraft, Joseph. 1978. A Rising Wave of Self-Indulgence. *Dallas Times Herald,* June 13, p. C3.

Kronus, Sidney. 1971. *The Black Middle Class.* Columbus, Ohio: Charles Merrill.

Krug, Mark. 1976. *The Melting of the Ethnics.* Bloomington, Ind.: Phi Delta Kappa.

Kunz, Phillip R., and Evan T. Peterson. 1977. Family Size, Birth Order, and Academic Achievement. *Social Biology* 24, no. 2:144–48.

Labov, William. 1972. *Language in the Inner City: Studies in the Black English Vernacular*. Philadelphia: University of Pennsylvania.

LaFrance, Marianne, and Clara Mayo. 1976. Racial Differences in Gaze Behavior during Conversations: Two Systematic Observational Studies. *Journal of Personality and Social Psychology* 33, no. 3: 547–55.

———. 1978. *Moving Bodies: Nonverbal Communication in Social Relationships*. Monterey, Calif.: Brooks Cole.

———. 1978b. On the Acquisition of Nonverbal Communication: A Review. *Merrill-Palmer Quarterly* 24:213–28.

Landis, Dan; Penny L. McGrew; and Harry C. Triandis. 1975. Behavioural Intentions and Norms of Urban School Teachers. In *Race and Education across Cultures*, Gajendra K. Verma and Christopher Bagley, eds. London: Heinemann, 117–44.

Larkin, Ralph W. 1979. *Suburban Youth in Cultural Crisis*. New York: Oxford University Press.

Larson, Heidi. 1980. Arab and Israeli Children Show That Play Habits Are Universal. *New York Times*, January 19, p. 20.

Latimer, Leah Y. 1986. Will Integration Hurt My Black Son's Education? *Washington Post*, April 20, p. C1.

Lawton, Dennis. 1968. *Social Class, Language, and Education*. London: Routledge and Kegan Paul.

Leacock, Eleanor Burke. 1969. *Teaching and Learning in City Schools: A Comparative Study*. New York: Basic Books.

———. 1977. Race and the "We-They Dichotomy" in Culture and Classroom. *Anthropology and Education Quarterly* 7, no. 2: 152–58.

LeCompte, Margaret. 1978. Learning to Work: The Hidden Curriculum of the Classroom. *Anthropology and Education Quarterly* 9, no. 1: 22–37.

Lefkowitz, Bernard. 1985. Renegotiating Society's Contract with the Public Schools. *Carnegie Quarterly* 29, no. 4:30, no. 1: 1–4, 6–11.

Lefkowitz, Monroe M.; Leonard D. Eron; Leopold O. Walder, and L. Rowell Huesmann. 1977. *Growing up to Be Violent: A Longitudinal Study of the Development of Aggression*. New York: Pergamon.

———. 1983. Symposium on "Consistency of Aggression and Its Correlates over Twenty Years." Presented at the annual meeting of the American Psychological Association.

Lerner, Barbara. 1972. *Political Impotence and Personal Disintegration*. Baltimore: Johns Hopkins.

Levin, Henry M. 1985. *The Educationally Disadvantaged: A National Crisis*. Philadelphia: Public/Private Ventures.

Levine, Lawrence W. 1977. *Culture and Black Conscience: Afro-American Folk Thought from Slavery to Freedom*. New York: Oxford University Press.

Levine, Marsha, ed. 1985. *The Private Sector in the Public School: Can It Improve Education?* Washington, D.C.: American Enterprise Institute for Public Policy Research.

Lieske, Joel A. 1978. Group Disorders in Urban Schools: The Effects of Racial Desegregation and Social Emancipation. *Urban Affairs Quarterly* 14, no. 1: 79–101.

Lightfoot, Sarah Lawrence. 1978. *Worlds Apart: Relationships between Families and Schools*. New York: Basic Books.

Lindsey, Robert. 1980. School Integration Looks More Than Ever Like a Lost Horizon. *New York Times*, August 24, p. E5.

Long, Nicholas J.; William C. Morse; Ruth G. Newman. 1976. *Conflict in the Classroom: The Education of Emotionally Disturbed Children.* 3d ed. Belmont, Calif.: Wadsworth.

Loury, Glenn C. 1985. The Moral Quandry of the Black Community. *Public Interest* 79:9–22.

Lubow, Arthur, and Jeff B. Copeland. 1978. How to Act Tough. *Newsweek,* July 10, p. 69.

Lundsgaarde, Henry P. 1977. *Murder in Space City: A Cultural Analysis of Houston Homicide Patterns.* New York: Oxford University Press.

McDermott, Raymond P. 1974. Achieving School Failure: An Anthropological Approach to Illiteracy and Social Stratification. In *Education and Cultural Process,* George Spindler, ed. New York: Holt, Rinehart, and Winston, 82–118.

———. 1976. "Kids Make Sense: An Ethnographic Account of the Interactional Management of Success and Failure in One First-Grade Classroom." Ph.D. diss., Stanford University.

McDermott, Raymond P., and Kenney Gospodinoff. 1979. Social Contexts for Ethnic Borders and School Failure. In *Nonverbal Behavior: Applications and Cultural Implications,* Aron Wolfgang, ed. New York: Academic Press, 175–96.

McGrath, Peter. 1978. The Middle Class Is Mad as Hell. *Washingtonian* 14, no. 1: 150–54.

McGrath, Peter, with Diane Weathers. 1985. Breaking the Code. *Newsweek,* October 21, pp. 84–5.

Mackay, Robert W. 1973. Children and Models of Conceptions of Socialization. *Recent Sociology* no. 5:27–43.

McLaughlin, Barry. 1982. *Language Learning in Bilingual Instruction: A Literature Review.* Washington, D.C.: National Institute of Education.

Maeroff, Gene I.. 1980. Inner-City Schools Show Signs of Progress. *New York Times,* January 16, p. Ed-1.

———. 1981. Discipline Leads Concerns in Poll on Schools. *New York Times,* August 23, p. 32.

———. 1986 Project Provides Vision and Values. *New York Times,* January 7, p. C1.

Manganyi, Noel C. 1977. *The Body, Alienation, and Racism.* New York: Nok.

Marek, Elizabeth A. 1985. Education by Decree. *New Perspectives* (Summer): 36–41.

Mark, Vernon H., and Frank R. Ervin. 1970. *Violence and the Brain.* New York: Harper and Row.

Marsh, Peter; Elizabeth Rosser; and Rom Harré. 1978. *Rules of Disorder.* London: Routledge and Kegan Paul.

Marty, Myron A. 1977. The Courts Are in the Classroom. *Chronicle of Higher Education,* December 12, p. 18.

Meier, August, and Elliott Rudwick. 1976. *From Plantation to Ghetto.* 3d ed. New York: Hill and Wang.

Merton, Robert. 1948. The Self-Fulfilling Prophecy. *Antioch Review* 8:193–210.

———. 1957. *Social Theory and Social Structure.* New York: Free Press.

Metz, Mary Haywood. 1978. *Classrooms and Corridors: The Crisis of Authority in Desegregated Secondary Schools.* Berkeley: University of California Press.

Millar, Susanna 1968. The *Psychology of Play.* Baltimore: Penguin Books.

Miller, Walter B. 1958. Lower-Class Culture as a Generating Milieu of Gang Delinquency. *Journal of Social Issues* 14, no. 3:5–19.

Mitchell-Kernan, Claudia. 1971. *Language Behavior in a Black Urban Community.* Berkeley: University of California, monographs of the Language Behavior Laboratory, no. 2, February.

———. 1972. Signifying and Marking: Two Afro-American Speech Acts. In *Directions in Sociolinguistics: Ethnography of Communication,* John Gumperz and Dell Hymes, eds. New York: Holt, Rinehart, and Winston, 161–79.

Mitchell-Kernan, Claudia, and Keith T. Kernan. 1975. Children's Insults: America and Samoa. In *Sociocultural Dimensions of Language Use,* Mary Sanches and Ben G. Blount, eds. New York: Academic Press, 307–15.

Montagu, Ashley. 1942. On the Physiology and Psychology of Swearing. *Psychiatry* 5:189–201.

———. 1967. *The Anatomy of Swearing.* New York: Macmillan Books.

———. 1986. *Touching: The Human Significance of the Skin.* 3d ed. New York: Harper & Row.

Moynihan, Daniel P. 1965. *The Negro Family: The Case of National Action.* Washington, D.C.: U.S. Department of Labor.

Mungham, Geoff, and Geoff Person. 1976. *Working-Class Youth Culture.* London: Routledge and Kegal Paul.

Muscatine, Alison. 1981. Chevy Chase Struggles over School Integration. *Washington Post,* August 25, p. B1.

Myrdal, Gunnar. 1944. *An American Dilemma.* New York: Harper and Row.

Nasaw, David. 1979. *Schooled to Order: A Social History of Public Schooling in the U.S.* New York: Oxford University Press.

National Academy of Education. 1979. *Prejudice and Pride: The Brown Decision after Twenty-Five Years, May 17, 1954–May 17, 1979,* Stephen K. Bailey, rapporteur. Washington, D.C.: U.S. Department of Health, Education, and Welfare Education Division.

National Advisory Commission on Civil Disorders. 1968. Washington, D.C.: Government Printing Office.

National Catholic Education Association. 1979, 1987. *Catholic Schools in America: Elementary, Secondary.* Montrose, Calif.: Fisher.

National Commission on Excellence in Education. 1983. *A Nation at Risk: The Imperative for Educational Reform.* Washington, D.C.: Government Printing Office.

National Committee for Citizens in Education. nd. *Violence in Our Schools. What to Know about It—What to Do about It.* Columbia, Md.: National Committee for Citizens in Education.

National Institute of Education. 1978. *Violent Schools—Safe Schools: The Safe School Study Report to the Congress,* vol. I. Washington, D.C.: U.S. Department of Health, Education, and Welfare.

Newby, Robert G. 1979. Desegregation—Its Inequities and Paradoxes. *The Black Scholar* 2, no. 1:17–28, 67–68.

Newsweek. 1979. A New Racial Poll. February 26, pp. 48, 53.

———. 1980. Suing to Prevent Schoolyard Crime. June 2, p. 58.

Noblitt, George W., and Thomas W. Collins. 1978. Order and Disruption in a Desegregated High School. *Crime and Delinquency* 24, no. 3: 277–89.

*Noblitt, George W., and Bill Johnston, eds. 1982. *The School Principal and School Desegregation.* Springfield, Ill.: Charles C. Thomas.

Ogbu, John. 1974. *The Next Generation.* New York: Academic Press.

Olweus, Dan. 1978. *Aggression in the Schools: Bullies and Whipping Boys.* Washington, D.C.: Wiley.

O'Malley, J. Michael. 1977. Research Perspectives on Social Competence. *Merrill-Palmer Quarterly,* 23, no. 1:29–44.

Omark, Donald R., and Murray S. Edelman. 1976. The Development of Attention Structures in Young Children. In *The Social Structure of Attention,* Michael R. A. Chance and Ray R. Larsen, eds. London: Wiley, 119–51.

O'Neil, Jean F. 1985. *Making a Difference: Young People in Community Crime Prevention.* Washington, D.C.: National Crime Prevention Council.

Pasteur, Alfred B., and Ivory L. Toldson. 1982. *Roots of Soul: The Psychology of Black Expressiveness.* Garden City, N.Y.: Anchor Press/Doubleday.

*Patchen, Martin. 1982. *Black–White Contact in Schools: Its Social and Academic Effects.* West Lafayette, Ind.: Purdue University Press.

Patterson, Orlando. 1978a. Hidden Dangers in the Ethnic Revival. *New York Times,* February 20, p. A17.

———. 1978b. Inequality, Freedom, and the Equal Opportunity Doctrine. In *Equality and Social Policy,* Walter Feinberg, ed. Urbana: University of Illinois Press, 15–41.

Pettigrew, Thomas F. 1971. *Racially Separate or Together?* New York: McGraw-Hill.

———. 1974. The Case for the Racial Integration of the Schools. In *Readings in Sociology.* 5th ed. E. A. Schuler et al., eds. New York: Crowell, 373–85.

———. 1975. ed. *Racial Discrimination in the U.S.* New York: Harper and Row.

Pettigrew, Thomas F. and Kurt W. Back. 1967. Sociology in the Desegregation Process: Its Use and Disuse. In *The Use of Sociology.* Paul F. Lazarsfeld, William H. Sewell, and Harold L. Wilensky, eds. New York: Basic Books, 692–724.

Phillips, W. M., Jr. 1971. Survival Techniques of Black Americans. In *Black Life and Culture in the United States,* Rhoda L. Goldstein, ed. New York: Thomas Y. Crowell, 153–64.

Piaget, Jean. 1926. *The Language and Thought of the Child.* New York: Harcourt and Brace.

———. 1932. *The Moral Judgment of the Child.* Glencoe, Ill. The Free Press.

———. 1951. *Play, Dreams, and Imitation in Childhood.* London: Heinmann.

———. 1968. Language and Thought from the Genetic Point of View. In *Jean Piaget: Six Psychological Studies,* David Elkind, ed. New York: Random House, 18, 91.

Pilling, Doria, and Mia Kellmer Pringle. 1978. *Controversial Issues in Child Development.* New York: Schocken.

Podhoretz, Norman. 1966. My Negro Problem—and Ours. In *The Commentary Reader,* Norman Podhoretz, ed. New York: Atheneum, 376–87.

Polgar, Sylvia Knopp. 1978. Modeling Social Relations in Cross-Color Play. *Anthropology and Education Quarterly,* 9, no. 4:283–89.

Polk, Ken, and Walter E. Schafer. 1972. *Schools and Delinquency.* New York: Prentice-Hall.

Poussaint, Alvin F. 1972. *Why Blacks Kill Blacks.* New York: Emerson Hall.

Powdermaker, Hortense. 1939. *After Freedom.* New York: Viking.

———. 1949. The Channeling of Negro Aggression by the Cultural Process. In *Personality in Nature, Society, and Culture,* Clyde Kluckhohn, ed. New York: Knopf, 473–84.

Powell, Gloria Johnson. 1973. Self-Concept in White and Black Children. In *Racism and Mental Health,* Charles V. Willie et al., eds. Pittsburgh: University of Pittsburgh Press, 229–318.

Proshansky, Harold, and Peggy Newton. 1968. The Nature and Meaning of Negro Self-Identity. In *Social Class, Race, and Psychological Development*, Martin Deutsch, Irwin Katz, and Arthur Jensen, eds. New York: Holt, Rinehart, and Winston, 198–218.

Prugh, Jeff. 1979. Forty-Two-Mile Bus Ride Leads to All-Black High School. *Washington Post*, December 26, p. A3.

Ramirez, M., and D. Price-Williams. 1976. Achievement Motivation in Children of Three Ethnic Groups in the United States. *Journal of Cross-Cultural Psychology* 7:49–60.

Raspberry, William. 1978. Blacks Are More Confused. *Dallas Times Herald*, April 4, p. C3.

———. 1979a. Boys: Endangered Species? *Washington Post*, March 19, p. A23.

———. 1979b. Pressure in the Classroom. *Washington Post*, May 3, p. A19.

Ravitch, Diane. 1978a. *The Revisionist Revised. A Critique of the Radical Attack on the Schools*. New York: Basic Books.

———. 1978b. The White Flight Controversy. *The Public Interest* 51:135–49.

Read, F. 1975. Judicial Evolution of the Law of School Integration since *Brown* v. *Board of Education. Law and Contemporary Problems* 39, no. 1:7–49.

Reece, M., and R. Whitman. 1962. Expressive Movements, Warmth, and Verbal Reinforcements. *Journal of Abnormal and Social Psychology* 64:234–36.

Reich, Michael. 1973. "Racial Discriminators and the Distribution of Income." Ph.D. diss., Harvard University.

Restak, Richard M. 1979. *The Brain: The Last Frontier*. Garden City, N.Y.: Doubleday.

Rich, Dorothy. 1985. *The Forgotten Factor in School Success: The Family*. Washington, D.C.: Home and School Institute.

Rickford, John R., and Angela E. Rickford. 1976. Cut-Eye and Suck-Teeth: African Words and Gestures in New World Guise. *Journal of American Folklore* 89, no. 353:294–309.

Rist, Ray C. 1970. Student Social Class and Teacher Expectations: The Self-Fulfilling Prophecy in Ghetto Education. *Harvard Educational Review* 40:411–51.

———. 1978. *The Invisible Children: School Integration in American Society*. Cambridge: Harvard University Press.

Rist, Ray C., ed. 1979. *Desegregated Schools: Appraisals of an American Experiment*. New York: Academic Press.

Robinson, Christine Emile. 1978. The Uses of Order and Disorder in Play: An Analysis of Vietnamese Refugee Children's Play. In *Plays: Anthropological Perspectives*, Michael A. Salter, ed. West Point, N.Y.: Leisure Press, 137–44.

Rochlin, Gregory. 1973. *Man's Aggression: The Defense of the Self*. Boston: Gambit.

Rodman, Hyman. 1963. The Lower-Class Value Stretch. *Social Forces* 42, no. 2:205–15.

Roebuck, Julian B., and Ronald L. Neff. 1980. The Multiple Reality of the "Redneck": Toward a Grounded Theory of the Southern Class Structure. *Studies in Symbolic Interaction* 2:233–62.

Rohter, Larry. 1986. From 6 New Benefactors, 425 College Dreams. *New York Times*, June 21, pp. 29–30.

Rosenbaum, James E. 1980. Social Implications of Educational Grouping. In *Review of Research in Education*, David Berliner, ed. Washington, D.C. American Educational Research Association, 361–404.

Rosenbaum, James E., and Stephan Presser. 1978. Voluntary Racial Integration in a Magnet School. *School Review* 86:156–86.

Rosenberg, Morris, and Roberta C. Simmons. 1972. *Black and White Self-Esteem: The Urban School Child.* Washington, D.C.: American Sociological Association.

Rosenfield, David; Daniel S. Sheehan; Mary M. Marcus; and Walter G. Stephan. 1981. Classroom Structure and Prejudice in Desegregated Schools. *Journal of Educational Psychology* 73, no. 1:17–26.

Rosenfeld, Gerry. 1971. *"Shut Those Thick Lips!" A Study of Slum School Failure.* New York: Holt, Rinehart, and Winston.

Rosenthal, Robert, and Lenore Jacobson. 1968. *Pygmalion in the Classroom.* New York: Holt, Rinehart, and Winston.

Rosnow, Ralph L., and Gary Alan Fine. 1976. *Rumor and Gossip: The Social Psychology of Hearsay.* New York: Elsevier.

Rubel, Robert J. 1977. *The Unruly School: Disorders, Disruptions, and Crimes.* Lexington, Mass: Lexington Books.

Rubenstein, Richard L. 1983. *The Age of Triage: Fear and Hope in an Overcrowded World.* Boston: Beacon.

Rubin, Lillian B. 1976. White against White: School Desegregation and the Revolt of Middle America. In *School Desegregation: Shadow and Substance,* Florence Hamlish Levinshohn and Benjamin Drake Wright, eds. Chicago: University of Chicago Press, 67–83.

Rubin, Nancy. 1980. Headstart Efforts Prove Their Value. *New York Times,* January 6, p. Ed.13.

Ruchkin, Judith P. 1977. Does School Crime Need the Attention of Policemen or Educators? *T. C. Record* 79, no. 2:225–44.

Runkel, Donnan B. 1977. When Iron-Clad Conviction Rusts out. *New York Times,* October 28, p. A31.

Rush, Sheila, and Chris Clark. 1971. *How to Get Along with Black People: A Handbook for White Folks and Some Black Folks, Too.* New York: Third Press.

Rutter, Michael, Barbara Maughan, Peter Mortimoe, Janet Outson, with Adam Smith. 1979. *15,000 Hours: Secondary Schools and Their Effects on Children.* Cambridge: Harvard University Press.

Sagar, H. Andrew, and Janet W. Schofield. 1980. Racial and Behavioral Cues in Black and White Children's Perceptions of Ambiguously Aggressive Acts. *Journal of Personality and Social Psychology* 39, no. 4:590–98.

Scanzoni, John H. 1977. *The Black Family in Modern Society: Patterns of Stability and Security.* Chicago: University of Chicago Press.

Scarr, Sandra, and Richard A. Weinberg. 1978. The Influence of "Family Background" on Intellectual Attainment. *American Sociological Review* 43, no. 5: 674–92.

Schafft, Gretchen Engle. 1976. "The Unexpected Minority: White Children in an Urban School and Neighborhood." Ph.D. diss., Catholic University.

Scherer, Klaus; Ronald P. Abeles; and Claude S. Fischer. 1975. *Human Aggression and Conflict: Interdisciplinary Perspectives.* Englewood Cliffs, N.J.: Prentice-Hall.

Scherer, Jacqueline, and Edward J. Slawski, Jr. 1978. *Hard Walls—Soft Walls: The Social Ecology of an Urban Desegregated High School.* Report to National Institute of Education.

———. 1979. Color, Class, and Social Control in an Urban Desegregated School. In *Desegregated Schools: Appraisals of an American Experiment,* Ray C. Rist, ed. New York: Academic Press, 117–54.

Scherer, Shawn E. 1974. Proxemic Behavior of Primary School Children as a Function of Their Socioeconomic Class and Subculture. *Journal of Personality and Social Psychology* 29:800–5.

Schoem, David. 1982. Explaining Jewish Student Failure. *Anthropology and Education Quarterly* 13, no. 4: 308–22.

Schofield, Janet Ward. 1982. *Black and White in School: Trust, Tension, and Tolerance.* New York: Praeger.

Schofield, Janet Ward, and H. Andrew Sagar. 1977. Peer Interaction Patterns in an Integrated Middle School. *Sociometry* 40, no. 2:130–138.

———. 1978. *Social Process and Peer Relations in a "Nearly Integrated" Middle School.* Report to National Institute of Education.

———. 1979. The Social Context of Learning in an Interracial School. In *Desegregated Schools: Appraisals of an American Experiment,* Ray C. Rist, ed. New York: Academic Press, 155–200.

Schwartzman, Helen B. 1978. *Transformations: The Anthropology of Children's Play.* New York: Plenum.

Seaford, Henry W., Jr. 1975. Facial Expression Dialect: An Example. In *Organization of Behavior in Face-to-Face Interaction,* Adam Kendon, Richard M. Harris, and Mary Ritchie Ked, eds. World Anthropology Series, Sol Tax, gen. ed. The Hague: Mouton, 151–55.

Sedlacek, William E., and Glenwood C. Brooks, Jr. 1976. *Racism in American Education: A Model for Change.* Chicago: Nelson-Hall.

Segrest, Melissa. 1978. Black Ownership Goal of Caucus Delegates. *Dallas Times Herald,* June 18, p. B1.

Sennett, Richard, and Jonathan Cobb. 1973. *The Hidden Injuries of Class.* New York: Knopf.

Serrin, William. 1979. NEA Says Teacher Burn-Out Causes Thousands to Leave Jobs. *New York Times,* July 6, p. A8.

Sewall, Gil; Jerry Buckley, and Jennifer Foote. 1979. Private School Boom. *Newsweek,* August 13, p. 83.

Shabecoff, Philip. 1980. U.S. Study Hints at More Jobless in Youth Ranks. *New York Times,* February 29, pp. A1, 15.

Shaftel, Fannie R., and George Shaftel. 1982. *Role-Playing in the Curriculum.* 2d ed.. Englewood Cliffs, N.J.: Prentice-Hall.

Shantz, C. 1975. The Development of Social Cognition. In *Review of Child Development Theory and Research* vol. 5. E. M. Hetherington, ed. Chicago: University of Chicago Press, 257–324.

Sheehan, Daniel S., and Mary M. Marcus. 1977. *Desegregation Report No. 1: The Effects of Busing Status and Student Ethnicity on Achievement Test Scores.* Dallas: Dallas Independent School District.

Shultz, Jeffrey, and Susan Florio. 1979. Stop and Freeze: The Negotiation of Social and Physical Space in a Kindergarten/First-Grade Classroom. *Anthropology and Education Quarterly* 10, no. 3:166–81.

Sieber, R. Timothy. 1978. Schooling, Socialization, and Group Boundaries: A Study of Informal Social Relations in the Public Domain. *Urban Anthropology* 7, no. 1: 67–98.

Siegel, Bernard J. 1970. Defensive Structuring and Environmental Stress. *American Journal of Sociology* 76, no. 1:11–32.

Silverstein, Barry, and Ronald Krate. 1975. *Children of the Dark Ghetto: A Developmental Psychology.* New York: Praeger.

Simoes, Antonio, Jr. 1976. *The Bilingual Child: Research and Analysis of Existing Educational Themes.* New York: Academic Press.

Slavin, Robert. 1980. Cooperative Learning. *Review of Educational Research* 50:315–42.

Smith, Louis M., and William Geoffrey. 1968. *The Complexities of an Urban Classroom: An Analysis toward a General Theory of Teaching.* New York: Holt, Rinehart, and Winston.

Smitherman, Geneva. 1977. *Talkin and Testifyin: The Language of Black America.* Boston: Houghton-Mifflin.

Sowell, Thomas. 1980. Flight Patterns. *Washington Post,* March 12, p. A21.

Speer, David C. 1972. Nonverbal Communication of Affective Information: Some Laboratory Findings Pertaining to an Interactional Process. In *Nonverbal Communication,* David C. Speer, ed. Beverly Hills: Sage, 33–48.

Spindler, George D., ed. 1970. *Being an Anthropologist: Fieldwork in Eleven Cultures.* New York: Holt, Rinehart, and Winston.

———. 1982. *Doing the Ethnography of Schooling: Educational Anthropology in Action.* New York: Holt, Rinehart, and Winston.

Spradley, James P., and David W. McCurdy. 1972. *The Cultural Expression.* Chicago: Science Research Associates.

Starr, Mark, and Frank Maier. 1985. Gang Warfare. *Newsweek,* January 28, p. 32.

*Stephan, Walter G. 1978. School Desegregation: An Evaluation of Predictions Made in *Brown* v. *Board of Education. Psychological Bulletin* 85, no. 2:217–38.

*St. John, Nancy H. 1975. *Desegregation Outcomes for Children.* New York: Wiley Interscience.

Stokoe, William C. 1976. Sign Language Autonomy. In *Origins and Evolution of Language and Speech,* Stevan R. Harnad, Horst D. Steklis, and Jane Lancaster, eds. New York: Annals of the New York Academy of Sciences, no. 280, 505–13.

Stumbo, Bello. 1978. Schools in Large, Urban Areas Unsafe for Teachers, Students. *Dallas Times Herald,* May 17, p. 2.

Sullivan, Allen R. 1974. Conflict Escalation or Reduction: An Exploration of the Function of Profanity in Schools." Unpublished.

Sutton-Smith, Brian. 1971. Play, Games, and Controls. In *Social Control and Social Change,* John Paul Scott and Sarah F. Scott, eds. Chicago: University of Chicago Press, 73–102.

———. 1976. *The Dialectics of Play.* Schoendoff, W. Ger.: Verlag Hoffman.

———. 1977. Games of Order and Disorder. *Association for the Anthropological Study of Play Newsletter* 4, no. 2: 19–26.

Szwed, John. 1975. Race and the Embodiment of Culture. *Ethnicity* 2:19–33.

Takaki, Ronald 1979. *Iron Cages: Race and Culture in Nineteenth-Century America.* New York: Knopf.

Taeuber, Karl E., and Alma F. Taeuber. 1965. *Negroes in Cities.* Chicago: Adine.

Taubb, William K. 1970. *The Political Economy of the Black Ghetto.* New York: Norton.

Taylor, Orlando, I., Leo Min, Arthur Spears, and Paul A. Stoller. 1974. *Problems in Cross-Cultural Communications: A Study of Blacks and Whites in the U.S. Army.* Washington, D.C.: Center for Applied Linguistics.

Taylor, Shelley, Susan T. Fiske, Nancy L. Etcoff, and Audrey Ruderman. 1978. Categorical and Contextual Bases of Person Memory and Stereotyping. *Journal of Personality and Social Psychology* 36:778–93.

Thompson, James J. 1973. *Beyond Words: Nonverbal Communication in the Classroom.* New York: Citation.

Toby, Jackson. 1980. Crime in American Public Schools. *Public Interest* 58:18–42.

Toffler, Alvin. 1970. *Future Shock.* New York: Random House.

Torbert, William R. 1981. Why Educational Research Has Been So Uneducational: The Base for a New Model of Social Science Based on Collaborative Inquiry. In *Human Inquiry: A Sourcebook of New Paradigm Research,* Peter Reason and John Rowan, eds. New York: Wiley, 141–52.

Twentieth Century Fund. 1983. *Making the Grade.* New York: TCF.

U.S. Bureau of Labor Statistics. 1976. Unemployment Declined in Metropolitan Areas and Central Cities in 1976—but Black Workers Made Few Gains. Press release. USDL 77-867.

Useem, Elizabeth. 1977. Correlates of White Students' Attitudes toward a Voluntary Busing Program. In *Conflicts and Tensions in the Public Schools,* Eleanor P. Wolf, ed. Beverly Hills: Sage, 69–104.

Valente, Judith. 1980. D.C. Board Backs "Academic" School for Top Students. *Washington Post,* February 27, p. C1.

Vincent, Joan. 1974. The Structuring of Ethnicity. *Human Organization* 33, no. 4:375–79.

Wang, Ming-mei; Moraye B. Bear; Jonathan E. Conklin; and Ralph Hoepfner. 1981. *Compensatory Services and Educational Development in the School Year.* Santa Monica, Calif.: System Development Corp. for the U.S. Department of Education Office of Program Evaluation.

Ward, Martha Coonfield. 1971. *The Children: A Study in Language Learning.* New York: Holt, Rinehart, and Winston.

Walder, O. Leopold; Leonard D. Eron; L. Rowell Huesman; and Monroe M. Lefkowitz. 1983. Alternatives to Aggression. Paper presented at the annual meeting of the American Psychological Association.

Warren, Donald L. 1975. *Black Neighborhoods: An Assessment of Community Power.* Ann Arbor: University of Michigan Press.

Wax, Murray L., ed. 1980. *When Schools Are Desegregated: Problems and Possibilities for Students, Educators, Parents, and the Community.* New Brunswick, N.J.: Transaction Books.

Weber, George. 1971. *Inner-City Children Can Be Taught to Read: Four Successful Schools.* Washington, D.C.: Council for Basic Education.

Wegmann, Robert G. 1977. Desegregation and Resegregation: A Review of the Research on White Flight from Urban Areas. In *The Future of Big-City Schools,* Daniel U. Levine and Robert J. Havinghurst, eds. Berkeley, Calif.: McCutchan, 11–54.

Weigel, Russell; Patricia Wiser; and Stuart Cook. 1975. The Impact of Cooperative Learning Experiences on Cross-Ethnic Relations and Attitudes. *Journal of Social Issues* 31, no. 1:219–44.

Weinberg, Meyer. 1977. *A Chance to Learn: The History of Race and Education in the U.S.* Cambridge: Cambridge University Press.

Weisman, Steven R. 1983. Reagan Seeks More Discipline in Schools. *New York Times,* December 9, p. A26.

Weisner, Thomas S., and Ronald Gallimore. 1977. My Brother's Keeper: Child and Sibling Caretaking. *Current Anthropology* 18, no. 2:169–90.

Wellisch, Jean B.; Anne H. MacQueen; Ronald A. Cairiere; and Gary A. Duck. 1978. School Management and Organization in Successful Schools (ESAA In-depth Study of Schools). *Sociology of Education* 51:211–26.

White, Ralph K. 1977. Interviews with Children and Parents in Three Desegregated Schools. A pilot study conducted by graduate students of George Washington University as part of the evaluation of Montgomery County Public Schools. Mimeo.

Wiggins, David K. 1980. The Play of Slave Children in the Plantation Communities of the Old South, 1820–1860. *Journal of Sport History* 7:21–39.

Wilking, Roger. 1977. The Changing Character of Blacks' Problem. *New York Times,* September 2, p. D10.

Williams, John E., and J. Kenneth Morland. 1976. *Race, Color, and the Young Child.* Chapel Hill: University of North Carolina Press.

Williams, Juan. 1979. D.C. Public Schools Losing Middle-Class Blacks. *Washington Post,* January 5, pp. B1, 6.

———. 1985. James Meredith: A Change of Course. *Washington Post,* February 23, pp. G1, 7.

Williams, Lena. 1979. Minority Students Given a Better Chance in ABC. *New York Times,* January 2, p. B2.

Williams, Melvin D. 1974. *Community in a Black Pentecostal Church,* Pittsburgh: University of Pittsburgh Press.

Williams, Robin M. 1977. *Mutual Accommodation: Ethnic Conflict and Cooperation.* Minneapolis: University of Minnesota Press.

Willie, Charles. 1973. *Race Mixing in the Public Schools.* New York: Praeger.

———. 1978. *Sociology of Urban Education.* Lexington, Mass.: Lexington Books.

Willis, F. N. 1966. Initial Speaking Distance as a Function of the Speakers' Relationship. *Psychonomic Science* 4:221–22.

Willis, Paul E. 1975. The Expressive Style of a Motor Bike Culture. In *The Body as a Medium of Expression,* Jonathan Benthall and Ted Polhemus, eds. New York: Dutton, 233–52.

———. 1977. *Learning to Labour: How Working-Class Kids Get Working-Class Jobs.* Farnborough, Eng.: Saxon House. New York: Columbia University Press, 1981.

Wilson, William Julius. 1980. *The Declining Significance of Race: Blacks and Changing American Institutions.* 2d. ed. Chicago: University of Chicago Press.

Wisdom, J. 1975. Random Remarks on the Role of Social Sciences in the Judicial Decision-Making Process in School Desegregation Cases. *Law and Contemporary Problems* 39, no. 1:135–49.

Wise, James. 1982. A Gentle Deterrent to Vandalism. *Psychology Today* 16, no. 9:31–32, 34, 36, 38.

Wiseman, Jacqueline P. 1974. The Research Web. *Urban Life and Culture* 3, no. 3:317–28.

Wolf, Eleanor P. 1981. *Trial and Error: The Detroit School Segregation Case.* Detroit: Wayne State University Press.

Wolfe, Tom. 1970. *Radical Chic and Mau-Mauing the Flak Catchers.* New York: Farrar, Straus, and Giroux.

Wolters, Raymond. 1984. *The Burden of Brown: Thirty Years of School Desegregation.* Knoxville: University of Tennessee Press.

Wood, Roy; Joanne S. Yamauchi; and James J. Bradac. 1971. The Communication of Meaning Across Generations. *Journal of Communication* 21, no. 2:160–69.

Woodson, Robert L. 1981. *A Summons to Life: Mediating Structures and the Prevention of Youth Crime.* Cambridge, Mass.: Ballinger.

Wollenberg, Charles M. 1977. *All Deliberate Speed: Segregation and Exclusion in California Schools.* Berkeley: University of California Press.

Word, Carol O.; Mark P. Zanna; and Joel Cooper. 1974. The Non-Verbal Mediation of Self-Fulfilling Prophecies in Interracial Interaction. *Journal of Experimental Social Psychology* 10:109–20.

*Yarmolinsky, Adam; Lance Liebman; and Corinne S. Schelling, eds. 1981. *Race and Schooling in the City.* Cambridge: Harvard University Press.

INDEX